TIME OUT

EMMA MURRAY

Boldwood

First published in Great Britain in 2020 by Boldwood Books Ltd.

Cover Design by Alice Moore Design

Cover Illustration: Everyday People Cartoons

A CIP catalogue record for this book is available from the British Library.

Paperback ISBN 978-1-83889-476-4

Hardback 978-1-80426-225-2

Ebook ISBN 978-1-83889-470-2

Kindle ISBN 978-1-83889-471-9

Audio CD ISBN 978-1-83889-477-1

MP3 CD ISBN 978-1-83889-474-0

Digital audio download ISBN 978-1-83889-468-9

Boldwood Books Ltd
23 Bowerdean Street
London SW6 3TN
www.boldwoodbooks.com

For the three great loves of my life: my husband, Sam, and our two daughters, Ava and Anya. (I can already hear the two girls arguing over whose name goes first.)

PART I

LONDON, PAST AND PRESENT

Motherhood is tough
But loneliness is far worse
Friends help us survive

1

LONDON, NOW

I'm not going to lie – I am nervous. It's not often you find your whole future determined by an innocent-looking blue and white icon on your computer screen. But Skype is not flashing yet, and so I wait impatiently with sweaty palms and a whirring mind.

I glance at the clock on the bottom right-hand corner of the screen. It is 2.05 p.m. on a hot, clammy Wednesday afternoon in late July. The waiting is unbearable. My agent, Harriet Green, is late. She's currently at a book event in New York and as usual she has no concept of the time difference. This is particularly annoying when I'm trying to schedule calls during my four-year-old daughter, Anna's, afternoon nap. I drum my bitten fingernails on my desk. If Anna wakes up soon, any chance of a real conversation will be scuppered.

With a quick swivel of my chair, I turn towards the small window of my tiny home office –i.e. the spare room, hoping for some kind of distraction. My husband, David, Anna and I live on one of those mean, narrow south-west London streets, in an area called Woodvale, which is neither woodsy nor in a valley. It is the sort of place that estate agents call 'quaint' or 'bijou' – in other words, totally overpriced.

Rows and rows of identical red-brick Victorian terraced houses cling to each other as they line the busy, impractically narrow roads. Despite being in a firmly middle-class postcode, the shrubs and pavements are almost always covered in a mixture of dog and fox shit, a recurring topic raised on 'Vale Mums', the secret local Facebook group administrated by fellow ex-antenatal group mum and Nazi sympathiser Tania Henderson. (I have no evidence to suggest she has ever been affiliated with the Nazis, but if her strident approach to parenting is anything to go by, I think I have a strong case to argue.) Personally, I think Vale Mums should come with the tagline, 'the home of First World problems'.

While I'm waiting for Harriet to figure out what time zone I'm in I swivel back to the screen and log into Facebook to check out Vale Mums for the latest 'news'. Much as I loathe the futile commentary and no-offence-intended grinning emojis, like reality TV, I find Vale Mums both appalling and fascinating in equal measure. A quick glance at the latest news feed tells me: Amanda has 'FINALLY' found the perfect cupcake recipe (I can safely sit back from the edge of my seat now); Karen 'desperately' needs to know how to remove limescale from her kitchen kettle (Google it, Karen!); and Bethany is ranting as usual about the amount of dog shit on the street outside her house (I think you'll find it's 'steaming dog shit' in this heat, Bethany).

So far so boring. As I am scrolling down to see if there have been any juicier entries, I see Rosalind's name pop up. Like Amanda, Karen and Bethany, I have never met Rosalind, but I'm willing to bet I know more about her than close members of her own family. Rosalind has three boys under the age of six ('Three boys! THREE!'). She is about to turn forty ('Any ideas for a fortieth celebration for a very tired mum?'); she currently has no childcare ('Help! My nanny has just quit – by text message!'); and her husband works in Dubai for three weeks out of every month ('Anyone else have a husband who works abroad?' Followed by face-screaming-in-fear emoji).

Rosalind is a frequent visitor to Vale Mums and seems to treat it as a sort of oracle. If one of her children has a high temperature, she goes on Vale Mums for diagnosis; if she wants to buy a gift for her husband, she asks the other mums for advice; and most recently, she posted a photo of a spider in her bathroom in her house and asked the mums to identify its type (answer: a house spider). I have concluded that Rosalind's posts imply that she is either very lonely or very bored, or perhaps a combination of the two.

Today, Rosalind's burning question is what to make her 'very fussy' two-year-old, Jacob, for breakfast. I suck my breath in through my teeth and shake my head in despair. Oh, Rosalind. Poor, naïve Rosalind. Never post a 'food' question on Vale Mums. You're leaving yourself wide open to all sorts of self-righteous comments from 'the Organics', a disturbingly large subset of Vale Mums led by aforementioned Tania Henderson.

To qualify as an Organic, you must feed your children only top-of-the-range organic food (preferably grown in your back garden, the more worms and muck the better) in order for your children to grow up happy, healthy and savvy enough to attract a partner with a trust fund. It goes without saying that being an Organic automatically makes you a better mum.

And so it is, with no small measure of trepidation, that I start to read the comments under Rosalind's 'breakfast plea' post. First to reply is Tania.

Shocker.

Hi, Rosalind! Why not make Jacob some organic porridge mashed with organic strawberries and blueberries? If the crop in your garden isn't doing well, there is great fruit picking at Johnson's farm in Surrey at the moment!

I sigh. This is vintage Tania. Like the other eight hundred people on Vale Mums, she knows full well that Rosalind has no childcare, an absent husband, and has barely slept in six years. Does Rosalind sound like the type of person who has the time to be cooking porridge or driving to fucking Surrey to pick fresh fruit, let alone grow fruit in her own garden?

But wait, another comment has just flashed up. It's Caroline, another member of the Organics crew.

Excellent suggestion, Tania! My LO [little one] also loves porridge with freshly picked fruit, but how about giving him some yoghurt too?

Although I find Caroline's allegiance to Tania vomit-inducing, I can't totally fault her response. Yoghurt is a handy stopgap; at least Rosalind can buy Jacob a few cartons of yoghurt from the shops. But I have given her too much credit. Another comment from Caroline flashes up.

Whoops! Just reread my last post and realised that I meant to say home-made yoghurt. Steer clear of the shop-bought variety – obviously. Too much sugar!

She signs off with a smiley emoji.

My fingers itch to respond. I rarely partake in this futile mum-off but I am too fired up to sit back and watch. I quickly write a response and post it before I can change my mind. I keep it simple. It's only one word.

Cheerios.

There will be reprisals.

I am distracted by the sound of an angry car speeding down my road – clearly ignoring the 20 mph signs plastered everywhere – in a race to get to the end of the street for fear it might have to pull in for the ten seconds it takes to allow another car past. My shoulders bunch in irritation. I can't stand speeding cars, especially when there are so many young children about. For the next couple of minutes, I fantasise about having my own speed gun, but because it is a fantasy, I switch it to an actual gun, a sniper rifle, and start mentally shooting at the car's tyres. Not for the first time, I wonder how I have become the type of person who fantasises about shooting out someone else's tyres. Shaking myself out of my reverie, I click back to Skype, but Harriet is still not online.

When I first met Harriet, roughly six and a half years ago, I was desperate. I had ditched my fancy marketing job in a fancy big bank – as well as my long-term lawyer boyfriend – to become a full-time writer, moved into a flat with a twenty-something hipster called Joss, who was far too cool for me, and spent six months and most of my savings writing a novel, before coming to the horrifying conclusion that the book was shit. And I'm not being too hard on myself here: it really was shit. If I was honest with myself, I knew fiction wasn't really my thing, the trouble being, I didn't know what was. So I popped six months of hard work in a box under my bed and started to freak out.

After I'd spent a couple of weeks stunned by my shockingly low bank balance, an email advertising the London Book Fair popped into my inbox. Without even thinking about it, I bought a ticket. Maybe I would meet some fellow writers there who were as miserable as I was. But instead of meeting other writers, I met Harriet.

To be honest, first impressions weren't great. Having spent hours going around smiling benignly at people representing different publishers on different stands, I was ready to give up. With aching feet and a self-critical voice in my head berating me for not having the confidence to strike up a conversation with one single person, I had headed outside for a breather. Lost in my own misery, it took me a moment to notice a woman gesturing to me.

'The time!' she said crossly. 'Do you have the time?'

She had long, shiny brown hair, sallow skin, and was smartly dressed in a beige cashmere coat, impatiently arranged leopard-print scarf, and expensive-looking tan mid-ankle boots. She would have been pretty if her mouth turned up at the corners, which I would soon find out never happened.

Flustered, I told her it was almost four o'clock, but she didn't move away. Instead, she took out a cigarette, put it in her mouth, and started talking.

'If I have to negotiate one more book deal with those tight-arse international publishers, I'm going to murder someone,' she said, in a public-school accent, through a cloud of smoke.

My head shot backwards: she was an agent! A real-life book agent. Exactly the person I needed to talk to.

The only problem was I had no idea what to say to her without sounding needy, so I just stood there, paralysed by my own desperation.

She took a deep drag, cocked her head to one side, and said, 'What do you do, then?'

And so I took a deep breath and told her. I told her everything about how I had given up my job in a bank to become a full-time writer, only to realise I was shit at fiction, and now I was seriously stuck.

When I had finished, she stared at me for a bit, grounding out her cigarette stub on the pavement. I didn't feel like this was the right time to point out that she was standing next to a bin.

'There's no money in fiction anyway,' she said, with a grimace. 'Have you ever considered ghostwriting?'

Immediately a red flag went up. Ghostwriting? Wasn't that just for lazy celebrities with giant egos and people who wanted to share their horrific stories of child abuse and sex trafficking? I couldn't handle the egos or the sad stories. Both would make me cry.

I was just about to tell Harriet that ghostwriting wasn't my thing when she said, 'I have a couple of professionals on my books looking for some help with their business books. You have experience working with corporate types, so you could be a good fit.'

And that was the start of my ghostwriting career – working with the same type of people that I had just spent almost a decade working with in a bank. It may not have been the writing I thought I was going to be getting into, but at least I was writing.

For the first couple of years, ghostwriting was good – really good. Turned out that these people were willing to pay big money to get out of having to write their books themselves. Sure, part of me had always hoped that one day my own name would grace a front cover, but still, I knew I was lucky to make a good living out of writing, and I decided to take every opportunity that came my way.

But then last year, it all stopped. Harriet told me in her offhand way that nothing was coming in, and I started to panic. I had heard of the plight of the freelance writer – either feast or famine – but I never thought it would happen to me. For the second time in my life, my bank balance was reaching a critical point, but this time there was much more at stake. I had a child due to start school soon, an overly inflated mortgage to pay, and a husband facing the real prospect of redundancy. We desperately needed the extra income.

So you can imagine how excited I was when, after months of zero contact, Harriet emailed me about a 'promising new book project'. Now I am prepared to do *anything* to get it.

More minutes go by and still nothing, so to stop myself biting my nails, I click back to Vale Mums to check the extent of the fallout of my 'Cheerios' comment. Eleven comments in less than five minutes. At first glance I can't make out the text for all the smiley emojis, a sure sign I've offended most of the people who have bothered to reply. I scroll down, bracing myself for the passive-aggressive onslaught. Someone called Danielle posts:

Saoirse – totally agree that Cheerios are so handy in the morning (smiley emoji) but thinking there are healthier alternatives maybe??? (Three more smiley emojis.) Besides, I'm fed up of stepping on them every time my LO chucks them on the floor! (Horror face plus crying laughing emoji.)

As judgements go, Danielle's isn't so bad. It follows a fairly standard format for the more decent members of Vale Mums – I'll pretend to agree with you, then add what I *really* think (couched in a plethora of emojis), and to take the sting out of judging you, I'll try to balance it out with something annoying about my own child.

A few other mums have posted in a similar format, but just when I think I have got off lightly, I reach Tania Henderson's post. As ever, her judgement is loud and clear.

Cheerios??? Have you READ the back of the packet? The amount of sugar! Soooo bad for our LOs (sad-faced emoji).

I sit on my hands to stop myself from replying in anger. After all, this is my own fault; I shouldn't have participated in the stupid exchange in the first place.

But then a familiar name pops up and a jolt of relief runs through me. Before I even read the post, I know I have been saved.

Harry had ice cream at 5 a.m. – with chocolate sprinkles on top.

I burst out laughing. It's from my best mum-friend and fellow secret Vale Mums addict, Bea, who has swooped in with a show-stopping comment to save me from any further judgement from the bloody Organics. Breathless with anticipation, I wait to see if anyone dares to reply. Some will think she is joking, and the ones who think she is serious won't be brave enough to take the chance. To be honest, *I'm* not even entirely sure if she's joking – you never know with Bea. Minutes go by and the feed stays quiet. It's a small victory, but one to celebrate none the less. I grab my phone to text Bea a 'thumbs up' but a loud tuneless sound stops me in my tracks. With a jolt, I realise that the screen is flashing. Harriet is finally calling me over Skype. I nervously push my unstyled and undyed, shoulder-length brown hair (a few bits of grey, but nothing to worry about just yet, according to Frank, my hairdresser) behind my ears, hurriedly making sure the camera is not pointing any lower than my face – so that Harriet can't tell that I am still in my pyjamas at 2.20 p.m. – and finally answer the call. Deep breath. Shoulders back. Here we go.

'Hi, Searcy,' Harriet says, leaning in so close to the camera that all I can make out is part of her chin and blindingly white lower teeth.

Oh, yes, that's one thing I forgot to mention: Harriet has never bothered to get my name right. My name isn't Searcy. It is Saoirse – Saoirse Daly, in fact. 'Saoirse' is an Irish name which means 'freedom', which is ironic given that freedom is exactly the thing I've lost since having Anna. As I don't live in my native Ireland any more, I have spent my whole life correcting people on the pronunciation, sometimes patiently, more often, not. When the talented young Irish actress Saoirse Ronan burst on to our screens with starring roles in the hugely acclaimed movies *Atonement*, *Brooklyn* and *Lady Bird*, I thought all my prayers had been answered. Finally, people would pronounce my name correctly – and certainly more people had. Apart from Harriet, that is, who still insists in calling me Searcy (I can only imagine she's a big *Game of Thrones* fan, given one of the lead characters is called 'Cersei'). Despite subtly pointing out the mistake on several occasions, sending her the phonetical spelling ('Seer-sha'), plus smiley-faced emojis to soften the blow of shitting all over her pronunciation, Harriet still insists on her own version.

So, our conversation has barely begun, and I am now both nervous and irritated. And desperate. Let's not forget desperate. I greet Harriet with a tight smile and a forced 'Hello', one hand clutching the computer mouse, and the other placed on my stomach in an effort to calm the churning inside.

Harriet leans back so I can see her full profile. In the background I can see the sad, beige curtains so typical of a cheap New York hotel room. She has dark circles under her eyes and the corners of her mouth are so severe they seem to be stapled down. I notice that a few dark hairs have appeared on her upper lip, which tells me she has been too frantic to go for a quick waxing or threading. For the first few minutes, she rants about the 'fucking shit American publishers' who don't understand the meaning of 'fuck off until you can come back with a better deal'. I drum my fingers on my desk impatiently. I have no time for her rants; frankly, it's a bloody miracle that Anna has stayed asleep this long. Finally, Harriet stops her tirade, and leans in closer to the camera.

'So anyway, I might have something for you,' she says. 'You have a young daughter, right?'

My mouth drops open. I would have been less shocked if she had asked me my favourite sexual position. My thoughts race. How does Harriet even know I have a child? I have never mentioned Anna, subscribing to that don't-talk-about-your-kids-to-people-who-don't-appear-to-have-any rule.

Evidently registering the shock on my face, Harriet shrugs and says, 'Facebook.' I nod numbly and stay quiet while she tells me that she has been 'doing some digging' and came across my profile photo on Facebook, which features myself and Anna. You know, the standard shot that looks like you're the happiest mother-daughter combo in the world, even though said daughter has just kicked you in the shins roughly five seconds before the photo was taken. But what does Anna have to do with this new exciting book project?

'Good, because I need someone to write a book about—'

And then the screen freezes.

'Noooooooooooooooo!' I shout at the frozen image of my agent's neck. Why is this happening? It isn't even a Sunday, when the whole world is online. It's a shagging Wednesday. OFF PEAK.

Then something far worse happens: the baby monitor starts to crackle. My ranting and raving has just woken up Anna, who has been napping in the next room.

I pick up the monitor and start to beg. 'Please go back to sleep, pleeease.' I wait and listen for the inevitable, 'MUUUUUMMMEEEEE' but nothing comes. Miracle of miracles, I have been granted a brief reprieve. I have two more minutes, tops.

Just then, the screen unfreezes, and the sound comes back.

'It's about motherhood,' Harriet says, through a yawn.

'Oh!' I say, surprised. This is a bit of a departure from the business books I have been ghosting, but it's not the worst topic in the world. I'm curious to know who I'll be working with. Maybe it's some celeb with shiny blond hair who needs a ghostwriter to help her show off her smug parenting skills, or some child expert, so super-busy he has no time to write his own ground-breaking theories to share with the world. I guess it makes sense for the ghostwriter to be a parent, too.

Then I listen while Harriet gives me the brief. In fairness, she is always good at giving these kinds of summaries – it's the only time she really comes to life. I listen while she talks about the way motherhood is treated in the media: everything from the cutie ads promoting babies as the best things to happen to you, from celebs who gush about their offspring to anyone who points a camera in their direction, to people like me, who save only the best bits for social media.

'My point is that people are rarely "real" about motherhood,' Harriet says. 'Granted, there are a few celebrities now who have vented a little about the usual sleep deprivation and tantrums, but it's all done in the name of comedy. Mothers paint this perfect picture on Facebook or Instagram and it's all bullshit. Parenting has become a competition, a contest to see who is raising their child the best. Mothers tear each other down over social media, and it stops the people who really need support and a shoulder to cry on from reaching out to others for fear of being judged. The publishers want an author who is honest about being a mother, both the positive *and* the negative. They've had enough of all those "My toddler is a sack of shit" and "Why mummy freebases every night before bath time". They want someone authentic, someone who will put themselves on the line and tell it like it is. Think of it as a warts-and-all account of being a mother, the impact it has, but with real meaning.'

Harriet turns away from the screen, which gives me the opportunity to think about what she has said. It is a refreshing take on motherhood, and it would be very interesting to explore the topic further with someone else. I just hope that I click with whoever it is.

Harriet's back with a silver e-cigarette dangling from her mouth.

'I'm definitely interested,' I say. 'Who's the client?'

Harriet exhales deeply and makes a face as though disgusted with what has just happened inside her mouth, before saying something that catches me entirely off-guard.

'There is no client, Searcy. This isn't a ghostwriting project. You are going to write it.'

And I am so stunned that I barely have time to register Anna slamming into the room, her blond-streaked chestnut hair splayed all over face, racing over to me as fast as her bare feet can take her. She jumps on my lap with a force that makes me wish I hadn't had that extra slice of quiche for lunch.

'What are you *doing*, Mummy?' she demands indignantly, which in her language means: 'How do you have the nerve to do something without my vital participation?'

Resigned to my fate, I reluctantly introduce Harriet to Anna.

'Hi, Anna,' Harriet says flatly, pronouncing it the American way with the 'A' as an 'Aw' sound, like 'Aw-na'. This is an affectation that seems to have travelled over here from the US, and, to be honest, it's annoying.

'It's Anna,' my daughter pipes up indignantly, emphasising the flat 'A' sound, as in 'apple'.

Then Harriet does something I've never seen before. The corners of her mouth twitch with what I think might be an effort to smile, but that's about as far as she gets. I hastily give Anna the computer mouse to keep her quiet, which will give me another ninety seconds, tops. Then, under immense time pressure, I quickly ask Harriet, 'Why me?'

'We're looking for someone ordinary; someone without any sort of reputation or history in the public eye... basically an everyday mum who has nothing to lose.'

I can't help but bristle at this. Ordinary, boring mum who has made zero impact on the world. It's hardly the most flattering description, is it?

'Full disclosure: it's not just you in the running, Searcy,' she goes on. 'You'll be pitching for it against a few other mums.'

Ha! Well, that's decided it. Why would I compete for a book that I have absolutely no interest having my name on? Besides, there's bugger-all money in being an author; everybody knows that. I might be desperate but there's no way I'm working for nothing. I shake my head, and open my mouth to tell her that it's really not for me, but a loud yelp comes out instead.

Anna, in a move that defies all logic, has just slammed the mouse down on my right hand.

'I can't do it, Harriet,' I say, hurriedly, trying to keep Anna from banging on my keyboard.

She sighs and raises her eyes skyward. 'You know the way I always tell you that you make more money as a ghostwriter than an author?'

I nod.

'Well, in this case, the advance is better than usual.'

Then she proceeds to tell me the figure, and although it's not as much as I would earn as a ghostwriter, it's certainly enough to give me pause.

'I'll think about it,' I say weakly.

'Good. I want the pitch in four weeks,' she says, pointing her e-cigarette at me.

'Say goodbye to Harriet,' I tell my daughter, far-too-brightly, as she bashes the computer keyboard once again.

Anna looks up, stares Harriet straight in the eye, and says, 'You have a moustache.'

Harriet instantly reddens. I dive for the mouse, and click it violently until the screen goes dark.

Then I burst into tears. After waiting so long for a new project to come through, I can't believe this is what I have been handed. I mean, my own daughter has just told my agent she has a moustache. I'm not exactly a ringing endorsement for Mother of the Year. What on earth makes Harriet think that I would be a good choice for a book on motherhood? I have barely been able to hang on to my sanity since I had Anna.

Anna shuffles off my knee, and looks at me curiously with her huge brown eyes – it's rare I let her see me cry in case she turns into an emotional basket case in the future (I read that can happen somewhere on the *Huffington Post*) – and then wanders off into her room, presumably to locate one of her millions of skinny princess dollies to torment (I'll be blamed for her inevitable eating disorder in later years).

Not a trace of sympathy or comfort, I think sulkily. After all I do for her, and she doesn't give a shite if I'm upset.

And then something happens to redeem my faith in difficult children. Anna emerges from her room with a grubby box of tissues – the one that fell down the side of her bed a good three months ago, which I haven't been bothered to dig out – crawls back on my knee, plucks a dusty tissue from the box, and wipes the tears from my eyes. It is like that Kleenex ad from the 1980s, where the little boy runs off to get his grandmother a box of tissues when he sees her crying while chopping onions. Anna's unusual act of kindness makes me cry even more.

I stand up and throw my arms around her to give her a big cuddle and she presses her head against my stomach. It is a lovely Facebook moment, and for a moment, I'm tempted to take a selfie. Look, everyone! My daughter and I have such a special bond. But just then, I feel a sharp, very painful pinch, just above my tummy button.

'Ouch!' I exclaim, trying to pull her away.

Anna doesn't move. And the pain intensifies.

'Agggghhhh,' I scream.

She looks up in fright and bursts into tears.

Still in pain, I move her away gently, and lift up my top, only to find two perfect tiny teeth-mark on my stomach. For no reason whatsoever, Anna has bitten me – hard.

We both howl.

2

I spend the next twenty minutes consoling Anna for biting me, even though she's the one who did it, until she sulkily agrees that I can be her mummy again. I explain to her that biting is not allowed, and that it hurts Mummy, and all the usual shite. She goes very still then, looks up at me with her still-watery brown eyes and says in a really thoughtful way, 'IPad, please.' I go and fetch it for her, like the good slave I am. 'And a snack,' she calls after me. But, of course.

After Anna is settled, I pick up the phone and call Bea, who I know is working from home today.

'Now that's enough broccoli, Harry. You'll get tummy pains,' she answers in a shrill, cheery voice.

'Relax, it's only me,' I say, grinning.

'Thank fuck for that. I thought it was my mum,' she says, through a yawn.

Bea's mother, the famous children's cookbook author Arianna Wakefield, is a health freak who constantly lectures Bea on childhood obesity and surreptitiously weighs Harry whenever she visits.

'What is Harry really eating?' I say.

'Pringles,' Bea replies. 'Actually, he's on his second box – the big versions.'

'Good man,' I say emphatically. 'Potatoes are good for him!'

'Exactly what I thought,' she replies.

'How come you have him?' I say.

Bea's fabulous nanny, Maria, works full time and is easily the most patient person I have ever met in my entire life.

'Maria's at a doctor's appointment,' Bea sighs. 'She's only been gone an hour and, frankly, it's an hour too long.'

There is a loud wail in the background, and then the rattling sound.

'More crisps?' I say.

'Yep, he's making his way through a six-pack now. That should keep him quiet for a few minutes.'

'Speaking of so-called unhealthy food, thanks for weighing in on Cheerios-gate earlier,' I say, with a laugh. 'That'll teach the Organics to be so bloody smug.'

'Who knew there could be so much sugar in just a handful of little 'O's,' Bea says in an exaggerated posh accent.

'I guess we've been killing our kids all this time,' I say, with a dramatic sigh.

'Yes, more guilt to add to the overflowing pot.'

We are quiet for a moment.

'Err, do you ever give Harry Cheerios for breakfast?' I ask.

This is the problem with Vale Mums: what these strangers say somehow feeds my insecurities as a mother. For example, I never thought twice about giving Anna Cheerios until the Organics started to 'educate' me.

'Are you kidding me, Saoirse? Harry has just eaten his own weight in crisps and had fucking ice cream with a half a tub of sprinkles at five o'clock this morning, what do you think?'

We roar.

When things go quiet again, I take a deep breath and tell her about the motherhood book dilemma. When I am finished, she lets out a big explosion of air and says nothing for a minute.

'Personally, I wouldn't be able to reveal to the world how I really feel about being a mother,' she says finally. 'Frankly, I'm shocked that social services haven't been round already. I almost called them myself today just for Harry's protection.'

I stay silent. Forget the terrorist organisations – it's social services Bea and I fear the most. Especially in those dark moments when trying to get our adorable screaming and kicking children into car seats or buggies. Exerting the odd bit of 'pressure' to persuade the apoplectic child to get his or her flailing legs and arms into the straps can cause some paranoia, especially when there are CCTV cameras and human witnesses everywhere.

Bea is still worried about the time she nudged Harry on the bottom with her foot to make him move faster when running for a flight at Heathrow airport. He had been screaming blue murder to be carried but she couldn't on account of her dragging her own small suitcase, as well as all his gear: backpack, large stuffed dog, and fucking Trunki, which he had refused to touch the second they arrived at check-in. Ever since the toe-on-bottom situation, she is petrified that the security cameras caught her in the act, and social services will be banging down her door.

'Also, I would be concerned about the response to the book. I mean, what if you wrote about swearing in front of children? We're all guilty of it when we're tired and the kids are in evil mode, but I wouldn't want the judgement for it. Could you handle the amount of negative comments you might receive?'

'Swearing is good for you,' I say automatically.

'Yes, I know *you* think so,' she replies smartly.

'It relieves tension and encourages honesty, which makes you a better and more loyal friend,' I chant.

'Where did you get that bit about friendship from?' she asks incredulously.

'Some meme on Facebook,' I say brightly.

'Fine, you think swearing is healthy, but what about when it comes to Anna? Are you really going to tell your readers what Anna said about Jesus Christ?'

'Saying "Jesus Christ" in front of Anna is simply blasphemy. That's different from swearing,' I retort defensively.

'Then why did Anna ask you the other day how could Jesus Christ be both a person *and* a "grown-up word"?' she asks, with a laugh.

Dammit, I'd forgotten I'd told Bea about that one. Snookered. Only one thing for it, I'll have to go down the self-righteous road.

'I stand by my belief that swearing is normal, healthy and human, but in any case, I'm not going to mention it in the book. Swearing is out of bounds.'

'See? You're doing it already. Censoring the human side of parenthood. Aren't you supposed to be the one who says the unsayable? Isn't the book supposed to bring empathy and comfort to the masses of mothers out there who think they are constantly doing a shit job?' she says, warming to the theme. 'Aren't you supposed to be giving two fingers to the smug Facebook mums who only ever post happy-clappy family photos and judge other mums for being less than?'

All good points, and I am cross with her for making them.

'Besides, you finally get to have your own name on a book. Perhaps it's time you came out of hiding,' she says.

I know she's right, but why does it have to be *this* book? The thought of putting down in black and white the struggles I've endured since Anna came along has me terrified.

'It means putting myself out there,' I say in a small voice.

'Yes, it does, but you can handle it, Saoirse,' she says, through a sudden crunching sound.

'Are you eating crisps?' I ask her.

'Are you joking? Do you think I could have wrestled them off Harry? No, I'm eating the carrots the little fucker refused to eat for his lunch earlier,' she says, taking another bite.

At that point, Harry starts screaming in a way that is designed to end all conversations. 'Right, I'd better head off and deal with Jurassic,' Bea said, with a heavy sigh. 'Jurassic' is her nickname for him. When he kicks off, his wails sound exactly like the tyrannosaurus from *Jurassic Park*.

Before she signs off, she says in her best commanding voice, 'Saoirse? I think you should go for it. Write the pitch.'

I hang up, feeling a bit better. I'm not convinced, but maybe I should give it more thought. Suddenly, I feel a rush of love for Bea, and I shudder when I think back to being a new mum and where I would have ended up if it wasn't for her.

3

LONDON, FOUR YEARS AGO

I first met Bea at a local antenatal group a month after David and I got married. Initially I had no intention of joining this type of group. I just didn't feel any real need to 'connect' with other heavily pregnant women. I had enough friends, thank you very much. Oddly enough, it was David who encouraged me to go. He reasoned that since I had moved to a part of London where I didn't really know anybody, and as I worked from home, I really should make an effort to make friends in the area.

I researched it just to please him really, but I wasn't happy with what I found out. 'I don't know, David,' I had said. 'It sounds like the sort of class where people get together after the baby is born just to bitch about their partners.' But David pressed on with his argument and we compromised: I would book the class as long as he came along with me. I deliberately chose the fast-track course. One day of talking about childbirth and babies sounded more manageable than the alternative: a weekly class spread over six weeks.

The meeting was held in our local church hall. It was all hard wooden chairs, chipped tea cups and broken biscuits. When David and I arrived, six of out ten chairs were occupied.

Years of living in middle-class suburban London has taught me how to behave when walking into a room full of strangers at a formal gathering:

nod politely, sit down, and wait for whoever is in charge to speak first. If you must talk, do so at a low murmur. And, most importantly, *never* look anyone directly in the eye.

For the church hall scenario, David and I went for the classic 'Hello' whisper and, as expected, tight-lipped smiles were given in return. And so we sat, eyes downcast like little children about to be caned, and collectively waited in silence for our birth practitioner to come in and break the ice for us.

Meanwhile, I took a sneak peek at my fellow mums-to-be and their partners. First impressions weren't great. There was the 'happy' couple – he in chinos and an expensive-looking public-school-boy blue shirt; she in a floaty, flowery dress with wide sleeves. They sat hips joined, him stroking her neat baby bump, while she gazed at him beatifically. Naturally, I hated them on sight.

Sitting next to them was another couple, who looked a lot younger than the rest of us. He in one of those broad-striped shirts worn by Essex boys and estate agents, frantically attacking the keypad of his iPhone; she with a gamine-style haircut, dressed in trendy dungarees with a cute orange T-shirt underneath. I reasoned that however nice they turned out to be, I couldn't ever be friends with them by virtue of the fact that they both looked so young that I felt ancient.

The remaining couple both wore thick black-framed glasses – he in tartan trousers, and she in a 'vintage' ragged pleated dress with a lace trim at the bottom. Nuff said. So, this is what I had paid good money for – a smug pregnant couple, a couple of tweens, and a geeky couple in bad clothes. Talk about slim pickings. I discreetly nudged David, nodding towards the group and raising my eyes to heaven. He frowned back; David has a real bee in his bonnet about my tendency to judge people on sight. I discreetly gave him the finger while pretending to scratch my cheek. Sometimes David is no fun.

Moments later, the hall doors opened again. A woman entered, striding across the room with such authority that I immediately presumed she was the birth class teacher. A hush fell over the group. It was as if we could all instinctively feel a powerful force in the room.

This new arrival was majestically tall. Where some women may stoop a little to compensate for their height, she did the opposite. For the first time ever, I finally understood the expression 'walking tall'. This woman almost luxuriated in her height, as if there were no limits to how far her neck would extend to support her head. And she was pretty too. Mid-length, straight, blond-streaked hair swayed and framed her smooth face. A small pair of spectacles perched on the end of a slightly too-long nose, which gave her a strangely old-fashioned but sexy look.

When this newcomer reached our group, she stood for a moment. We waited with ready smiles, exchanging 'a-ha' looks, bonded by the shared knowledge that our teacher had finally arrived. But instead, the woman sat down on the empty seat opposite me, without giving any of us a second glance. It was only then that I noticed her small bump – the only part of her that looked out of proportion to her super-fit body shape. The word 'Amazonian' did not do this woman justice. She could probably shoot out that baby during a spinning class and not even blink. In fact, I wouldn't be surprised if the baby was born with a decent set of pecs. I vowed to hate her immediately, mostly because she was probably my age and looked younger and prettier, but also because, unlike me, she clearly hadn't been stuffing her face with Mackey Ds and pizza for the majority of her pregnancy.

Just then, Michelle, our real teacher, rushed in, apologising for her late-ness. She welcomed us to the class and cheerily ordered us to introduce ourselves and, as a breaking-the-ice tactic, to tell the group our guilty plea-sures. So far, so cringe-worthy. We all did the polite 'oh no, I couldn't possi-bly' thing until Floaty Dress raised her hand and waved her manicured fingertips at the teacher.

'Hi, my name is Tania,' she said in a posh, all-girls boarding-school accent. 'And my guilty pleasure is eating full-fat yoghurt.' She burst into giggles, with a hand covering her mouth in faux embarrassment.

'That's totally true,' her husband (turned out his name was Giles – of course it was) responded, laughing in an equally trust-fund accent. 'She ate a *whole* tub last night.'

Tania punched Giles in the arm playfully, and we all had to pretend to smile at this hideous stage show. I started to feel a bit sick.

As Tania had taken both the 'guilt' and 'pleasure' out of the exercise, I found myself hastily revising the one I had in mind – masturbating to erotic fiction when I was supposed to be working. So instead I just said, 'Watching spoiled rich kids on reality TV.'

It was Gamine's turn next. Her name was Odette and she and her boyfriend, Claude, were from France. As we were all about to learn, that was about as far as Odette's English was going to take her. It appeared that Claude was equally clueless. All credit to Michelle, she spent a few patient minutes trying to explain to Odette what she meant by a 'guilty pleasure'. Finally Odette got it, exclaiming, '*Ah, oui! Le chocolat!*' which was also lame but at least relevant.

Geeky mum-to-be introduced herself as Maddie, and she told us in a heavy Yorkshire accent that her guilty pleasure was watching kids' movies. I stifled a groan. There weren't going to be too many laughs in this group.

And then it was Amazon lady's turn.

'My name is Bea,' she said, in a strong South African accent, 'and I like to swipe right when I'm taking a bath.'

I was the only one to burst into uncontrolled laughter. Bea looked at me and smiled. I smiled back. Suddenly we were co-conspirators in this dull situation. Things were looking up.

An awkward hush fell over the group for a few moments. I noticed Tania and Maddie exchanging raised eyebrows, while poor Odette looked totally befuddled. 'Wat deez zees mean?' she asked, hands raised questioningly in the air. Michelle shook her head quickly as if trying to erase the image of a naked Bea ordering sex from a cyber menu. Completely ignoring Odette, she thanked everyone for 'sharing' and then busily launched straight into her spiel. In hushed tones, she reminded us all of the 'gift' we had been given, eyes watery and twinkling as she described the beauty of childbirth, otherwise known as 'the most special moment of your lives', and how much she envied us for our magical lives ahead.

As Michelle wittered on about caring for the baby – she demonstrated nappy-changing using a hard plastic doll with entirely smooth genitalia – I drummed my fingers on my bump impatiently, and smiled as I got a big kick in return. Even my unborn child was bored out of her half-formed skull. When was Michelle going to get to the drugs? That's all I wanted to hear about: the pain relief during labour.

And then, as if on cue, Bea's deep voice rang out in a tone that meant business. 'Can we talk about the drugs now, please?'

Michelle paused for a moment, her frown line deepening, and with barely controlled impatience, replied, 'Yes, of course. I will be covering pain relief in the second part of the day.'

Bea looked at her watch. 'Is there any chance we can cover it now? I can't actually stay for the rest of the class.'

Our eyes met again, and I gave Bea a slight nod. I couldn't take much more of this rubbish either.

Barely trying to hide her irritation, Michelle described the different types of natural pain relief: water birth, hypnobirthing, massage, aromatherapy, etc. I allowed myself an undisguised yawn, earning a dark look from Michelle in return. David gave me a look that said, 'Stop behaving like a naughty child and pay attention,' and I wrinkled my nose at him in response. When was Michelle going to get to the epidural? And then suddenly, our teacher clapped her hands and announced a tea break.

What?

As everyone started to rise from the chairs, Bea spoke up.

'I think you have forgotten to talk about the epidural,' she said in a voice that could cut through granite.

Everyone sat down again.

Michelle looked awkward. 'Well, epidurals aren't for everyone,' she said, wringing her hands. Both Tania and Maddie nodded their heads vigorously at this.

'Well, an epidural may not be for everyone but it is certainly for me,' Bea countered, looking hard at Michelle.

'And me,' I squeaked, bravely siding with my new friend. If we were going down, we were going down together.

Bea shot me a grateful glance and I instantly felt rewarded for my courage.

Michelle sidestepped any further discussion by recommending that Bea have a 'little think' about the epidural, and Bea simply scowled back at her. Flustered, and clearly forgetting about the tea break, Michelle moved on to Tania.

'Soooo, let's talk about breast-feeding,' Michelle said in a high nervous pitch. 'Tania, what are your thoughts? Remember, there is no right or wrong answer.'

Bullshit.

Tania flicked back her hair in the manner of an American high-school cheerleader who has just humped the quarterback, and said, 'Of course, like any mother who wants the best for their baby, I am all for breast-feeding. I actually can't wait. Oh, and just to let you know, I have engaged a doula for the childbirth AND I'm having a water birth. No drugs. *Au natural* for me.'

I had never hated anyone more.

Maddie and Odette (once Michelle had explained to her what breast-feeding was by grabbing her own breasts) agreed that breast was best, and then with a big deep breath, Michelle turned to Bea.

Bea smiled pleasantly and answered, 'I have zero intention of breast-feeding.'

I looked at her open-mouthed. She was the bravest person I had ever met.

Tania went for the jugular first. Didn't Bea know that there were greater health benefits for breast-fed babies? Didn't she know that breast-feeding was the best gift a mother could give to her baby – the chance of life-long immunity to illness?

Without waiting for Bea to answer, Maddie joined in, thus pledging her allegiance to Tania. Didn't Bea know that a breast-fed baby has less chance of suffering from allergies? Or that it's the best way for a baby to bond with its mother?

Bea sat with her head cocked, as though she had heard it all before, and when she was finally allowed to speak, she said simply, in a slightly amused voice, 'I believe that everybody has the right to make their own choices. What I choose to do about breast-feeding is simply my own business, and nobody else's.'

After she said that, I felt the beginnings of a girl crush creeping up on me. When you're at a certain age, it is so much harder to find someone with whom you instantly feel any sort of affinity. I just knew Bea and I would hit it off, and I couldn't wait for the tea break to come so I could take her off into a corner and make her my new best friend purely on the basis of slagging off the other judgemental Jennies in the class.

But just when I thought the break was finally going to happen, Maddie opened her stupid big mouth again.

With a quick adjustment of her thick-rimmed glasses, she said snootily, 'And what about the father of your baby, Bea? Does he not get a choice?'

Bea went from sanguine to angry in a nanosecond. She whipped round at Maddie and replied angrily, 'The father of my baby lost his choices when he started fucking someone else when I was six months pregnant.'

Jesus. Nobody knew where to look after that.

Shaking her head impatiently, Bea gathered up her coat and bag, and, much to my dismay, marched straight out of the church hall.

I thought I would never see her again.

4

LONDON, NOW

It has been three hours since my chat with Bea and, despite her encouragement, I'm still not sure what to do about the motherhood book. I should probably talk to David about it, although he's been so distracted with work lately that I'm not sure what good it will do. I glance at the clock and my heart quickens when I realise it's almost six o'clock. David will be home in ten minutes! Over the last hour, I have managed to prise Anna away from her iPad long enough for us to make pizza together (pizza bases bought, *not* made from scratch – fuck you, Organics!) and every available surface is covered in tomato sauce, grated cheese, and half-chewed pieces of pepperoni.

Anna has also taken the time to venture into the freezer and busily scattered the contents of a giant bag of frozen peas all over the white wooden floor. Immediately I go into frantic mode. Skating over the thawing peas, I deposit Anna on the wipe-clean kitchen chair and give her back the iPad, which she greets with a squeal more appropriate for a long-lost family member. Then I race around like a lunatic, sweeping up the peas, hastily cleaning surfaces, and slotting all the dirty dishes into the dishwasher out of sight.

You see, David and I live in the type of house where socks never go missing and no UFOs (unidentified frozen objects) live in the freezer. In fact, nothing is ever mislaid, and everything is very clean. Every wall and surface in our tiny terraced house is so white, I sometimes have a sudden urge to put on sterile rubber gloves for fear of getting anything dirty.

Just as I close the dishwasher door, I hear a key turning. David's home. I tell Anna loudly to go and say hello to her daddy, but she sets her little mouth in a firm line and turns up the volume on her iPad. Sighing, I go to meet David in the hallway.

David walks in and wipes his feet (twice on each side) and then turns to close and lock the door behind him. He kisses me briefly but distractedly on the lips, his eyes scanning the hallway, searching for anything that might be out of place. As he picks up a tiny bit of muck off the floor, he asks me how my day has been. Shit, I want to tell him, but I can't because, as I've learned over the years, David is absolutely useless until he has 'settled back in' after a hectic day at work. Sometimes I feel I'm the modern-day equivalent of the 1950s housewife but without the nice dress, the make-up and the cooking ability. And so I wait.

I wait while he takes off his shoes and places them carefully on the mat. Then I watch him as he takes off his light jacket and flings it on the bottom of the stairs, which never fails to wind me up. For a man so fastidious, how on earth has he not learned to hang up his fucking coat? Sometimes I find myself measuring David's behaviour by flashes of annoyance. For example, David dropping his coat on the foot of stairs rather than hanging it in the coat cupboard. *Flash!* David picking up a few groceries for me but then leaving the shopping bags just inside the front door, rather than going the whole hog and putting them away in the kitchen. *Flash!* David folding the laundry but leaving Anna's clothes for me to put away ('I don't know where all her stuff goes!'). *Double flash!*

I hate feeling so irritated by these little things, and I do my best not to bring up how much they bother me, but the problem is all those flashes tend to build up into one big catastrophic flash, and then the fireworks begin. Don't get me wrong, there are flashes of love too: David who always wants to know about my day, without giving much thought to his own; David who tries so hard with his only daughter, even though she carelessly rejects his affections time and again; and David who always takes my side during debates with difficult clients or rows I have with rude people (like the ones I always have with those arseholes travelling solo, who insist on using the wide Tube gates, the only ones accessible to people in wheel-chairs, carrying suitcases, and wheeling buggies). Yet lately these flashes of love have become clouded by the flashes of annoyance, and it's exhausting.

I follow David into the kitchen and watch his futile attempt to give Anna a kiss on one of her flushed chubby cheeks. Over his shoulder, I see Anna is fully engaged on the iPad, watching one of her favourite videos, which involves other children opening small pieces of plastic. David's chances of a good reception from her are nil but, in a way, I admire him for persevering. As predicted, before David can make contact, Anna gives him 'the hand'. Wounded, he raises his head, and looks to me for support. I shrug. Although I admire his efforts, frankly, he should know better than to try to go near Anna when she's on the iPad. It's like trying to cuddle a lion when it's mauling fresh kill.

Sighing, David walks over to the fridge and takes out some cheese.

I choose this moment to fill David in about my call with Harriet and the book on motherhood.

'And then Anna bit me...' I say plaintively, finally finishing offloading my tales of woe.

'Let's see,' he says, through a mouthful of cheese. David always eats cheese when he comes home from work – another part of the ritual.

I lift up my top to show him the teeth-mark.

'Wow, that's a new low,' he says, glaring at Anna. 'Still, her teeth-marks are pretty straight; hopefully she won't need braces,' he adds thoughtfully.

I glare at him in turn.

'What is she now? Irrational nutcase-turned-cannibal?' he says, noticing my fury and very sensibly backtracking.

Ever since our daughter has 'turned' from angel of the universe/daddy's girl to crazy psycho with intent, David has become increasingly frustrated and mystified by her behaviour. Suddenly, she doesn't want her daddy any more – it is all about Mummy. This suits neither of us as I am more than happy for him to do bath time and story while I do the nice quick and easy 'night night'! This new development has caused endless tension and stress at bedtime when Anna screams her lungs out if her daddy so much as glances in her direction.

'It's just a phase,' I have explained to him over and over.

'Phase, my bollocks,' he replies angrily. 'It's been going on for two years! If we were living in the US, she'd be on prescription drugs and have her own therapist.'

'So, do you think I should the pitch for the book?'

'Why wouldn't you?' he says in a nonchalant way that makes me want to start throwing things.

'Have you not been listening to me? It's a fucking disastrous topic – motherhood, for fuck's sake!' I hiss, the day's stress accumulating so now I'm ready to explode.

'Don't swear in front of Anna!' David says in his most self-righteous tone. This only fans the flames as, out of the pair of us, he is definitely the more sweary.

'Fuck off, David, you hypocrite. Anyway, she's on the iPad – she can't even hear us!' I say.

As if on cue, Anna looks up with big sparkly eyes and says, 'Fuck!'

David and I look at each other, and with well-practised neutral expressions, reply, 'That's a grown-up word, Anna.'

Anna stares at us with utter contempt, and returns to her essential viewing of two small Canadian girls re-enacting the story of *Frozen* with three tubs of slime and a shopping trolley with eyes.

'Anyway, you were saying about the pitch...' David says, his voice muffled as he bends over to rearrange the cutlery in the dishwasher. *Flash!*

As patiently as I can, I explain to my husband why my experiences of being a mother are not something I want to share with the world.

'But you've been a mother for four years. You must have something to say!' David answers, carefully washing his hands in the kitchen sink with half the hand wash, before plucking the yellow towel from its place on a hook above the sink for drying off his hands.

Every towel is colour-coded in our house according to its function. Green is for placing vegetables on after they have been washed (and, for the record, I had never washed a vegetable in my life before I met David); white is for drying the surfaces; blue is for mopping up the odd spill on the floor; and yellow is for drying our hands after we wash them in the kitchen sink.

Don't get me started on what goes on inside the cupboards. It's like *Sleeping with the Enemy* on speed.

'Yes, I am a mother in the technical sense, but I'm shite at it,' I say through gritted teeth, so Anna doesn't hear. 'How can I write about something that I'm no good at? I would be like a travel writer who is afraid of public transport, or a mountain climber with a fear of heights, or a prostitute who has taken a vow of celibacy.'

But what I really mean is that I'm afraid – absolutely fucking terrified – to reveal how hard I find being a mother; how every day of my life is an enormous test in patience, love and restraint, and how ashamed and guilty I feel when I fail that test over and over again.

David crosses to the oven, straightens the oven gloves, which are dangling at a slight angle, and seemingly satisfied that order has been at last restored, turns back and looks at me thoughtfully.

'How much does it pay?' he asks.

I tell him and his eyes light up.

'But this isn't about the money!' I say, pleadingly.

'Listen, Saoirse, I know this isn't the book you thought would have your name on, but sometimes it has to be about the money,' he says.

I know he is right. We need the money. With salaries slashed and lay-offs sweeping through David's company, and my rainy-day savings all but gone, I know we need the extra cash.

To top it all off, our 'compact' three-bedroom house is located in what estate agents call 'a black hole' when it comes to schools. This means that getting Anna into a decent local primary school is nigh on impossible, leaving us to face the horror of sending her to the 'special measures' school down the road – the one beside the chippy, where all the parents light up their joints under the 'No smoking' sign in the playground – or, even worse, the prospect of private-school fees.

Anna scuppers any chance of further conversation with a shriek of panic. 'No Wi-Fi!' she screams over and over, and then, 'Dadd-eeee!!!' With a superhuman leap, David crosses the kitchen and takes the iPad off her to remedy the situation as fast as he can, clearly grateful that Anna actually wants him for something. Within seconds, Wi-Fi has been restored and all is right with the world ('You can go now, Daddy'). Clearly forgetting what we have just been discussing, David announces that his mother has been in touch and wants us to visit this weekend.

Irritated by the dismissal, I say, 'Oh, for fuck's sake, do we have to?'

And he says, annoyed, 'Yes, Saoirse, she hasn't seen Anna in weeks, and we should visit her. She's my mother.'

And with every fibre of my being, I bite back my knee-jerk response, which would have been, 'Well, she's not your *real* mother.' Instead, I just take a deep breath and look away.

I don't hate many people – for long periods, anyway – but Rose is one of those people that I struggle to relate to on any level. While David admits to not having a close relationship with his adoptive mother, he still feels duty-bound to visit her, especially since his father died a few years ago. Rose, now in her mid-seventies, is still in annoyingly good health.

So once a month we all pile into our clapped-out Ford Focus and drive the two hours to Rose's damp, cream pebble-dashed semi in Oxfordshire to go through the charade of pretending we all like each other.

I watch this little charade play out every few weeks; the polite greeting at the door, the impatient smile thrown at Anna whenever she has the nerve to speak or, God forbid, cry or scream; the endless offers of cups of tea; and finally, after an excruciating two hours, the curt farewell, the door closing firmly behind us before our goodbyes have faded from our lips.

After I begrudgingly agree to visit my mother-in-law, a tense silence follows, only to be broken by David complaining about the amount of mouldy fruit in the fridge. *Flash!* Being around him is getting harder and harder. It never used to be this way. In fact, it's hard to believe we have been together six years. It's becoming more difficult to reconcile the man I first met with the one he has now become.

Things were different before Anna came along. *We* were different. In fact, I am struggling to remember how we fell in love in the first place.

5

LONDON, SIX YEARS AGO

I first met David in my local curry house, which handily happened to be right underneath the East London flat I was living in. It was a cold, rainy night, and I was dressed only in my favourite crimson fleecy pyjamas. I had popped downstairs to Vinda-YOU for my usual Friday-night curry and this time I had decided to stay and eat in its lovely velvetiness and soft lighting, rather than getting a takeaway. My achingly trendy flatmate, Joss, had a 'friend' round, and the creaky bed springs and over-exaggerated moans (him) were getting to me.

I threw a long coat over my pyjamas, grabbed my laptop and popped downstairs for some food and inspiration.

A year before, I had broken up with my boyfriend, Hugo, the man I thought I would marry. Hugo was a sparkly blue-eyed Cambridge graduate who came from the type of family who wore wellies and tweed caps, and holidayed in the Lake District. After a year of being together, I was 80 per cent sure Hugo was 'the one', and as I'd never been 80 per cent sure about anything I felt those odds were good enough.

When I told Hugo I was going to leave my fancy banking job to pursue my dream of being a writer, he was horrified and spent weeks trying dissuade me. After all, we were the 'power couple' that were 'going places'. I tried to listen, but while I had thought my future was with Hugo, I couldn't see my future without me as a writer.

After I left Hugo and chucked in my lucrative job, I gathered up all my savings, answered an ad on Gumtree and moved into a tiny two-bedroom flat above a curry house, Vinda-YOU, in East London.

My new flatmate, Joss, was the first hipster I had ever met. Young and trendy, she wore a uniform of leggings or skinny jeans, with long-sleeved tops underneath T-shirts emblazoned with clever messages that I didn't understand. On her feet she wore a range of battered ankle boots. Her dyed-red hair was perpetually piled on top of her head and sometimes she wore thick-rimmed glasses to offset the look. To my eyes, she was fantastically dressed but utterly unemployable, so I was surprised to hear that she worked for a government research centre, in the missing persons department.

As she was too cool to hang out with the likes of middle-aged me, save for the odd Monday night when we both crashed out in front of the TV, our paths rarely crossed. It was the perfect arrangement, apart from the sagging couches, creaky beds and the perpetual smell of curry.

So, there I was, in my mid-thirties and single, living in a dingy cheap-as-chips flat, sharing with a 'young person'. As for my love life, I wasn't going to give it another thought. Besides, the Hugo episode had taught me that 80 per cent of being 'the one' wasn't enough, and perhaps one day I should try to find that extra 20 per cent. Little did I know that I was about to meet the man who would fast become the love of my life, my 100 per cent.

* * *

When I pushed open the heavy glass door of Vinda-YOU, I was relieved to see only one other customer there: a man sitting by himself. He looked up briefly as I walked in and then went back to his poppadoms. Good. I could do without the distraction of loud conversations. I deliberately sat down at a table for two in the far corner of the room, just in case this other customer started yabbering on his phone.

Vijay, the manager, came by with his notepad and pen, greeted me by name and asked me if I wanted 'the usual'. I made a mental note to stop coming here so often – he'd be sending me a Christmas card next.

While I was waiting for my food, I started to type, content to feel the smooth keys under my fingertips. And just as I was getting into the flow, to my intense irritation I was interrupted.

'Is this seat taken?'

You've got to be kidding me.

I looked up to find the same man – the other (and only) customer – standing by the chair opposite me.

So annoyed was I by the interruption that I really didn't take him in. Instead I just glared at him in response, hoping he would take the hint and piss off. But he just kept standing there, calmly waiting. I resigned myself to the fact that I would have to reply in some way.

'I'm sorry, but I'm really busy,' I said, and waved my hand violently at the laptop screen just to reinforce how busy I was. He remained unfazed.

'I see that,' he said. 'But I make it my business to eat with complete strangers in restaurants, and it would be disappointing if you are the first one to turn me away.'

I laughed. I don't know why. I think it was the way he said it: as if he was making the most reasonable and logical request and I was the one who was being the stick-in-the-mud. Besides, when I looked at him more closely, I saw he had nice brown eyes, neatly cut dark brown hair, and dimples. I'm a sucker for dimples. Hugo was blond with no dimples. So I thought, why not? I gave in, and agreed he could join me for dinner. His name was David Addington and he was intense. Looking back, I would say that he wrenched rather than swept me off my feet. Our first conversation wasn't so much small talk between strangers as an interrogation. Every time I answered a question I felt like he was ticking off some sort of mental wife-suitability list in his head. He quizzed me on my age, my job, my living situation, boyfriends/husbands/ex-husbands, kids, religion, and family background. At one point I wondered if he was considering me as a candidate for surrogacy. But there was something sexy about this first exchange – it had been a long time since someone took such an interest in me – and I found myself responding to him, almost daring him to see how intimate our conversation would become.

Then it was my turn, and with every answer he gave, I ticked off a mental list of my own. Age? Thirty-eight. Job? Works in technology for a social media company, i.e. not a loser – tick! Lives by himself in a house in south-west London (homeowner – tick!). Several exes but has never made it up the aisle. When I asked why, he gave me an intense look and said, 'I have very high standards,' which made me feel a bit wobbly.

When the topic of kids came up (this was a bit of a deal breaker, as I did want kids, eventually), he said he would like just the one. As I hadn't really given the number much thought, I didn't go into this further. I remember just feeling relieved that he was open to the idea, which was ridiculous, given that this was the *first* time we had met. We were the same religion (this would please my mother no end – tick!), but he regarded himself as a committed atheist (this would not please my mother – I vowed to keep that one to myself) and I was a lazy Catholic.

The family background part took some time to explain. Mine was pretty straightforward (only child, father died when I was little) but his was more complex: adopted as a baby by Derek, an engineer, and Rose, a primary school teacher, a middle-class couple living on the outskirts of Oxfordshire.

At the time I couldn't put my finger on why I was so drawn to him, but later on I figured that it was a mixture of charisma and fragility. He exuded charisma from every fibre of his being. Not conventionally good-looking – medium height, receding hairline, lips too-full for his angular face – his attractiveness lay in his single-mindedness. He was a man who knew what he wanted.

We talked until the lights dimmed and the chairs were placed on the tables. When Vijay's polite coughs turned into impatient hand gestures, we finally got the hint and left. At the bottom of the stairs to my flat, David took my number as if it was the most natural thing in the world.

After that, things moved pretty fast, mostly because we were both older and couldn't be bothered with 'playing the game'. David couldn't give a toss about the 'three-day rule', and texted me first thing the following morning to arrange another date. I found his keenness flattering and refreshing – how nice to meet a guy who was above all the gameplay bullshit.

From the get-go, we saw each other as often as we could.

One of the things I loved most about David was his sheer fearlessness and impulsivity. We could be on our way to a restaurant, and he'd take my hand and lead me into some beautiful, historical building that I'd never seen before, or dance me into a salsa class that he had happened to find out about the previous day. He had a keen love of art, theatre, food and music, and during that happy period we really made the most of what London had to offer. Being a stay-at-home-and-reading-a-good-book kind of person, I found his enthusiasm opened my eyes. I had gone from being a resident to a tourist, and I loved every moment of it.

Everything was new with David. The food – who knew I liked Korean food, and spicy sushi, or even spicy anything? – the music, the theatre... everything was fun and spontaneous, and I loved it. I used to be a korma girl and now I was a vindaloo. He was just so refreshingly passionate about everything, including my career change. I had been so used to people like Hugo telling me I was crazy to fulfil my dream as a writer that it came as a pleasant surprise when David told me how much he admired me for pursuing my ambition. Because of him, I became even more driven, determined to make a success of it.

Another thing I liked about him was how he took care of me. I had always been fiercely independent. With Hugo, I was always the one who took charge, made dinner reservations, organised nights out and so on. But now David insisted on doing all those things instead. It was a relief for someone else to take charge for a change, for me to be at the centre of someone else's universe.

To my surprise, even Joss liked David, calling him 'not too bad for a geek', which was the ultimate compliment, coming from her. When David was over, the two of them would start all these tech conversations, which I couldn't give a shit about, so I wasn't really surprised when they ended up exchanging business cards on the day I finally moved out of the flat.

Living with David was hard in the beginning. While he was kind, protective, funny, and a good chef, it turned out that he was a neat freak, and frankly, it was killing me. Everything I touched seemed to send him into a frenzy: the dishwasher was wrongly stacked, the dish towels were being used for the wrong function, and the groceries were not being put in the right part of the fridge.

Following one spectacular row about the socks that had come out of the wash furled rather than unfurled, I'd had enough. I gave him two choices: to stop being so bloody anal, or to be single for the rest of his life.

Following that episode, David started to ease up (in David terms) a little around the house. This meant that he sort of went underground when it came to the tidying. In other words, he became a stealth control freak. Instead of whingeing about the disorderly dishwasher, he rearranged it when I wasn't around, or at least would wait until I had left the kitchen. The same went with his wardrobe, the exact alignment of the bathroom towels, and a whole host of other household items that I didn't give a shit about.

This arrangement suited us both: he still had the freedom to exert his control-freakishness, and I didn't have to deal with the nagging. In return for these small allowances, I tried to make more of an effort to use the right dish towel for its specific function, unfurl the socks before washing, and of course take my shoes off in the house. But the biggest concession David made was to allow me to have my bedside table the way I wanted it –messy and cluttered. This meant I could stack up my books to toppling point, bring my work notes to bed to read, and display my box of tissues without fear of retribution.

For a time, there was peace. Instead of spending every single moment together, we became more independent. A major foodie, David would take off on a Saturday or Sunday afternoon to browse London's trendy food markets, and I would trot down to our local café with a good book; both of us perfectly happy in our own company for those few hours.

When I discovered I was pregnant after a year of living together, we married quietly and uneventfully in a civil ceremony in a beautiful historic town hall in central London with my mother and Rose, David's mother, as witnesses. After watching Rose clean the sparkling silver cutlery with her napkin, sending back her glass because 'it had smudges on it', and lamenting the fact that there was no tablecloth on the ornate glass table, I finally understood why David was as anal as he was. As my mother muttered later, 'It's not from the wind he got it, Saoirse.'

After the wedding, things settled between David and me; there was a good sense of being properly bonded together. We were nicer to each other, and more willing to let the little things go. This feeling of contentment lasted right up until Anna was born. But I hadn't predicted that a newborn was just the catalyst necessary to send David back into control freak high-frequency mode, or that I would become a certified nutcase, for that matter. Not long after we brought Anna home from hospital, I told the man I had just married that I wanted a divorce.

6

LONDON, FOUR YEARS AGO

Looking back, I realise the trouble between David and me began from the very first moment we saw Anna. It had been a long labour and, in the end, she was suctioned out. To be honest, she wasn't the best-looking baby I'd ever seen. As I recall, after a good minute of silence, the dialogue between myself and David went something like this:

David: 'What's wrong with her nose?'

Me: 'Poor thing, she looks like a boxer that's been through at least eight rounds in the ring.'

Husband: 'Well, she didn't get that nose from me.'

Me: 'What are you trying to say?'

Husband: 'Well, your nose has always been on the large side.'

Me: 'What? Since when? Fuck off.'

A moment of tense silence.

Me: 'I knew I should have had a caesarean. Those babies always come out without a mark on them.'

Then the nurse, who was busy doing things to my vagina that I have since blocked out, interjected firmly that our baby's face and head was only swollen on account of her being suctioned out, adding, 'The swelling will go down over the next couple of days.'

As soon as she had left the room, I burst into tears. 'Thank God she's going to get better-looking,' I sobbed. 'I thought she was going to get the shit kicked out of her in school.'

I held her closely to me and watched her poor swollen eyelids flicker as she slept in my arms. In that moment, I was overwhelmed by sensations I had never felt before. For the first time in my life I felt I was capable of murder. I would kill for her without blinking. I also realised that I would choose her over my husband in a heartbeat, which is exactly what ended up happening. Then things got really bad.

It took precisely three days for the newborn baby 'glow' to wear off. I had read all about the impact of sleep deprivation and the roller coaster of emotions associated with the 'new mum' experience, but I had absorbed this in an abstract sense. I mean, I wasn't naïve – I knew it was going to be tough – but *I* was tough. Uncertainty was my friend. I had moved to London from Ireland by myself in my twenties and travelled the world as a marketing expert. I had walked out of my well-paid job and a long-term relationship with Hugo to pursue my dream of writing full time; and I had managed to get through living with David and all his weird quirks.

I was hardy, independent and up for a challenge. I was a *survivor*. Of course, a new baby was not going to change that. But nothing prepared me for the sheer sense of possession I felt as soon as I held my little girl in my arms for the first time. Never before had I had something that was totally and utterly mine. David was a mere bystander, an unwanted irritation. Besides, I knew that I loved her far more than he ever could.

It took me about three days to realise I had absolutely no idea how to look after her – not the first clue. It turned out that David was as clueless as I was. For some reason, David kept asking me questions that 'as a woman' he thought I was supposed to know.

'Saoirse, why is she crying?'

'I have no fucking idea, David.'

'Saoirse, how do you change a nappy?'

'I have no fucking idea, David.'

'Saoirse, why is Anna not sleeping?'

'I have no fucking idea, David.'

'Saoirse, why is she not breast-feeding properly?'

'I have no fucking idea, David. All I know is that my boobs are in absolute agony, and I hate every second of it.'

By the time David had finished his two weeks of paternity leave, we were throwing things at each other, with the odd brother/sister-type fisticuffs thrown in. Anna was in the Moses basket beside our bed and every stir and sniffle had me racing to her side. I resented David for sleeping so peacefully while I became more and more sleep-deprived.

It also didn't help that David had reverted to his super-control-freak ways, but this time targeted at all things baby related. If Anna spat her dummy out and it landed on the cushion, it had to be sterilised straight away or if she spat up (even the tiniest amount) on her Babygro, it had to be washed instantly. He insisted on us both washing our hands before either of us could pick her up. If all that wasn't enough, David became an authority on breast-feeding, giving me 'pointers' as to which way I should hold Anna. When I sobbed that I couldn't do it as the pain was so bad, he piled on the guilt, trotting out everything that the breast-feeding Nazis had said in the antenatal group, coupled with whatever bullshit he had picked up online.

Between David's fussiness, my chafed and bleeding hands, the disastrous breast-feeding, and the sleep deprivation, I knew it was only a matter of time before I murdered him and buried him under his sparkling white floorboards. What the hell was happening to us? Before Anna came along, I was the only one who had mattered. He was the one who took care of me – spent hours listening to my crashing anxieties and terrible fears, and was my absolutely favourite person to have dinner with. We joked about being 'the same person', and spent many happy minutes wondering if there was really such a thing as a soulmate. I never thought that specialness would ever die away, but here we were, teetering on the brink.

I hoped that things might improve when David went back to work, but they only got worse. More resentment built as I watched him enjoy his usual forty-minute shower-and-shave routine when I would be lucky to have a shower at all. I hated him for leaving the house with only his wallet and keys to think about, when I had to remember to pack all the millions of items Anna needed. The bottom line was that *nothing* had changed for him: life had just trotted smartly on. But I had been left behind.

The final straw came when David announced one sunny Saturday morning over breakfast, when Anna was three weeks old, that he was off to the other side of London to check out a new food market. He might as well have told me he was visiting a whorehouse.

'What? You're going out?' I shouted at him in disbelief. 'All day?'

I was aghast. This had been the first week I had looked after Anna all by myself and I was ready for the nuthouse. I hadn't exactly told David, but I had dreams of a long uninterrupted shower and blissful snoozes between feeds. There was no fucking way he was going out to wander around some poncy market while I did another full shift of baby duty.

'I don't know what you're so upset about,' he said, irritatingly calm. 'I mean, I've been working all week, and I could do with a break.'

Big mistake.

'What? And you think I've been sitting on my arse all day? I'm up all night. She barely fucking sleeps. You, on the other hand, get to sleep all fucking night because of your precious job, which, by the way, you're *lucky* to have because you get to go to the toilet alone, you get to have lunch in peace, and you can have an *adult conversation.*'

I stopped to take another breath. The floodgates had opened and they were releasing three weeks of pent-up angry lava. There was no stopping me now.

'I, on the other hand, haven't brushed my teeth for weeks; barely get time to eat, and I'm walking in circles every day like a gormless Irish setter because she refuses to sleep in her fucking Moses basket. Oh, and my tits are on fire,' I continued, wanting to punch him very hard in the nuts.

David gave me a dark look. 'Well, what am I supposed to do about all of that? I can't feed her because you're doing that. I can't walk her in her pram because I'm fucking working all day; and even when I am home, I can't help out because she screams blue murder every time I try to hold her,' he said angrily.

In the mist of the red fog, I knew there was some truth to what he saying. Every time he tried to pick her up she screamed, and part of me knew I was to blame for that. I did feel very strongly that Anna was mine and only mine. But then Anna, who had been sleeping upstairs, started to wail and all logical thought went straight out the window.

'Do you know how you can help me, David? You can start by *not* going to that *shit* food market and giving me a fucking break by taking care of *your* daughter for at least five minutes,' I said, feeling the heat of rage prickling my skin.

David took one look at my red, twisted face, glanced at the baby monitor, which had reached 'apoplectic' on the sound measurements, turned on his heel and walked straight out of the kitchen.

For a moment, I felt relief. Finally, someone else was going to pick up Anna and change her nappy. Maybe I would get that snooze in after all.

But then I heard the jingling of what sounded suspiciously like keys, and then the sound of the front door slamming.

I raced out of the kitchen into the hallway in total disbelief. Instead of tending to Anna, David had taken his keys and walked straight out of the house.

Then I snapped.

Leaving Anna in hysterics, I ran out of the front door, wild with fury. I could just about make out his retreating form halfway down the street.

'Fuck you, David!' I screamed. 'I want a fucking divorce.'

And do you know what he did? He turned around, gave a salute of acknowledgement, and then gave me his middle finger in response.

I turned round so violently that I almost slammed into our elderly neighbour, Joseph, who had been standing just outside his gate, obviously coming out for a bit of a snoop. I am convinced Joseph was a headmaster in his previous life. He has that sort of officious air.

'Everything OK, Saoirse? I heard a bit of commotion out here,' he said, in the manner of someone used to handing out detention.

'All fine here, Joseph,' I said, breezily. 'Just some hooded youths having an argument.'

I was sure that Joseph was just the sort of man who blamed everything on hooded youths. My gamble paid off and Joseph spent a few seconds tutting about the youth of today and so on and so forth. I made my excuses – 'Crying baby, Joseph. Must dash!' –and raced back into the house.

As I held Anna's poor frantic mouth to my breast, feeling jolt after jolt of pain with each suck, the determined anger suddenly began to abate. I hung my head over my suckling newborn and cried and cried.

After that row, our relationship changed from loving husband and wife to two people who just happened to be married. I moved into the spare room with Anna and avoided David whenever I could. It was easier than I thought. We existed in different time zones, after all. I would be up with Anna every two hours at night, while he was sleeping in our bedroom, and I would be asleep when he got up for work. Often I was in bed when he got home at 7 p.m. In the space of a few weeks, we had gone from best friends and lovers to flatmates who didn't much like each other.

I desperately needed a shoulder to cry on. I had told my husband, the father of my baby, that I wanted a divorce, for goodness' sake, and I was struggling just to get through the day. Very few of my work friends had kids, and I had lost touch with the ones who did. All the visitors I'd had when Anna was first born had faded away and moved on with their baby-free lives. Although I had met David's friends on many occasions, I didn't feel close enough to any of them to reveal how badly I was struggling.

The shame of admitting that I couldn't do what millions of women had been doing over the centuries was too much. I had tried to open up to my mother about Anna's dreadful night sleeping, and she had told me uselessly, albeit kindly, that things would get better. She had offered to come over and give me a hand, but I declined, mortified that my own mother would see her fiercely independent daughter in such a state. After all, my mother had raised me practically by herself, and worked full time. How could I confess how desperate I felt?

I had so many friends yet nobody I could really confide in. Unconsciously I had divided up my friends into groups for different purposes. I had my banking friends for drinks and larks; my writing friends for work discussions; and my Irish friends for relationship advice. The only problem was I hadn't got a friend to rant to about babies *and* shit husbands. I felt totally isolated.

Even Jen, my oldest and best friend from Ireland, couldn't relate to my new circumstances. Jen and I had been 'best friends, best friends, never ever break friends' since our first year at primary school. As I was an only child, Jen was the closest I had to a sister, and I clung to her through every formative stage of adolescence. When Jen tried on make-up for the first time, so did I. When Jen tried her first alcoholic drink at the age of fourteen

– bravely breaking The Pledge, a vow Catholic children take to abstain from alcohol before the age of eighteen – I was right along with her. If we were sinners, we sinned together. When Jen had her first kiss (with tongues), I grabbed the nearest hapless fella and did the same.

And that was how it was, all the way up until I moved to London. For all her daring, Jen was a home bird and had no intention of leaving her native Ireland. Besides, she had got herself a job as a personal shopper for the Irish glitterati and there was no way she'd give that up. Before I had Anna, Jen would come over and stay with us every couple of months. Thankfully, Jen and David always got on well, Jen finding David's 'quirks' hilarious rather than ominous ('he's a bit of a neat freak but not in a serial killer sort of way'); and David rating Jen as a 'good house guest' because she 'makes her own bed', 'doesn't slam doors' and 'doesn't leave coffee-stained mugs in the sink'.

Yet things started to change between me and Jen when I had Anna. For as long as I have known her, Jen has never wanted children, going so far as calling them 'shit factories'. I remember once having a deep and mean-ingful discussion with her about it when we were both pissed. David and I had been talking about trying for a baby and it had made me realise how much I wanted one. Jen had looked thoughtful for a bit, and said, 'It's tough to describe, but there has never been any part of me that wants children. I don't seem to possess the same feelings about babies that other people have. It's just the way it is.'

And because of the way she explained it, I didn't feel sad or sorry for her. I respected her: she felt the way she felt, and that was it.

What I hadn't bargained for was how much our friendship would change when Anna was born. I would see the texts from her flashing up but barely had time to read them, let alone reply. How could she ever under-stand what I was going through? Keeping Anna alive was as much as I could cope with. Even if I had wanted to text Jen back, I was too sleep-deprived to write anything coherent.

One particularly bad day, the landline rang at 6.30 p.m., just as I was about to put Anna in the bath. I ignored it. The only thing worse than a landline ringing when there is a new baby in the house, is the cheery and over-enthusiastic knock of the postman when both mother and baby are desperately trying to get some sleep. Then the landline rang again. Swearing prolifically, I wrapped my naked daughter in a towel and walked begrudgingly downstairs to pick up the phone. It was Jen.

'Hey, stranger! I've been trying to get in touch with you for days,' she said, traffic noises in the background.

'Oh, hi, how are you?' I replied, trying to keep hold of the receiver and a wriggly baby at the same time.

'Fine, fine. You'll never guess what happened in the pub just now. Do you remember Liam from uni? The one who we all used to fancy? Well, I just bumped into him and he asked me out on a date. Told him I'd think about it. What do you think? He's not as good-looking as he used to be. I mean, sexy, svelte twenty-year-old Liam with the trendy blond hair is now early forties, chubby, balding Liam, but he's still a nice guy, you know?'

While she babbled on, I was suddenly struck with a terrible feeling of clarity. I didn't give a *fuck* about some guy I couldn't even remember, or her love life, for that matter.

Stifling my frustration, I said as nicely as I could that I needed to get Anna to bed, and would it be OK to call her back a bit later. And that would have been the end of it, except at that moment Jen decided to quiz me about motherhood in a way she obviously felt was amusing.

'What? Sure, it's only six thirty,' she laughed. 'My mother used to have me up until all hours, on her lap in front of the telly.'

'Well,' I said, trying to match her lightness of tone, 'if I don't get Anna into bed by seven o'clock, she will get overtired and will be up on the hour every hour, and then I will be fit for the nuthouse!'

'Oh, Saoirse,' Jen laughed, 'you're *such* a first-time mum!'

It was those words that neatly summarised the growing chasm between us. The great kids versus no kids divide. Jen, one of the only people in the whole world who had always 'got' me – knew what I was thinking before I opened my mouth and always said the right thing when I was feeling bad about myself – suddenly didn't get me any more.

YES! I wanted to scream. I *am* a first-time mum. I live with the fear and guilt of this new role every waking minute. Do you know, Jen, that every night before I go to sleep I lie awake in bed ticking off all the ways I might harm Anna or how she might be harmed by others? No? Well, I could slip and fall and drop her down the stairs, or I could forget to put the brake on the buggy and she could roll right into traffic, or I might accidentally drop her out of the sling when I'm bending down. Do you know why I haven't set foot in the car since I had Anna? It's because I am *afraid* of crashing it and killing her.

And don't talk to me about other people, Jen, because they all have the potential to harm my child. A thug might pull out a knife and try to stab her. Or the postman, who I've had a right go at for knocking too loudly every bloody morning, might decide this is the house he wants to mail bomb. Or a terrorist might mow her down in our local shopping mall. Don't you see, Jen? I am plagued by the non-stop nagging guilt that I am in the wrong job. I have been made head of security for this beautiful little girl but nobody has given me the training. All in all, I am FAILING my baby, Jen. Did you know that? Your best friend from the age of six, who has never failed at anything in her life, is flunking out, and worst still, she can't talk to anybody about it.

The thoughts raced but the words stuck in my throat. I knew she could never understand. In the end, Anna's tired wailing brought the call to a swift conclusion. I told Jen I'd call her later, but I never did. After the Jen disaster, I felt an overwhelming compulsion to find some like-minded people – some proof that I was not the only one who was struggling. In short, I needed the type of group that would sit around and bitch about their partners. Despite my initial dislike of the antenatal crew, I decided in desperation to attend the next meeting: the three-week baby meet-and-greet. Maybe they weren't as bad as I had first thought. How wrong I was.

7

LONDON, FOUR YEARS AGO

When I arrived at the gloomy church hall, Tania and Maddie were already there with their babies. Tania's baby boy is called Heath, and Maddie's little girl is called Gardenia. Both of them were happily breast-feeding. There was no sign of Odette. I would find out later that she had hot-footed it back to France for the birth and hadn't been seen since. I forced myself to smile a greeting and then spent the rest of the time feeling like the new girl at school who didn't know anyone.

To me, it seemed as though they both had it all worked out. Each of them had read every single baby book on the market, competitively swapping baby tips. Tania, who had no more qualifications than the rest of us in motherhood, would say things like, 'I find Gina a miracle worker when it comes to the sleep routine,' while Maddie would parry, 'Really? I have to say Gina didn't work for me, but Tilly's advice was invaluable.' And so on. Their babies were only waking once in the night – the ultimate badge of honour for new mums. They had cracked the parenting code and had been awarded the holy grail of mostly uninterrupted sleep.

When I dared to venture how tough breast-feeding was, Tania cooed sympathetically, while laying a nurturing hand on my shoulder, which I instantly wanted to bat away, while Maddie cried, 'Persevere! It's the best thing for your baby – the greatest gift a mother can give.' To which I replied, 'I think the gift of sleep is probably more valuable,' and they cooed and clucked and exchanged sympathetic looks, bonded together in the knowledge that they had got it right and I had got it wrong.

But maybe I was being too sensitive. Fine, they had the baby thing sussed, but what about their partners? Surely, there were moments where they wanted to drive a stake through their new-daddy hearts too?

'Oh, Giles has been so fantastic,' Tania gushed. 'He *loves* being a dad. Totally *obsessed* with Heath!'

Maddie's response was so similar that I dare not bore you with it.

And then they brought up Bea, and I started to feel a flicker of hope. Had they seen her? How was she doing? But all they wanted to do was bitch about her: how rude she had been in the antenatal class, and imagine just walking out like that...

I ignored them until they stopped.

'So, what's Anna's sleeping pattern like?' Maddie asked, nodding at Anna's flickering eyelids.

'Non-existent,' I said, hoping a short response would shut her up. But it didn't end there. In an effort to 'cure' Anna's 'poor sleeping habits' Tania announced grandly that the rest of the coffee meeting should be devoted to finding 'sound sleeping strategies' to help 'poor Saoirse' deal with her 'challenging baby'. That's when I finally had enough.

Channelling Bea, I stood up and said with just the right amount of sarcasm, 'But Anna *is* in a routine. She wakes up five times a night without fail. She's regular as clockwork. As a shit sleeper, she is bang on cue.' As their mouths fell open, I got up, flicked my hair and pushed Anna's pram out of that stupid, echoey church hall for good. I made a decision never to see those two smug cows again. It was hard enough that they had triumphed where I had failed.

Incidentally, the day after that disastrous meet-up, David bumped into Giles, Tania's husband, on the Tube. Giles told David that he and Tania hadn't slept since the baby was born, and had to hire a night nanny to get them through the nights. All this 'sleeping through the night' stuff was bullshit. Tania hadn't cracked the code, she had faked it. She was that girl in school who pretended to get her period or lose her virginity first just so she could lord it over her impressionable friends. And I had fallen for it hook, line and sinker. But rather than feeling angry about the pretence of it all, it had made me feel sad and hopeless. Is that what everyone did, then? Make up some bullshit story about how great they were at parenting to hide the fact they were struggling? Was I the only idiot that was upfront and honest about how tough I was finding it?

I retreated further into my isolation. I ignored all the baby-group meet-up emails and trudged around the narrow streets with Anna every day, trying to get her to sleep. I had the world's most exciting and cosmopolitan city on my doorstep and it had shrunk to the size of half an acre. If I ventured any further, I would feel threatened. I started to shop online rather than face the ordeal of the supermarket. My biggest fear was Anna crying in public. Crying attracted attention, and I couldn't bear it. Every tut or glare decimated my confidence.

Prior to having Anna, I had enjoyed the anonymity of London life. It was the antithesis of Ireland, where two degrees of separation can get a little bit claustrophobic. It was liberating to know that nobody knew or really gave a shit about you. You could walk onto the Tube one day dressed as a half-alien half-human playing the banjo and the most you might get is an impatient rustle of the *Metro* newspaper. But put a baby into the mix and the invisibility cloak no longer exists.

Whenever I was out in public, I felt as though people were watching and judging, waiting for me to slip up. It took me three days to work up the nerve to take four-week-old Anna on the bus, a simple ten-minute ride to the local shopping centre. I had timed it with the precision of a hitman. I had just breast-fed her and changed her nappy, and if I hurried, I would be back at home in time for her next feed. The thought of breast-feeding in public was terrifying.

When I got on the bus it was packed. I was so anxious that I must have bumped the wheels of the buggy into half the passengers there, trying to get to the space where you could park your buggy. Two minutes later, Anna started to cry – her hungry cry. Shit, I had only just fed her. I began to panic. There was no way I was getting my tits out on the bus. I pressed the red stop button several times with shaky fingers. I had to get off the bus and feed her. With every glance of annoyance from my fellow passengers, my anxiety grew. The bus didn't stop. I pressed the button again and just as Anna's screams and the tuts from the passengers reached fever pitch, the bus finally pulled over. I manoeuvred the buggy towards the back door – except there was no back door. This bus only had one door for entering and exiting and it was right up at the top by the bus driver.

And so as other people were trying to get on the bus, I was trying to get off. There were red-faced apologies from me as I tried to squeeze the buggy past all the passengers standing in the aisle, and copious amounts of swearing from them.

But then something miraculous happened. A voice rang out, an oddly familiar voice. 'Move the fuck out of the way. There is a lady here trying to get her baby off the bus, you utter pricks!' And there was Bea, standing tall at the entrance of the bus in all her Amazonian glory, her baby strapped to her chest. As if sensing there was little point in arguing with her, the grumbling passengers started to part ways and let me through. As I moved closer to her, I dared not look her in the eye for fear I would burst into tears.

Bea took one end of the buggy and helped me off the bus. Miraculously, Anna stopped crying and my heart rate started to slow. But as soon as Bea went to get back on the bus, I burst into tears. I couldn't help it. I needed someone to talk to. Bea took one look at me and gestured to the bus driver to carry on.

Feeling silly and awkward, I brushed away my tears and peered at Bea's little baby strapped to her chest.

'He's lovely,' I said, and even though nobody ever gives a shit about anyone else's baby but their own, I really did think Harry was a particularly lovely boy: huge blue eyes and perfect skin, just like his mum. You just knew he was going to be a looker when he was older.

Bea glared at him, and said in her strident tones, 'His name is Harry, and let me tell you that he wasn't so fucking lovely at four o'clock this morning, or indeed the other five times he woke up.'

I can't really explain it – perhaps it was the honesty and the swearing – but I had another surge of emotion. She fished around in her changing bag and handed me a baby wipe.

'Sorry,' I said, wiping away the tears. 'You must think I'm a fucking nutcase.'

'Not at all,' she said, putting her hand on my shoulder. 'You're just exhausted, the same as all of us new mums.'

'A few days ago, I asked my husband for a divorce,' I confessed, weepily.

She cocked her head on one side, then looked down at her watch and announced, 'Right, come on then – we're getting pissed.'

It was 11 a.m.

Bea guided me to a pub I had never seen before. It was empty and grotty – perfect for the situation. Bea marched up to the grumpy-looking bartender and ordered us a bottle of Prosecco. As the bubbles settled in my stomach, I told her everything: how I felt totally out of control; how I was failing as a mother; how I had no fucking idea what I was doing; and what a loser David thought I was as a result. I told her about all David's weird habits and how hard he was to live with, and how I didn't want him around me any more. I even told her about Jordan, David's slutty boss, who I was pretty sure had a crush on him. I have never told anyone else about Jordan.

To this day I have no idea how long I ranted on for, but I do remember that Bea sat there and listened, and that both our babies mercifully slept for most of it.

When I had finally run out of steam, Bea set down her glass of Prosecco, adjusted her glasses and began.

'You think you're a shit mother,' she said.

I nodded vigorously.

'Is your baby neglected, deprived, or starved?'

I shook my head emphatically.

'Do you ever hit or shake your baby?'

'No!' I said, shocked. 'But in my darkest moments, I can think of places I'd rather be,' I confessed, ashamedly.

'Like where?' she said.

'Prison,' I replied, just as she was taking another sip.

Bea spat out some of her drink.

'Prison? Why?' she laughed, grabbing one of Harry's wipes to mop her face.

'In prison you get to sleep, and you get your meals cooked for you. I would *kill* to have someone else make my food,' I said dreamily.

'Well, maybe you'll get there after all!' Bea quipped.

Another thought occurred to me.

'Hospital!' I said, brightly. 'A nice relaxing stint in bed, but it would have to be the right sort of injury to keep me there for a couple of weeks. Nothing too serious.'

Bea looked thoughtful.

'Broken limbs would be too inconvenient...' she said, brow furrowed.

'Yes, definitely no broken limbs,' I replied gravely, delighted she was playing along. 'Like some sort of mystery disease that is totally curable but takes at least two weeks in hospital to treat.'

Bea nodded vigorously.

'And have you given much thought to shorter breaks away from your screaming baby?' Bea said, in the manner of a concerned interviewer on a morning chat show.

'I have indeed, Bea,' I replied, enjoying my role of interviewee. 'I can safely say, I'd rather go to Ikea on a Sunday, have six root canals done at the dentist, and have an MRI a day rather than be with my newborn baby 24/7.'

Bea laughed until she cried, and suddenly I felt better than I had in ages.

The bartender chose that moment to come over, tutting noisily as he cleared away our glasses, clearly disapproving of our daytime drinking. For once, I didn't give a shit about the judgement.

Bea continued to cycle through the rest of my woes. She told me that David was probably feeling just as lost, clueless and out of control as I was. She told me to stop being so possessive over Anna and to give David a job.

'Men need to feel useful. Get him to do something that involves just him and Anna. Put him on bath-time duty every night,' she ordered, taking a large draw of Prosecco.

In reference to David's neat freakery, she told me to start laying boundaries in the same way I had when I had first moved in with him.

'He has regressed because a tidy house is the only thing he can control. Give him back some control by acknowledging how chaotic life with a new baby is and share that feeling together,' she said, sagely.

I knew she was right – about all of it. I had to stop thinking of David as being 'fucking useless', as I had told him, and start involving him more with Anna. I also knew I had to have a serious chat with David about the obsessive tidiness. I had got through to him before and I could do it again.

But Bea wasn't finished yet. 'About Jordan...' she began.

I stiffened. Even when someone else said her name it made me feel a little sick. Noting my reaction, Bea corrected herself. 'Would "Jordan the slut" be a more accurate moniker?' she said.

I smiled. Yes, Jordan the slut was much better.

I won't go into it, but a few weeks into our relationship, when I thought we were the most loved up, David had gone on a date with Jordan, who then was just a girl from work. He only told me about it after we were married. David insisted nothing had happened between them. They had gone out for dinner, and that was it. When I asked him why he had done it, he told me that he just wanted to see 'what else was out there' before he committed fully to me. He told me that after the date, he knew that I was the one for him. It sounds trivial but the whole episode bothered me, and still does, especially as Jordan is now David's boss.

Bea looked thoughtful. 'Listen, you have to move past the Jordan-the-slut thing,' she said. 'It was a long time ago. If he says nothing happened then you have to believe him.'

I nodded. I knew she was right. I couldn't bring up Jordan every time we had a row.

I let out a huge sigh of relief. All my problems had just been put into total perspective by someone I didn't even know. It was then I realised with a bit of a jolt that Bea knew everything about me and I knew nothing about her. I was mortified. There was nothing worse than someone going on about themselves all day. I determined to correct the balance immediately. This is what I learned about my new friend.

Bea was from Cape Town in South Africa and worked as an events manager for a South African beer company, which she planned to return to as soon as she finished her maternity leave. She lived in a two-bedroom duplex with Harry just a few streets away from me. As we ploughed through our second bottle of Prosecco, I drunkenly fired all sorts of questions at her, to which she responded in her refreshingly direct manner.

'How do you look so fantastic?' I slobbered, admiringly. 'I feel and look like shit.'

'Because I have a full-time nanny called Maria,' she said. 'I do the nights and she does the days.'

'You're sooooo lucky,' I replied, grabbing her shoulder and shaking it, just to emphasise how lucky she was.

'Well, I don't pay for her,' she said. 'My mother covers all the fees.'

My mouth dropped open. Bea was the luckiest person I had ever met.

'Ha! Don't be too envious,' she replied, evidently registering my shock. 'The only reason she's paying for the nanny is because during a particularly sleep-deprived moment, I threatened to put Harry up for adoption,' she laughed. 'My mother is also a health freak and a member of the "breastapo". She is barely talking to me since I decided to give Harry formula from the get-go.'

This led to a juicy if belated post-mortem of the antenatal group meeting where we had first met. Bea was thrilled to hear that Tania was also having a hard time with her baby and not surprised in the least that she had pretended otherwise. 'The judgemental mothers are always full of shit,' Bea said, reflectively.

But as much as I was enjoying the gossip, there was something I really wanted to ask Bea. As it was personal, I was hesitant to cross any lines and jeopardise our budding friendship. Prosecco bottle number three soon niftily removed those boundaries.

'So, tell me,' I whispered, conspiratorially. 'Who's the baby daddy?'

Bea stiffened, gave a tight smile, and put her glass down.

'Sorry, sorry, totally none of my business,' I said, cringing. Why had I used the term 'baby daddy'? I had never said anything like before that in my life!

Bea softened and smiled. 'Don't worry, it's just a topic I don't like to discuss.'

I apologised again and hoped she didn't hate me.

'But I can tell you, in a nutshell, that we had been together for a long time, then I got pregnant and he had an affair. He is not in my life and he never will be.'

'I'm sorry,' I said, again. 'I'm a bit pissed and...'

She smiled kindly and suddenly clapped her hands.

'Now, let's get one more bottle before we hit the road.'

As she got up to go to the bar, Anna started to cry as if she was being pricked heavily with safety pins. I looked at my watch. Holy shit, it was half past three. Anna had slept through two feeds. She must be starving.

I hurriedly went to undo the clip on my maternity bra strap and froze, putting my hand to my mouth.

'What's wrong?' Bea said.

'Jesus, I can't breast-feed her,' I said. 'I've been drinking for over four hours. She'll be pissed if I feed her now.'

'Oh, don't worry about it,' she said airily, rooting in her bag. 'I always carry a spare.'

And with a flourish, she produced a ready-made bottle of formula, otherwise known as the 'devil's milk', according to the antenatal group.

'I can't give it to her,' I said, panicking. As if sensing there wasn't a meal coming any time soon, Anna's crying hit supersonic. 'She's only ever had breast milk. She won't like it.'

I didn't say what I really meant: that I would be a bad mother if I gave my four-week-old baby formula instead of breast milk. I could already feel the judgemental whispers from Michelle, the antenatal teacher: 'Don't do it – breast is best.'

'Try,' Bea said gently.

Doing my best to shake off the voices, I took it.

Balancing a frantic Anna on the crook of my arm, I slowly moved the teat of the bottle towards her tiny open mouth, all the time thinking about the fruitlessness of it all. There was no way after four full agonising weeks of breast milk that she would accept a lesser product.

Anna clamped down on that fake teat with an enthusiasm I'd never seen before, and sucked the bottle dry. Usually she took over an hour, if not more, to feed on my poor enflamed, agonised nipples. While I was relieved the crying had stopped, I had never been so offended in my life. What a little traitor!

'Now,' Bea said, carefully, 'I know your preference is breast-feeding but you can do both. You can breast-feed her during the day, and get David to give her a bottle at night. That might help her sleep for longer at night, give him a job, and give you a rest,' she said authoritatively.

I nodded weakly. Bea was right: if I went on like this, I would lose my mind as well as my marriage.

As if he had heard his name, Harry woke up, wailed, and inhaled his bottle.

Bea and I decided to call it a day. Slightly unsteady on my feet, I settled Anna into her pram, and tucked her in.

We walked back together, tipsy and high on the potency of our new friendship.

And that's how Bea and I became best friends.

8

LONDON, NOW

It is Thursday night, and if I'm going to write this stupid pitch for the motherhood book, I need to get some ideas down on the page. I place my fingers on the keyboard and there they stay for the next few minutes. Finally, with panicky resolve, I spin off a few paragraphs to test my 'honest mum' skills.

I write about the joy we felt when I got pregnant, the wonders of the birthing process, how happy we were when we saw our beautiful daughter for the first time, and how much her arrival brought us closer together as a couple. I end with the following passage:

> When we leave the hospital, we carefully place our sleeping living doll into
> her car seat, and head for home. We are filled with indescribable euphoria.
> We have a baby now – we are three instead of two. And she is everything.
> So happy are we that we don't talk on the drive back. I know that my
> husband is as filled with joy as I am and I don't want to break the spell.

There, I've written something. As I am reaching to turn off the desk lamp, David walks into the room and peeps over my shoulder. 'Is that it then? Have you started the pitch?'

Automatically feeling self-conscious, I grab the mouse to remove what

I have written from sight. While I have no problem with complete strangers reading my work, I feel very exposed when someone I'm close to reads it.

'Oh, come on!' David says, covering my hand with his. The mouse stalls.

I sigh and, still seated, swivel my chair over to give him enough space to read. He bends down and stares intently at what I have written. I look down at my bitten fingernails.

Eventually, he turns to me and says, 'It's certainly well written.'

Well, that's something, I think, but, watching him rub his chin, I know there is more to come.

'And...?' I prompt him.

'Well...' he hesitates and frowns, opening and closing his mouth as if he can't decide whether he should say something or not.

I lose patience.

'David, spit it out!'

And then he does.

'Well... it's total bullshit, isn't it?'

And of course, he's right. It is bullshit. It's nothing like what really happened. But it's late, and I'm tired and fed up with thinking about this stupid pitch. So, without saying a word, I switch off the desk lamp with unnecessary force and stomp noisily out of the room.

He follows me into the bathroom, hands raised like a priest about to address a congregation and asks me what's wrong. I ignore him. He asks me again, and I tell him to fuck off. As we both know from experience which way this conversation is headed, I decide to remove myself from the inevitable fireworks and go into our bedroom. This time he is wise enough not to follow.

I turn on the bedroom light and immediately I freeze. Something is missing from our room and I can't put my finger on it. I scan the room. Everything is still as it should be, yet the symmetry is off. What is it?

Then I spot it. The entire contents of my bedside table are missing, save my bedside lamp. Usually, the surface is covered in books, bookmarks, earplugs, an alarm clock, and a box of tissues – what David refers to as my 'table of shit', one of his very rare concessions to my untidiness – but now the table is totally bare.

The hairs on the back of arms start to rise and my heart begins to thump faster.

The thought of David deliberately swiping all my comforting clutter away makes me physically sick. In that moment I realise that I would have preferred it if a sociopath had broken into the house to play mind-games with me, or even that I was the one losing my mind, than to accept the fact that my husband, the father of my child, has done this to me. All the repressed flashes merge and the fireworks begin.

After the big row that follows, I toss and turn, and must eventually doze into a fitful sleep, until something jumps in my chest and I find myself bolt upright.

Anna.

Anna shouting.

I shoot out of bed so fast, I wouldn't have been surprised if I'd jumped clean out of my nightdress. I race down to the end of the corridor, but the funny thing is I feel like I am not moving fast enough. My legs are going, but I don't seem to be getting anywhere. It is like a horrible reverse Road Runner cartoon.

Just as I am about to push open the door, the shouting stops. YESSSSSS, I think to myself. No need to go in – whatever it is, she's over it. But just as I visualise getting back into my warm, cosy bed, making as much noise as possible (to punish David for sleeping through the whole experience, and for being an arse), the guilt starts to creep in. What if there is an axe murderer in her room? Or what if she has been stolen? I'd never forgive myself if I don't at least look in on her.

When I open the door a crack, she is sitting up in bed, her huge eyes staring at me, illuminated by the glow-clock in her room. I let out a small shriek. She may still be alive but she is also looking extremely creepy.

'What is it?' I hiss at her, guilt and fright giving way to relief that she is alive, and then anger that she is looking far too lively for... what time was it anyway? The glow-clock tells me it is 2.45 a.m. Fuck.

'I had a bad dweam, Mummy,' she wails.

Sighing, I kneel down on the fluffy rug beside the bed and stroke her forehead.

After a good half-hour of reassurances – 'No such thing as girls turning into blueberries'; 'It's all make-believe' – she is still nowhere near settling down. I tuck her in and prop all her cuddly toys up on the railing of her toddler bed so they look like an adoring furry audience, but when I go to leave, she starts to wail again.

I am beginning to lose my reason. It is time to lay down the law.

'Now go to sleep, Anna,' I say, firmly.

'No, thank you, Mummy,' she says politely. As much as I love her for finally using her manners, there's nothing more irksome than a four-year-old politely refusing a desperate request to go to sleep at 3.15 a.m.

'Seriously, Anna. It's very late – you're going to be a very tired little girl in the morning,' I say, trying to keep the desperation out of my voice. Once she senses weakness, I'm done for.

'I'll be fine,' she says dreamily.

'Well, I won't,' I wail, finally losing it. 'I'm going to be knackered, and I need my sleep!' I add silently, and Mummy had a fight with Daddy and is on the verge of being a single mother.

Anna started humming 'The Gummy Bear Song', the only song that's actively banned in our household because of its lethal catchiness.

I try to fight the red mist, but it is too late in the night and I don't have the strength. I take a deep breath and get out the big guns.

'Anna, if you don't close your eyes and go to sleep now, there's going to be NO treats tomorrow,' I say, through enamel-chipping gritted teeth.

She stops singing.

My heart begins to sing.

She looks me dead in the eye, and says, 'What about marshmallows?'

To which I reply with a happy note of triumph, 'Nope!'

Looking unsure, she tries again, 'What about chocolate biscuits?'

And I give her the same cheery answer. We are on the home stretch now.

She cycles through all her usual treats and I give her the same joyous response. Suddenly, she lets out a great big yawn and her eyes start to flicker. Good, good. And then her eyes snap open again, and she says, 'What about pears?' and actually gives herself a little hug.

'You hate pears!' I say, incredulous, which is absolutely true, although I have been continuously trying to get her to eat them by disguising pears as 'treats'.

'You always say pears are a tweat, Mummy! That means I don't have to eat them ever again!' she says, breaking back into a cheery rendition of 'The Gummy Bear Song'.

Eventually, I do what every mother does when they have been defeated by their toddler. I draw back the covers, get into bed with her and, teary and humiliated, doze off into a restless sleep.

9

LONDON, NOW

The next morning, I wake up alone in Anna's toddler bed with a churning feeling in my stomach, crusty eyes from angry, unspilled tears, and a sore jaw from clenching my teeth. Classic aftermath symptoms from a row with David. I don't want to relive it but I can't help feeling angry that all the 'no-go' topics have come to the surface yet again – the burden of our finances (David: 'If you got a proper job maybe I wouldn't be so stressed all the time!'); David's escalated habits (Me: 'Why are you so bloody anal? What is wrong with you?'); and the fairly regular argument about sex (David: 'I can't remember the last time we had sex,' and me: 'David, nobody has sex any more – we're fucking MARRIED WITH A CHILD!').

The worst thing about our arguments is their utter repetitiveness. The lack of originality is more painful than the mud-slinging.

I spend some time unscrunching myself, having slept in a bed half the length of my body, before wearily stepping out onto Anna's purple, fluffy floor mat. I can hear breakfast noises from the kitchen below and I am grateful David is with Anna and nowhere near me. I treat myself to a longer shower than normal (three minutes rather than two), which makes me feel half-human again. As I emerge, I stand on the bathmat soaking wet and drip for two whole minutes (David can't cope with a wet bathmat) as small revenge for David's incurable pettiness. Finally dry, I encase myself in a towel and get dressed in my usual uniform of jeans and T-shirt, yawning throughout.

'Mummy, I can't find the wemote!' Anna wails as I walk slowly into the kitchen and hand her the remote. The front door slams shut. Good. After the row last night I'm not in the mood to play happy families with David. After several rounds of *Peppa Pig,* accompanied by a 'lethal' bowl of Cheerios and some fruit and toast that inevitably remains untouched (I don't know who I'm kidding – Anna always has a shite breakfast), I dress Anna as one of the less slutty Disney princesses – I'm too tired to battle with her to get into her normal clothes – and then we begin my favourite 'put your shoes on' game. As it always does, the game ends in a furious, barely disguised muttering of, 'Put your fucking shoes on.' Thank fuck it's Friday and Anna has nursery today. If I have any chance of doing anything about this pitch, I need some peace and quiet.

I pack Anna into the car, and off we go to Rocking Horses nursery, with Anna singing 'Uptown Funk' in the back, although the way she says it, 'funk' sounds a lot like... a grown-up word. Five minutes later, I pull up on the street alongside Rocking Horses and for the umpteenth time, I am astonished that the building hasn't been condemned by the council. It looks like the sort of premises used for public information films from the 1970s, the ones where children ignore all the red 'Beware!' and 'Danger!' signs in order to creep under the barbed wire to have a bit of a lark with live electricity. Why is Anna going here? Because all the decent nurseries have been booked up by savvy mums like Tania Henderson, who put their babies' names on the waiting list when they were mere foetuses.

So, Rocking Horses it is. Anna started there part time when she turned one and, at the time, despite its grim appearance, I would have happily trotted over blazing hot coals to find some care for Anna just so I could hang on to my sanity for a couple of hours.

Over the years, Anna and I have perfected the hazardous walk to the nursery door, which in itself is a feat in self-preservation. I pull open the rusty iron gate, and the two of us run through lest it swing back on our legs, which has happened quite a few times already. As is our ritual, we cover our ears as the huge gate crashes behind us. No injuries today; our calves will live to fight another day. We gracefully dodge the dog poo through the

narrow passageway that leads to the nursery building itself, and as usual
Anna points out the barbed wire strung across each of the high walls.
Concentration camp or kids' paradise? Nobody can really be sure.

As we approach the cheerily painted sludge-brown door, my heart sinks
as I see the familiar round-shouldered shape of Misery waiting outside
with her daughter, Mara. I curse my strict time-keeping skills. If I'd only
been a few minutes later, nursery would have been open, and I would have
avoided the awkward small talk we are now obliged to engage in. As it is, I
will have to face her for at least five minutes, a very long five minutes at
that. As soon as Anna clocks Mara, she races over to say hello. It is fairly
typical of Anna to befriend someone whose mother I actively despise.

Misery is the type of person who sucks any trace of energy from you the
closer you get to her. I can actually feel my feet dragging on the ground as I
walk over to where the kids are busily playing a game of 'peel the paint off
the decrepit nursery door'. I think it's fair to say that relations with Misery
have become more strained since the disastrous playdate incident a year
ago. Even though I try to avoid playdates – and, frankly, even using the term
'playdate' – Anna's incessant repetition of, 'Can Mawa come to my house?'
finally got the better of me. So, with huge reluctance I invited Mara over to
play, and her mother spent the entire afternoon lecturing me about the
dangers of modern technology. Apparently using the iPad was akin to
throwing sulphuric acid into the child's eyes, and the TV was simply a plot
to brainwash young minds into heroin addiction. That sort of thing.

So, when Anna fetched the remote at teatime and niftily navigated to
her recorded programmes to watch *Dora the Explorer* for the fiftieth time
(the ballerina one), the other mother turned a grim shade of puce, huffing,
'Oh, do we have TV during teatime, then?'

To which I responded, in my most upbeat passive-aggressive voice, 'Yes,
we do.' The rest of the tea was spent with Mara staring open-mouthed at
Dora, her meal totally untouched, with her mother desperately trying to get
her to focus on her food, muttering all the while that the TV was 'killing
Mara's appetite'. Honestly, did this woman not know the rules? Judge all
you want, but at least have the grace to do it behind my back.

In case you haven't already guessed, Misery is also one of the Organics
crew and prolific on Vale Mums. Her commentary is endless and her

wisdom boundless. When new, sleep-deprived mums desperately looking for support tearfully post their struggles with breast-feeding, Misery is the first to share her own perfect record just to make those poor mums feel doubly shit about themselves: how she herself breast-fed for eighteen months, loved it, and would have regretted it if she hadn't persevered.

When another mum posts that she really wants to go back to work, but feels guilty about putting her six-month-old son in full-time nursery, up pops Misery again. She tells the eight hundred members of Vale Mums that she herself 'waited a year before putting my son in nursery and I only work part time. What's the point of having children if you never see them?' And it doesn't stop there. Don't get Misery started on the number of paedophiles in the area. A slave to the paedophile register, she makes it her business to publicly 'out' paedophiles on social media. At least once a week, she names and shames someone in the area who has been listed on the sex offenders list.

Don't get me wrong, Misery aside, I like most of the Rocking Horses mums. They always say hello, and if I bump into one of them on the street, they stop to exchange a friendly word or two. 'Polite' is the word I would use. Which is all very fine and nice. But while I'm happy to engage in the odd bit of small talk, there are days where I could do with something a bit less 'nice'. I often look at these mums and think, wouldn't it be such a relief if one of you would just let rip and go on a big rant about your troublesome toddler? Tell me about the time little Eddie shit in the bath and smeared it all over the walls, or how Josie punched you in the face so hard you thought she'd broken your nose. Stop feeling so self-conscious and tell me something real. Above all, do not use the words 'challenging' or 'tricky' when you're describing your toddler's appalling behaviour. Sentences like, 'Well, Jasper's behaviour has been a bit challenging lately,' are prohibited. Try using language like, 'Jasper was such a shitbag yesterday that I wanted to throw him out the window.' And while you're at it, try swearing for a bit. It may not sound pretty but it sure is cathartic.

In fact, tell me I'm not the only one who has to lock herself in the bathroom for a couple of minutes lest I lash out at my daughter in frustration; and tell me that I'm not the only mother who is humiliated down to her very core when her child throws the mother of all meltdowns in a supermarket. I promise I won't judge your parenting skills and I promise that whatever story you tell me, I will better it. That's the conversation I want to have when I'm pushed to the very limit as a parent, and yet apart from with Bea, that dialogue simply never takes place.

And it's not for the want of trying. Last year, when Anna turned three, and David was on a work trip, I decided to get eight of the nursery mums and their kids over for a barbecue. I thought getting a few drinks into the mums might encourage them to loosen up a bit. Officially, the party was from two until five o'clock. The last of our guests stumbled out of our house at 11 p.m.

On the face of it, the party was a huge success. Just like the popular children's book *The Tiger Who Came to Tea*, the mums ate all the food in the cupboards, and drank all the drink in the house (including copious amounts of 'Daddy's beer'). By five o'clock, the alcohol had done its work, the kids had been collected by nannies or partners, and the mums were in no rush to leave. Deep and salacious conversations were taking place in every corner of the house; guilty secrets were being shared – the types that would never have been revealed sober. One mum announced she was going to sell her troublesome toddler on eBay, with no refunds or returns, while another went one better and said she was going to sell her husband. Others competed by sharing murderous thoughts about their spouses, or their silent yearnings for an everlasting holiday from their children.

They were those glorious rare conversations that seldom take place within a group of near-strangers, the ones that create and cement the bonds of friendship. And when the last of my red-faced and incoherent party guests stumbled ungainly out of the front door, I hugged myself with the knowledge that I had finally found people who felt exactly the same as I did. But as it turned out, just like the tiger in the book, these jolly party guests never came back.

Instead, things almost went back to the way they always had. Polite nods and small talk at the Rocking Horses' gates, but no acknowledgement of the party whatsoever. It was almost as though it had never happened. But one thing did change after the party: the false promises. The hand on the shoulder, the intense stare into the eyes, followed by, 'We *must* go for a coffee,' or 'We *must* catch up for a cheeky glass of wine,' or my personal favourite, 'You and David *must* come over for dinner one night.' Yet when I suggested dates, I would be gracefully dismissed with a wave of a hand. 'Sorry, love, those dates simply don't work. But, honestly, we *must...*'

I couldn't figure it out. Hadn't we all bonded that night in my house? Weren't we now supposed to be friends? Why bother suggesting a coffee or a night out when you don't mean it?

One night, over a second bottle wine at her flat, Bea attempted to clear it up for me. 'It's a middle-class London thing. Happens all the time. You can have the most intimate conversation with someone you barely know one minute, and then they scarcely acknowledge you the next. Londoners of a certain age and social standing don't feel obliged to form new friendships because they form their friendship groups earlier in life. By the time they reach our age, they don't really need anyone else.'

Which, if it was true, was probably the most depressing thing I had heard in a long time. Surely Bea's theory couldn't be right.

'Bea, I've been living here for years and I've always found it easy to make friends with Londoners from all walks of life,' I told her adamantly.

'Ah, yes, but that was before you became a new mum,' she said. 'People have more to hide. Everyone's so petrified of being found out that they haven't a clue how to raise their children that they've stopped sharing their stories. Different vibe.'

But I wasn't convinced. Maybe the Rocking Horses mums 'just weren't that into me'.

In any case, I can tell you one person who certainly wasn't that into me and that was my Rocking Horses nemesis, Misery.

Today, Misery is wearing her usual drab garb: the army-green canvas all-weather raincoat, big shit-kicker boots, and over-long stripy Oxfam scarf in faded mustard. A what-may-have-once-been-cream-but-is-now-a-dirty-beige woolly hat sits atop long, thin (or 'streely', as my mother would call it) light brown hair, which spills forlornly halfway down her hunched shoulders. She looks like a cross between a homeless person and 'Sadness' from the kids' movie *Inside Out*.

Yet, here we are – the only two people at the nursery door – and social custom dictates that one of us should at least wave a hand in greeting. Just as I prepare to do this, she surprises me by speaking.

She cocks her head in a self-important way, blows her greasy fringe away from her eyes out the corner of her mouth like a defiant teenager, raises her eyebrows and says, 'Cheerios?' in a sarky way.

For a moment I am nonplussed, and then the penny drops. Of course, Misery would have seen my Cheerios comment; she does nothing else but troll people's posts all day long. Well, she picked the right day for a battle. After last night's fight with David, and Anna's night horrors, I am in no mood to discuss the pros and cons of breakfast cereals.

'Yes, Cheerios,' I say, evenly. 'Anna loves them.'

I say the name 'Anna', loudly, fervently hoping that she will overhear and come over and save me from this pointless conversation.

To my shock, Misery says, 'Mara loves them too.'

I can't believe my ears. One of the Organics gives her child a sugary cereal? How can this be? Suddenly, I feel an odd sense of kinship with Misery. Maybe we are not so different after all.

'But she's not allowed to have them,' Misery adds, destroying any previous notions I may have had about her. 'They are full of sugar, you know. She has home-made yoghurt instead.'

Before I can give her the finger, the nursery door opens, and the manager Heather sticks her head out. 'Come on in,' she cries in thick staccato Glaswegian.

Heather is one of those people who should not be working around children. Not because she's a paedophile but, like David's mother, Rose, she simply doesn't like them. The difference is that unlike Rose, Heather is both open and unapologetic about it, which is both refreshing and concerning. Heather regularly complains to anyone who will listen about 'the headaches' she gets from 'all the noisy children' and that she has to have a 'lie down' on the couch in her office when it all gets too much.

Everyone – parents and staff alike – is terrified of Heather and with good reason. If Heather takes a dislike to a parent – usually one who ventures an opinion about how the nursery is run – she will phone that parent incessantly if the slightest thing happens to the child at nursery. Instead of simply administering Calpol to a child suffering from a mild cold, she will call that child's parent at work and demand the child be picked up because that child is 'ill' and shouldn't be at nursery. As nobody wants to be on the other end of that conversation, we all make sure we stay on the right side of Heather. I, in particular, have made sure I am at least halfway up her arse. The thought of having to take Anna home from nursery sooner than I need to fills me with horror.

The only time Heather is forced to interact with parents is when endless paperwork (usually another hike in nursery fees) needs to be signed or when a parent is taking their child out of Rocking Horses for good. (Trying to take your child out of nursery is like trying to resign your gym membership – very, very difficult.)

Having said that, Heather's administration skills are impeccable and she runs the nursery so efficiently that it sort of makes up for her lack of personal skills.

I sidle past Heather, giving her a cheery arse-licking 'Good morning'.

'Is it?' she replies aggressively as she steps into her office.

Then I walk Anna to her rotting pre-school room, and prepare for what I like to call 'the cut and run', which is basically a speedy exit that leaves no time for clinginess or sobbing on either side. I give Anna a quick kiss good-bye, do the 180-degree swivel towards the door, and switch the turbojets on.

As I reach the car, I spot one of the nursery mums, Nell, coaxing her son, Tristan – or 'the spitter', as Anna calls him – to get out of his car seat. Nell is one of the mums who went to my barbecue party, and was easily the most entertaining. After the seventh bottle of Prosecco, she pulled me into the bathroom to tell me that it was a miracle she had got pregnant at all, given her sexual preference for 'taking it up the arse'. Then she laughed hysterically, pulled down her pants, and did a wee in front of me. She was the best drunk I had ever met, and a real contender for a lasting friendship – or so I thought. But like the rest of the mums who I felt I had bonded with, Nell is part of the 'we must' brigade. If she tells me one more time how 'we must' go for coffee, I'm going to scream.

Looking flustered, she gives me a quick wave. She has Tristan by the hand now, and is walking my way.

'Someone's not too keen on going to nursery today!' she says brightly.

That 'someone' spits on her shoe, but we both pretend not to notice.

'He'll be fine once he gets in,' I say, following the standard script for nursery small talk.

'Oh, yes, it's always the way. Always act up for us but great for other people!' she laughs.

So far, so benign.

I give her a quick nod, and reach for the car door. There's literally nowhere to go from here. But to my surprise, she puts her hand on my arm.

'Do you know, Saoirse, I have been given two free tickets to *Billy Elliot, The Musical*, and my husband refuses to go. Can you believe that?' she says, with a frown.

Intrigued by this line of conversation, I turn and give her my full attention.

'Why won't he go?' I say.

'He hates musicals,' she replies.

And then we say at the exact same time, 'I mean, who hates musicals?'

Then we laugh in a conspiratorial way that makes my heart beat a little faster. Is it possible? Are we bonding?

Feeling emboldened by our new camaraderie, I say, 'Well, if you're looking for someone to go with, I'm happy to volunteer. I've always wanted to see *Billy Elliot*.'

Nell looks at me in such shock that you'd think I had just invited her to swingers' party. Clearly, I have misread the situation – again.

'Oh, no, I didn't mean...' she falters. 'I'm sure I can persuade my husband to go...'

Deciding to brazen it out, I wave away her embarrassment and tell her not to worry, and I'm sure her husband will enjoy it once he gets there. And then she says, 'Oh, yes, I'm sure he will.'

Tristan hurries on the awkward goodbyes by spitting on Nell's other shoe. She tells him off this time, probably grateful for the distraction. I give her a quick wave as I get into the car, but she doesn't notice. It's only when I go to put my foot on the brake that I notice a large globule of white saliva dripping down the side of my black boot. The little shit.

Trying to put the most recent social fail out of my head, I drive home quickly, conscious I have very little time to get started on this bloody pitch.

An hour later, I am staring at a blank Word document. I will the words to come but I'm exhausted from last night, and I can't seem to clear the fog in my mind. I start to panic. After another hour of typing and deleting, I leave my tiny office and head downstairs to try to clear my head. I put on a wash and have a cup of tea. It is 11 a.m. I need to pick up Anna at 3 p.m. I march back upstairs to my office with shoulders-back resolve and force myself to face the dreaded screen once more.

But it's no good. Fighting my best instincts, I click into Vale Mums, where I am surprised to find no further comments have been made on my Cheerios post. Clearly, Misery wanted to say her piece to my face rather than cyber-judging. Besides, Rosalind has posted a question asking about childcare during a family holiday abroad and all hell has broken loose.

Misery:

WHY would you need childcare on a family holiday, Rosalind? Just curious (plus confused emoji).

'Because she needs a FUCKING break,' I mutter angrily at the screen.

One by one the rest of the Organics chip in with similar comments, ranging from 'Gosh, the only real quality time I get with my children is on holidays!' to 'Sooo many friends have had terrible experiences with their children at those holiday clubs abroad – really would tread carefully.'

Rosalind ends the discussion, defeated.

Thanks, mums! You're probably right. I'll hold off on putting them in a holiday crèche for now.

Three of the Organics post patronising 'thumbs up' emojis in response.

Shaking my head in anger, I switch back to the empty page, willing myself to concentrate. Right now, I'm furious. Maybe I can channel some of that into my writing.

A flash of an opening sentence suddenly appears in my mind and I quickly place my fingers on the keyboard to capture it before it flits away. And then the landline rings and the thought is gone. I shout loudly in frustration.

The only people who call me on the landline are the gas and electricity people, and David's mother, Rose, because she's too tight to call me on my smartphone.

As none of the above are of any particular interest to me, I ignore it. If someone really needs to contact me they can leave a bloody message. But then the phone rings again. I swear as loudly as I can, snatch up the phone, and say, 'WHAT IS IT?' in the angriest voice I can muster. On the other end, there is a pause, a little sigh of disapproval, and then a harsh clipped voice that I immediately recognise, and my heart sinks.

It's Heather from Rocking Horses.

Fuck.

'Saoirse, you need to pick up Anna. Now.' Heather spits, staccato-like.

'What's happened, Heather? Is Anna sick?' I say as nicely as possible, trying to claw back any favour I have ever won from her.

Unless Anna has thrown up all over the place, developed a bumpy rash, or broken at least two of her limbs, she can stay where she is.

Heather coughs self-importantly, sucks in her breath and grandly announces, 'Your daughter has *harmed* another child.'

Shit. That's not good. That other kid was probably at the mercy of one of Anna's numerous meltdowns. However, I'm standing firm. Unless that other child is en route to A&E, there is everything still to play for.

With unnecessary drama, Heather goes on to tell me how Anna 'worked herself up into a state' after some kid snatched a doll from her. Apparently, she threw herself onto the floor, kicking and screaming, and another child (an 'innocent passer-by') inadvertently tripped over the frenzied body of my daughter and fell against a table, where said child suffered a cut on the forehead.

'Oh, my goodness!' I say, with, I hope, just the right amount of concern to talk Heather out of sending my child home early. 'That's terrible! Does the other child have concussion or need stitches?'

Heather replies, slightly less confidently, 'Well, no, the child just needed a plaster.'

I have her now.

'The thing is that I'm working, Heather, and it would be quite difficult for me to pick up Anna so early in the day,' I say in a wheedling voice that makes me lose all respect for myself.

But Heather digs her heels in.

'I still need you to get her,' Heather replies in aggressive mode.

The gloves are off. No more nicey-nice.

'So, just to clarify, Anna didn't hurt a child deliberately, and everyone is fine so why can't she stay where she is until home time?' I ask, not even trying to keep the frustration out of my voice.

'Anna has locked herself into the staff room and she is refusing to come out,' Heather explains gruffly, without a trace of accountability.

And this is where I lose it.

'Let me get this straight. My daughter is trapped in an E.coli-riddled windowless room, and you and your staff of eight are unable to get her out. Have I got that right?'

'Well, yes,' replies Heather, as if this sort of thing happens all the time.

And then with relief and a strange sense of enjoyment, I give myself full licence to let the tensions of the last twenty-four hours verbally rain down on that child-hating nursery Nazi. When I have used up every swear word I have ever learned, I finally run out of steam.

Heather responds in an irritatingly polite voice that I'm to pick up Anna in the next twenty minutes or she will call the police and report me for verbal abuse. Suddenly, I'm very, very tired.

I tell her with as much dignity as I can muster that I am on my way. Weary and defeated, I get back into the car with angry tears once more prickling my eyes.

Heather is waiting for me outside the nursery door, arms folded, and wearing a look that says, 'Don't even think about fucking with me.' I ignore her and head straight to the staff room where two teenagers masquerading as nursery staff are peering through the keyhole, whispering softly, presumably in an attempt to coax Anna out.

I close my hand into a fist and knock softly on the door. 'Anna, it's Mummy. Turn the key and come on out. I'm taking you out of here and I'm never bringing you back.'

I turn around and glare at Heather when I say this last bit. Heather may be tough as nails when it comes to threatening parents, but I know her weak spot. Her whole career as nursery manager depends on meeting a certain quota of high-paying customers and if one parent pulls out, her arse is on the line.

Suddenly, I hear the sound of metal on metal and I shift my attention back to the door. It opens slowly, and there is Anna, her huge eyes looking even bigger than normal, and her cheeks red and muddy with tears. I hold my arms out and she runs into them. For once, Anna and I are on the same side. I pick her up and triumphantly carry her out of shitting Rocking Horses, with the pride of a firefighter carrying a child from a burning building.

Heather follows me out of the nursery, shouting like a true jobsworth, 'But your paperwork! You need to fill out paperwork if you are taking her out for good!'

'Fuck the paperwork!' I cry in return, which makes absolutely no sense as I'll obviously have to sign something to make it all legal. But right now, I'm not in the mood to be responsible.

So I keep walking, hugging Anna more closely as I exit Rocking Horses for good, slamming that crappy ham-stringing gate behind me for the last time. It is only when I get home and Anna becomes, well, Anna again, it occurs to me that I have shot myself in the foot, big time. I have a pitch I haven't started yet and no childcare. Shit.

After an hour of me trying to persuade Anna to watch her iPad, do some colouring, or play with her dolls – and failing at all three – she finally settles on playing games on my smartphone. I wrestle it off her just long enough to get Bea's number and call her on the landline. I am too fired up to start work now. I need to get everything that's happened out of my system, including my row with David.

'And then David compared me to Elsa from *Frozen*!' I wail, in full flow.

'Why? Because of your good looks and magical powers?' Bea jokes.

'No, because he reckons I'm a fucking Ice Queen when it comes to sex.'

'But you're married with a child,' Bea shoots back indignantly.

'That's what I said!'

If I'm being honest, sex with David has been fairly low on my list of 'things to do' lately, or more accurately, ever since Anna came along, but calling me an 'Ice Queen' was a low blow all the same.

'Then he had a go at me about not earning enough. Talk about putting the knife in. He told me he couldn't believe he had married someone who had no assets.'

There is the sound of a ringing phone in the background.

'Don't you need to get that?' I say.

'Nah, they'll call back,' she replies, casually.

Bea is in the office today but has no qualms about picking up the phone for personal calls. One time, she let me drivel on for about five minutes before telling me she was in a meeting with her boss. She is the queen of late starts and early lunches. I have no idea how she gets away with it, but I'd say with her straight talk and a gaze that could slice you in two that they're all petrified of her.

'So, what did you say when he said that thing about the assets?' Bea says.

'I pulled up my top, grabbed my tits and said, "THESE ARE MY ASSETS".'

'Nice,' Bea responds, admiringly.

'Then I called him a neat freak and told him never to touch my stuff again,' I continue, getting myself all worked up once more.

'And what did he say to that?' Bea asks.

'He said that he had every right to do whatever he wanted, given it was HIS name on the mortgage,' I reply angrily.

'Low blow,' Bea replies, with just the right amount of sympathy.

I sniff in response, feeling very sorry for myself.

'Did you say anything to piss him off?' Bea asks craftily.

Dammit, she knows me too well.

'Not really,' I say breezily, hoping she won't pursue it any further.

'Did the whole Jordan thing come up?' she says.

Fuck. The jig is up.

I sigh. 'OK, yes, I brought up Jordan.'

'Bloody hell, Saoirse, Jordan was years ago, and nothing even happened between her and David,' she says, sounding exasperated.

'So he *says*,' I reply petulantly.

Now Bea sighs.

A wave of fatigue rushes over me. I'm so damned tired.

'And to top it all off, I have just liberated Anna from Rocking Horses,' I continue, wearily.

I spend some time filling Bea in and, as usual, she says just the right thing. She tells me that Anna is better off without that 'shithole' nursery anyway, and that she's sure Heather is only a nursery manager because the position for 'prison executioner' has already been filled. She finishes with, 'You were totally right to get her out of there.'

All the Rocking Horses talk reminds me of Nell and the social fail. I fill Bea in and she says, 'Remind me, which one is Nell? The one who wants to sell her child on eBay or the one who takes it up the arse?'

This is what I love about Bea: she has never met any of the nursery mums, yet she remembers all the right details about them.

'The one who takes it up the arse,' I reply.

Bea pauses for a moment. 'You'd expect her to be a bit less uptight under the circumstances,' she says thoughtfully.

I burst out laughing, and the tightness in my chest starts to relax, only to be replaced by an overwhelming feeling of crashing exhaustion.

'I need a break, Bea,' I say quietly, rubbing my eyes. 'From David.'

'And from Anna,' Bea adds.

I take a deep breath to stop my voice from cracking. The truth is that I feel trapped – suffocated by Anna's hourly meltdowns and David's insufferable fussiness. At least once a day I feel the need to just get away from the pair of them, and the only thing stopping me is guilt. When I trust myself to speak again, I say in a forced jocular tone, 'Chance would be a fine thing!'

'Well, actually...' Bea says in her 'plotting' voice, 'why don't you get away? It's summer. You're not paying for nursery any more. Why don't you stay at The Cube for a week or two to get some space and focus on writing the pitch?'

'What the fuck is The Cube?' I say.

'Oh, it's just this summer house in Wexford that my mother bought years ago. Haven't I mentioned it before?'

I sigh. This is typical Bea. This sort of thing happens all the time. It's like she has this whole other life that she thinks she has told me about but hasn't. I only found out a couple of years ago that her mother was the famous health nut Arianna Wakefield; and to this day, she has never told me who Harry's father is. Now here she is dropping in the fact that she has some almost certainly fabulous summer home in Ireland.

With some effort to keep the weariness out of my voice, I say, 'Well, tell me about this house then.'

'It's all rugged cliffs and crashing waves. Very romantic. Real Maeve Binchy stuff. My mother uses it as a retreat when she's writing her "cookbooks".'

I can almost see her doing the air quotes.

'Wow, it sounds amazing,' I say wistfully. 'But I can't, much as I'd love to. Who would look after Anna?'

'That's the easy part. Maria will take her when David's at work. Harry will love having his partner in crime around for the day.'

I think about this for a minute, a glimmer of hope rising. Anna adores Harry's nanny, Maria, as much as she adores Harry. A week or two, though. It seems an awfully long time.

'I can't leave Anna,' I say, feeling defeated. 'Not only have I never left her before, but she fucking hates David at the moment.'

'Well, then, a bit of time together will be good for them,' Bea says. 'Besides, they will have a better chance of bonding without you being there.'

Deep down, I know she's right. Anna wants me and only me at the moment; maybe if I'm out of the picture she will start to lean on her dad a bit more.

'Listen, Saoirse, you need some time to yourself, and some space from David. I bumped into him the other day and he was telling me how much pressure he is under at work. Maybe a break from each other is a good thing: you can focus on your work without the extra strain of his neat-freak side, and he can focus on getting this bloody deadline out of the way in relative peace.'

I sigh. Bea has always been good about understanding David's 'quirks' when he is in stress mode. Not for the first time, I am grateful that she is the type of friend who sees arguments from both sides. Despite my frustrations with David, I don't want to hear anyone else slagging him off – that's my job and mine alone.

Even though I know she's right, the anxiety keeps on rising. Going away by myself seems utterly out of reach. I can just hear the Organics now, 'How *could* you leave your four-year-old daughter for a couple of weeks? How selfish!'

'It would be different if it was just a day or two,' I mumble. 'But a week or two...'

Then something else occurs to me. 'My mother!' I say.

'What about her?' Bea says, puzzled.

'Even if I did take you up on your offer, I can't go back to Ireland and not stay with her – she'll murder me.'

'Well, don't tell her,' Bea says practically.

'I'm sure she has my phone tracked,' I say in dismay. 'She'll know exactly where I am.'

I must be the only forty-year-old whose mammy tracks them on Google maps.

'So, tell her you're going to Wexford and ask her to spend a couple of days with you.'

Oh, that's good, I think. My mother would love the idea of getting away to the country and nosing around someone else's fabulous house. After Bea spends a few more minutes making a convincing case for abandoning my husband and only daughter, I end up promising that I'll at least think about it. Then I grab one of those children's snacks that pretends it's healthy by virtue of the fact that it has 'fruit' emblazoned on the packet, and check on Anna. She is exactly where I have left her: in my office, sitting on the sofa bed, legs crossed, eyes tuned to YouTube Kids. My heart swells with love for her. How could I ever think about leaving her? Look at her! She's such a sweetheart!

'OK, Anna?' I say, merrily.

'Snack,' she growls, through the corner of her mouth, tearing her eyes away from the screen just long enough to say, 'Now!'

'Grand,' I say, and place it carefully beside her, gingerly stepping backwards and edging out of the room. Not for the first time, I wonder if it's normal to be so terrified of your own child. Maybe I'm suffering from Stockholm Syndrome. I look at my watch. There is just enough time to call my mother to see what she thinks about a potential break in Ireland.

My mother, Brenda (Irish to the point where even the stereotype is a bit understated), was a primary school teacher, and now teaches English to 'foreigners' in Dublin. Her hobbies include all things social media related. I find more out about her over Twitter than I do when I'm talking to her on the phone. If you were to compare my mother to an animal, you would probably choose a terrier: short, wiry, energetic, and snappy.

My mother's mobile phone rings at least six times before she answers – unusual for her, given it lives in her back pocket, despite the number of 'falling down the loo' incidents.

'What?' she says, sounding breathless and distracted.

I groan. There are only two explanations for my mother when she's like this. She's either on the toilet or on eBay.

'Are you on the loo again?' I ask, immediately fearing the answer.

'No, no. I'm on the eBay,' she says impatiently. 'I have three people watching the 'Marital Miracle' I have put on and I want to see who bids the most.'

'For fuck's sake...' I mumble, but she picks up on it anyway.

'Language!' she barks.

'Sorry,' I say, contritely. 'For *feck's* sake.'

'Better,' she says, approvingly.

I'm becoming more and more uncomfortable with my mother's latest online entrepreneurial ventures. Ever since she discovered that anybody could sell anything on eBay (or '*the* eBay', as she likes to call it), she has set herself the challenge of sourcing the most unusual items to auction guided by the 'one man's trash is another person's treasure' philosophy. In the beginning, it had all seemed fairly harmless: rubbish items picked up at bargain-basement shops in the poorer parts of Dublin, which she sold for a few pence more on eBay. Most of it was animal related: jockstraps for dogs; a little wooden coffin for a dead hamster; or a weird metal contraption designed to protect the virginity of your cat.

I take a deep breath and try to sound interested.

'I'm afraid to hear the answer, but what on earth is the "Marital Miracle"?' I say.

'Well, it was Father Casey who gave me the idea when I was cutting his hair the other day,' she says, in what I refer to as her 'storytelling' voice.

I give a silent groan. My mother doesn't know the meaning of the word 'nutshell' when it comes to short answers.

'But you're not a hairdresser,' I say.

'Sure, didn't I cut your hair for all those years when you were younger?' she says, indignantly.

Yes, I think silently, and a crooked fringe and a bowl haircut do not a hairdresser make.

'It's very simple, Saoirse,' she begins, giving a sniff of self-importance, something she does when she has something significant to say. 'Father Casey gave a sermon about marital disagreement at mass the other day – the church with the twenty-five-minute mass. *Not* the church with the priest who loves the sound of his own voice. Sure, you'd miss your Sunday dinner if you went to mass there, it's that long...'

My mother's determination to find the world's shortest mass comes a close second to her eBay fixation. She treats her mass attendance with the same Murphy's Law mentality as the most dedicated of lottery ticket buyers. If she misses just one mass then you can be sure that would be the one week where she would have received the grand prize of everlasting salvation.

'Anyway...' I say pointedly, to move her along. There is no stopping her when she goes off on one of her tangents.

'Right, yes, Father Casey and the sermon. I'll keep the story short, Saoirse, because I only have five minutes to go on this auction and I have a million things to do when it's over.'

I clench my free hand in frustration. Keeping a story short? Chance would be a fine thing.

Apparently, my mother had hijacked poor Father Casey as he was shaking hands with the parishioners after mass and told him he could do with sorting out that 'shaggy mop on top of his head'. Clearly bewildered and confused by this short but snappy pensioner, Casey had allowed himself to be led into the back room of the church where priests get ready before mass. There, my mother had 'magically' produced a pair of scissors and proceeded to chop away merrily, drilling Father Casey about his sermon.

'And it was while Father Casey was telling me the extent to which married couples disagreed, that the idea came to me, like a big flash of lightning.'

She pauses for effect. My mother loves nothing better than a big build-up to her stories.

'Jesus, Mother. Will you get on with it?' I snap.

It's almost Anna's teatime and I need to get cracking before she starts getting 'hangry'.

'Don't be taking the Lord's name in vain,' she snaps back.

This time I don't apologise. But she can't stay mad at me for too long because she is desperate to tell me her big story.

'Anyway, it was the scissors that gave me the idea about how I could help married people solve their disagreements,' she says triumphantly.

I think that if I had a pair of scissors now, I'd put myself out of my misery rather than put up with the rest of this story.

'It was then I decided to make two boxes; one for him and one for her. In each box is a rock, a bit of paper, a pair of small scissors, and a haiku,' she says confidently.

'A haiku?' I say, bewildered.

'Yes, Saoirse,' she says in her best 'teaching foreigners English' voice. 'A haiku is a Japanese poem,' she explains, importantly.

'I know what a haiku is!' I say, annoyed. 'Since when do you know how to write a haiku?'

'One of my Japanese students, Noboku, is into them. Sure, they're only three lines, Saoirse. Any eejit can do them.'

I massage my left temple with my fingers, trying to shake off the feeling that I have entered into some parallel universe where my mother is now a haiku-writing marital peacemaker.

'So you're telling me that you're selling these boxes to couples on eBay as an aid to solve marital disagreements,' I say slowly.

'Exactly!' she replies delightedly. 'I've called it the "Marital Miracle". It's a brilliant way to make decisions. Say you wanted David to look after Anna one night but he has already made plans for the same evening. You would each take out your Marital Miracle box and choose either the rock, the paper, or the scissors. So if you took out the paper, and David took out the scissors, then David would win because *scissors cut paper*. Then he would head out for the night and you would stay at home to look after Anna.'

'And what's the haiku for?'

'It's there to help you to reflect on your relationship,' she says cheerfully.

'And then you put these boxes on eBay,' I say tiredly.

'*The* eBay,' she replies. 'They're flying off the shelves, Saoirse. You wouldn't credit it!'

Before I can respond, she gives a delighted shriek.

'It's gone, Saoirse! The latest Marital Miracle box is gone to bidder "Engorged2013". I've just made eighty-five euro and I only put it on for ninety-nine cents. Would you credit that? "Engorged" swooping in, in the last five seconds. Good man,' she says, thrilled with herself.

Quietly appalled, I congratulate her on her 'big win', as she likes to call it. Given her mood, I decide that this is probably a good time to break the news that I'm considering a trip to Ireland by myself to work, and staying two hours' drive from my family home.

There is a bit of silence and I can picture her doing that narrow-eyed head-cocking thing that she always does when she's faced with something she doesn't want to hear.

Then the questions begin. Minutes go by as she quizzes me on everything from Anna's childcare ('Are you sure you can trust Anna with that wan Maria?) to David ('And what's David going to do without you?') to my accommodation in Wexford.

'Now what did you say the house was called again?' she says officiously. I can hear the busy click of her mouse.

'The Cube,' I say. 'I don't know much about it, but—'

'"The Cube is an all-glass architectural miracle perched on the cliffs of Wexford, about a two-hour drive from Dublin,"' she reads in a higher pitch than normal. 'I've just looked it up on the Google!'

I don't bother to comment. Of course, the house is fabulous. Nothing surprises me when it comes to Bea.

'Saoirse, it's been featured in *Property Dreams*,' Ireland's answer to property show *Grand Designs*, 'and has won architectural awards and everything. It's fantastic!'

My mood lifts. Suddenly this trip is becoming more real and, despite my trepidation, I'm starting to feel excited about it.

'You can join me for a couple of days towards the end of the first week,' I say.

'You're feckin' right I will,' she responds.

I spend the next few minutes trying to extricate myself from my mother's incessant questions about The Cube, but before I sign off I ask her one question.

'Mum, what did the haiku say in that Marital Miracle box you just sold on eBay?' Despite my scepticism, I am curious to see my mother's perspective on relationships.

She clears her throat, and in her best staged voice, says solemnly:

Love keeps us going
We will always be as one
Never fall apart

'Not bad,' I tell her. I feel an unexpected lump in my throat. It makes me wonder if David and I will go the distance. I swallow hard as I say goodbye.

* * *

It is 6.30 p.m. when I hear the key in the door. Anna and I are on the tiny kitchen sofa, chuckling away at *Ben and Holly's Little Kingdom*, the one with the town mayor who is clearly modelled on Boris Johnson. I hear the clatter of David's shoes as they hit the ground, and I brace myself for The Big Sulk. This means no verbal communication or eye contact until a resolution has been made. Our longest record of silence has been three days, and quite frankly, I look back on that episode with a certain degree of fondness. Sometimes it's nice to have a bit of peace and quiet; freedom from all David's nitpicking and toe-clenching habits.

Based on past history, I presume he will go and hide in our bedroom to sulk for a bit longer. Well, let him. So, imagine my surprise when he strides straight into the kitchen and presents me with a stunning bunch of yellow roses.

David never buys me flowers. He thinks they are 'utterly useless and a total waste of money'. Such is his strength of feeling that he actually included it in his wedding vows.

But here I am, in total shock, holding a gorgeous bouquet of flowers, and my eyes start to fill up.

As if sensing a lovely emotional moment to ruin, Anna immediately grabs the bouquet and starts pulling off the heads of the flowers.

Well used to Anna's senseless delinquent behaviour, David and I immediately spring into action. He goes to take the flowers from her, while I wave the iPad in a threatening way just above the bin. Defeated, Anna retires sulkily to the couch, grabs the iPad off me and starts punching the code in with unnecessary force.

David and I exchange smiles. Nothing better than a good bit of teamwork when it comes to taming Anna.

He comes closer and kisses me on the lips. 'I'm sorry, Saoirse. I shouldn't have said all those things last night. And I shouldn't have moved all your stuff. I'm tired and stressed and sometimes I don't even know what I'm doing...'

And suddenly all the fight goes out of me. I see his face lined with exhaustion, and I think about how much pressure he is under at work, and although it isn't easy, I try to see things his way. We hug briefly and I do my best not to think of the next time we fall out, and the time after that. I suppose we could actually sit down and talk through everything, like we used to, but it's been so long since we communicated properly that it all just seems like too much hard work. A wave of sadness rushes over me. It's not the way I wanted us to end up, bickering and point-scoring all the bloody time. Maybe a break will give me the space I need to reflect on everything. I take a deep breath and tell him I have taken Anna out of nursery – for good – and then about Bea's offer to me to spend a couple of weeks by myself to work out of her holiday home in Ireland. To my surprise, he is totally fine with it – all of it. In fact, almost suspiciously fine with it.

'It's a good idea! You need the break. Anna and I will be fine. Won't we, Anna?' he says, loudly enough to get her attention.

Anna gives him her best death stare.

I try and fight the anxiety I feel about leaving Anna alone with David, but deep down I know I need to try to let go. He's her father and he needs to spend time with her.

'I'm glad you got her out of Rocking Horses,' he says. 'It was a total shithole.'

I laugh and the sound takes me by surprise. Then David does something else that hasn't happened in a very long time: he wraps his arms around me, and gives me a lingering warm kiss. I can't remember the last time we kissed outside the bedroom, and it gives me a tingly feeling I haven't felt in months. Eventually, we break away and David tells me he's going upstairs to change out of his suit.

Bathing in an unexpected warm glow, I set about getting a vase for the flowers. As I am cutting the ends off the stalks with a scissors, I hear the sound of David's phone buzzing. A text flashes up and catches my eye.

David – Call me. I have what you need. J.

It is followed by three lipstick kiss emojis.

Somewhere in the distance, I feel the scissors leave my right hand and clatter onto the kitchen floor.

David is having an affair.

PART II

IRELAND, PRESENT DAY

Value Your Freedom
Careful not to cross the line
Live without regret

10

The plane touches down in Dublin. As I walk to baggage reclaim, my left hand feels a little empty without Anna holding it. Without her, everything moves faster, and before I know it I'm in a cheap rental car driving through the misty rain down the M11 from Dublin to Wexford.

Two hours later, my GPS has shat itself about fifteen mins from Wexford city centre trying to find The Cube, which has no postcode and real address apart from being known locally as 'that glass thing on the hill'. Thankfully, Bea has provided me with wonderfully specific instructions ('Do NOT turn left at the sign that says, "The Cube" – turn right first and THEN left,' etc.) so, I am not completely at sea.

Eventually, I find myself driving slowly up a gravel dirt road inches from a large cliff before rounding a corner. And there in front of me, set about fifty metres from the wild cliff grasses, looms The Cube. I switch off the engine and just sit there for a moment. It's a building that deserves to be stared at. Of course I've seen it online but the photos don't do it justice. It is mostly made up of glass with gigantic floor-to-ceiling windows, supported by bricks that look as though they have been carved from the cliff itself. Its roof is perfectly flat, and it is indeed cube-shaped. I had thought that such a modern structure might have looked out of place against such a rustic background, but the glass has made it delicate, unimposing, and unobtru-

sive. It is a building comfortable in its surroundings and it gives me a sense
of comfort and indescribable peace that I haven't felt in a long time.

I step out onto the gravel, wrestle my suitcase from the tiny boot and
make my way towards the large front door, which looks like it has been
carved out of the nearest tree trunk. Using the keys that Bea has given me, I
open the door and step into a cool, airy open-plan L-shaped space covered
in creamy-white marble slabs. I close the door, drop my case, and start to
explore.

I walk by snuggly couches swathed with soft, furry blankets and throws
with gorgeously colourful cushions, before reaching a state-of-the-art
kitchen gleaming with stainless steel, offset by a sparkly black kitchen
island and three brightly coloured high stools. The mix of the soft furnish-
ings and the modern touches gives the whole place a lovely, warm,
comforting feel. I stroll back towards the front door, intent on exploring the
two bedrooms, and I am not disappointed. The master bedroom is a cheery
sky-blue with a soft fluffy white carpet and a king-sized bed covered in
fancy cushions. Bea's mum certainly has impeccable taste. I walk into the
spacious en suite bathroom, with its sparkling white tiles and beribboned
wicker baskets, and immediately lift the toilet lid. A ripple of pleasure
passes over me as I admire the impeccably clean toilet bowl. Between
David's forty-minute dumps (me to David: 'Why the hell don't you *look
behind you* after you flush?') and Anna's speedy-but-messy affairs ('But I *did*
flush, Mummy, I pwomise!'), I can't remember the last time I went to the
toilet without using a toilet brush first. I sit down on the gleaming seat and
allow myself a smile. It's the happiest wee I've had in ages.

As I come back into the bedroom, I realise that the master bedroom,
just like the rest of the rooms, is all-glass. I spend several minutes trying to
find cleverly hidden curtains or blinds, and just as I start getting a bit
nervous about being entirely on view to passers-by, I spot a small remote
control on one of the bedside tables. I click it with a degree of apprehen-
sion, wondering if this is the moment I trigger an alarm, but I'm relieved to
see blinds made of dark blue fabric fall effortlessly from an innocuous-
looking bar just below the ceiling. I throw myself on the bed and rest my
head on the soft cushions.

Peace.

Broken moments later by the sound of my phone ringing in my pocket. Sighing, I fish it out and reluctantly tap the answer button.

'I see you've arrived,' my mother says officiously.

I open my mouth to ask her how she knows I've just got here and then, knowing the answer already, I promptly close it again.

'Yes. The Cube is fabulous!' I tell her, unable to keep the excitement out of my voice.

Although my mother has already memorised every detail from viewing the house online, she is still keen to hear from me, so I go to great lengths to tell her all about it.

But of course in her world nothing is perfect so she has to find fault. She starts with the marble floors.

'Marble floors – they're awful cold in the winter. Must cost a fortune to heat the place.' And then moves on to the automated blinds.

'Sure, those things break all the time – very gimmicky and impractical.'

And finally, the location itself. 'That house is very close to the edge of the cliff – sure, it's that flimsy it might be blown into the sea!'

Feeling a little deflated, I say to her churlishly that given her views on the house she probably won't want to visit a freezing cold, gimmicky, unstable house after all.

She pauses a moment and says breezily, 'Ah, no, I'll definitely come and stay. Sure, what else would I be doing now I'm almost finished teaching for the summer?'

Then she tells me she'll be down towards the end of the week, which gives me a few days to get started on my writing.

After the call, I stare at my phone for a bit. I know I need to check in with David to let him know I have arrived safely and to see how Anna has survived her first full day with Bea's nanny, Maria. I know I should, but I need a moment.

David.

Since I found out about the affair a few days ago, I have managed to imprison all thoughts of David and his slut-boss, Jordan, to one tiny corner of my mind. My mother once told me that when she broke the news to me about my father's death, my first reaction was to take a photo of him from the mantelpiece and put it in a shoe box, which apparently I reserved for 'secret things'. As my mother had said, 'It's almost as if you were tucking the trauma away in a safe place so you wouldn't have to deal with it.'

Maybe I'm doing the same thing with David, but I am too numb to make any real sense of anything at the moment or maybe I just don't care enough.

Between throwing myself into packing for this trip, dealing with Anna full time, rounding off lots of domestic chores and admin, and providing endless instructions to Bea's nanny, Maria ('One of Anna's biggest fears is stew'), I haven't given myself a moment to dwell on it. I even managed to get through a visit to Rose's place in Oxfordshire ('In my day we didn't have iPads to stare at. We were just as happy with Poohsticks and conkers') without taking it out on David on the drive home.

Between more of David's late nights 'at work' and my strategically early bedtimes, I have barely seen him. It's like we've gone back to the baby days: the times where we barely saw each other and had gone from married couple to flatmates. But at least back then my flatmate hadn't been shagging someone else. He would have been too exhausted, for a start.

And then there's Anna. My stomach gives a lurch and suddenly I want to hold her as tightly as she'll let me and stroke her soft downy cheeks. I start to feel claustrophobic and jump off the bed, trying to shake off the beginnings of waves of emotion. I am determined not to let the fog engulf me. With a half-run, I fling open the sliding glass doors in the kitchen and trudge through the slanted wiry grass and spongey earth towards the cliff edge. Dusk is falling and I watch high up as the waves crash together in violent symphony against the jagged rocks below.

Standing a couple of feet from the edge I take the deepest breaths I am able.

I start to feel calmer as the pure, cold air fills my lungs and then the relief as I release it slowly. The air is so good here. I breathe deeply some more and focus on flooding all negative thoughts out of my mind.

When I feel calm again, I turn to go back to the house when I slam straight into someone else. The bump is so violent that I ricochet backwards and only for a hand pulling me to safety, I would have been part of the angry sea below.

Shaking, I look at the short, stout woman in front of me, who is still holding my hand. Although the light is poor, I see that she is in her mid-sixties with the type of uneven cropped red hair that looks as though she might cut it herself. She is wearing cropped pink trousers, white trainers, and a zip-up white hoodie. Her dark-green eyes are full of concern.

'Jesus, love! You nearly went over the cliff there,' she exclaims in a broad Irish country accent. She still hasn't let go of my hand and I realise I don't want her to. Her hand feels soft, maternal and reassuring.

'Thanks for saving me. I didn't see you behind me at all!' I reply, feeling less shaky now I am back on solid ground.

We stand there for a moment looking at each other, and then I remember that I am in Bea's back garden, and I wonder why she is there too.

I introduce myself and explain that I'll be staying for a couple of weeks.

'May I ask who you are?' I say.

I do a quick list of possible names in my head. What with her age and her rural accent, I'm guessing she is bound to be called one of the following: Brid, Brigid, Breda, Kitty, Nan, Nell, Nora, or Margaret.

'I'm Catherine,' she says, and adjusts her grip on my hand to a formal handshake before finally dropping it.

I feel an embarrassing sense of abandonment when she lets go of my hand.

Her name is Catherine. That'll teach me to generalise, I think.

'But everyone calls me Kitty,' she adds.

Ha! I allow myself an inwardly smug grin.

Not wanting to accuse her of trespassing, I ask her if she looks after the house and grounds when it's unoccupied. She gives me a hard look, narrows her eyes and says, defensively, 'I don't need permission to come up here. This isn't *The Field*, you know!'

Christ.

The last thing I need is to get into a tense discussion about Irish boundary laws with a woman who is most certainly eligible for a free bus pass.

'So, what takes you to this *field*?' I try again.

She breathes through her nose and looks away towards the moody sky. Moments go by and I'm beginning to regret asking her the question. When she finally looks back to me, her eyes are full of tears and I have no idea what to do. Do I give her a hug? Ask her what's wrong? Or do I go all 'English' (Agggh! Emotion from strangers!) and pretend I haven't noticed?

I choose the latter.

'It's a great view, isn't it?' I say, waving my hand vaguely. I hope that this tactic will give her a chance to recover, and I am relieved to see her discreetly dabbing her eyes with the sleeves of her hoodie.

'That it is,' she says, wistfully.

She takes a deep breath and gives her head a little shake, and then surprises me by asking about Bea. Of course, apart from giving me directions and the code for the Wi-Fi, Bea has followed her usual 'need to know basis' approach when it comes to useful information. In other words, she hasn't said a thing to me about Kitty.

'Bea's on great form,' I say.

'Poor Bea,' Kitty says, shaking her head. 'I haven't seen her or her mother in The Cube for a long time.'

Now I've heard Bea described in many ways over the last four years, but 'poor' isn't one of them.

But before I can dig any deeper, Kitty is asking about Harry and if Bea has found a 'new fella', and it suddenly dawns on me that Kitty feels sorry for Bea because she's a single mum. She's probably been gossiping to Bea's mum about her.

I suddenly feel defensive on behalf of my friend so I take great pains to tell Kitty that Bea is doing *brilliantly* – in a 'thank you very much' kind of way; that she has a great social life and a fantastic job; and that Harry is a *gorgeous* child. And all the time I am defensively gushing about my best friend, she stands there and listens, head cocked with a half-smile on her face.

When I'm finished, she just mutters, 'Ah, glad to hear she's doing so well.'

We stand there for a moment.

'Where are you living yourself?' she asks.

'London,' I say.

'Your accent has a touch of the West Brit,' she says suddenly. 'Where are you from?'

I feel like I've been punched in the stomach. Granted I'm married to a British man and my daughter is half-British and I've been living in the UK for twenty years, but where other more pretentious Irish people have failed, I have ALWAYS hung on to my Irish accent. To be called a 'West Brit' – or someone who secretly yearns to be British – is absolutely out of order.

'I'm from DUBLIN,' I semi-screech at her.

She regards me for a moment and then mutters something that suspiciously sounds like, 'Same thing.'

I'm beginning to go off Kitty. Just as I open my mouth to bid Kitty goodbye, she says, 'Are you a swimmer?'

Weary now, I shake my head.

'Can you swim, I mean?' she says impatiently.

I tell her that I can swim but avoid it where possible.

'Grand,' she says. 'Every morning around eleven o'clock, a group of us gather on the beach just at the bottom of the cliff steps over there.'

She grabs my arm and practically marches me over to the very back right-hand corner of the garden and sure enough, there is a row of large steps that have been carved out of the cliff.

'You should join us for a swim in the sea one day,' she says.

I laugh and shake my head, thinking of nothing worse than throwing myself into the icy waters of the frothing Irish Sea.

As if reading my thoughts, Kitty says, 'It's nice and calm when the tide comes in. It'll put a bit of colour back in your cheeks.'

I politely thank her for the invitation but just as I'm about to demur for the second time, she clasps my hand and says softly, 'It's good for the soul, Saoirse,' and gives me a look of such sympathy that I have to turn away. 'Whatever worries are clouding your mind, the sea will clear them.'

'I'll think about it!' I say brightly, blinking away unexpected tears.

'Do!' she says, dropping my hand for the final time, and with a brusque wave, I watch as she walks quickly out of the garden and onto the gravel road.

When I get back into the house, I go straight to the kitchen, pick the yellow kitchen stool, and pour myself a very large glass of wine. I think about Kitty and wonder how she knew about all my worries, and then I drink another glass and stop thinking about Kitty altogether. Full of boozy

Dutch courage I calmly text David to tell him I have arrived safely and to ask him to give Anna a big hug from me. I thought that saying goodbye to Anna would be heartbreaking, but she managed to make the whole distressing experience far less traumatic by kicking me up the arse for absolutely no reason. Apparently I chose the wrong moment to bend over and pick up my suitcase.

Two minutes later, I receive a chatty text telling me that Anna has had a blast with Maria the nanny and her 'partner in crime', Harry. Apparently, Anna hasn't mentioned me at all, which is a relief. I don't want her to miss me as much as I miss her. David signs off with his customary five kisses (it has be five – no other number will do) and, teary-eyed, I shut down my phone. No point in replying when he's probably sending the same kisses to someone else as well.

11

The next day is Saturday. I wake up at 7 a.m. with a heavy heart and a touch of a hangover. There is no reason for me to be awake at 7 a.m. – I have nothing to get up for. No Anna demanding Cheerios and then changing her mind twenty seconds later; no David (that cheating bastard) grumbling about the disorder of the fridge or the countless other domestic concerns that I couldn't give a shit about. This is freedom, but not the way I wanted it.

Desperately in need of distraction, I grab my phone to check Vale Mums, hating myself for my weakness.

Scrolling down, I see that chief Organic, Tania Henderson, has been on again, this time complaining about the 'screaming foxes' outside her house late the previous night. Apparently, the foxes woke up her little boy, Heath, who goes to bed at seven o'clock every night. Lots of sympathisers to this post, plus the odd crying emoji. So far so tame. Then Caroline – Tania's biggest fan – has to ruin it all by posting,

Tania – how DO you get Heath to bed at 7 p.m.??? My Sebastian refuses to go to bed until 8.30 p.m.!

Cue the inevitable patronising-yet-obvious tips ('Have you tried reading him a bedtime story?', 'What about some soothing music?' and 'A warm glass of milk before bedtime does wonders!') from Tania and the other smug mums just desperate to share their code-cracking strategies with 'poor Caroline'.

Feeling grateful to be irritated rather than depressed, I fling my phone down on the soft quilt and decide to get of bed. It may be a Saturday, but I have work to do. So I heave myself up and walk heavily to the bathroom. I wash my hair without removing all the stray hairs from the plughole, and deliberately leave the wet towels on the floor. Then I brush my teeth with my electric toothbrush and let the toothpaste drizzle onto the holder to make a nice gummy stain. Finally, I get dressed, leave the bedroom without making the bed, and pad across the cool marble tiles *without wearing any slippers*, before going to the kitchen to make myself some breakfast. Gratified to find a well-stocked fridge and cupboard, I decide on impulse to make myself a fry-up – one of David's most hated dishes (he can't bear the splashes of the oil on the hob) – and eat it all up contentedly at the kitchen island, facing the window that looks out over the back garden and the cliffs only a short distance away.

It is a glorious morning: bright, sunny and calm, with clear blue skies populated with low-hanging white clouds. After breakfast, I deliberately leave the dishes in the sink, mix up the cutlery drawers just for fun, and then throw open the sliding glass door to the back garden, and step outside into the cool sea breeze. Finally, a lovely sense of calmness rushes over me and I feel inspired. Before it slips away, I go back indoors to the bedroom momentarily and come back with my laptop, intending to get started on the pitch, only to find Kitty standing in my kitchen, dressed in just a swimsuit and flip-flops, her hand clutching a beach towel.

I give a little squeal of fright and my laptop almost falls from my grip.

'So, are you coming then?' she says, with the confidence of someone who has made a firm prior engagement.

'What do you mean?' I ask, stunned that this woman is now standing half-dressed in my kitchen as if it's the most normal thing in the world.

'Swimming!' she says impatiently.

'Kitty, I never said I was going to go swimming today,' I reply, trying to keep calm.

'But sure, it's a beautiful day!' she says, genuinely surprised. 'Why would you miss it?'

'Kitty,' I say her name again with the vague hope that she will actually listen to what I'm saying. 'I am not going swimming. I have to work.' I hold up my laptop and sort of shake it at her in the hope that she will finally get the message and feck off.

She stares at the laptop and then back to me. 'Well, OK then,' she sighs disappointedly, as if I have just pulled out of a very important commitment. She makes her way towards the door and steps back out into the garden.

My heart sings in relief.

She turns and I give her a cheery wave goodbye and I watch her stout figure walk steadily towards the stone steps she showed me the previous evening. Just as reaches the steps, she turns and calls out, 'I'll try you again tomorrow so.'

My stomach plummets.

Trying to shake off the worrying feeling of being stalked, I set up my laptop on the kitchen island, and start to type. I type about the guilt, and the shame and the isolation I felt after Anna came along, how my world shrank to the size of an acorn, and how everyone else seemed to know what they were doing but me. I write about my bitter, resentful feelings towards David and how unsupported I felt. When I have finished writing I feel exhausted, and slightly worried. I have poured my whole soul onto a couple of pages and it's tough to think that they might turn into a book, which will, one day, be out in the world for anyone to see. But I can't think like that now – I have to take it one step at a time.

Although I'm tired, I am reluctant to walk away from that lovely 'in the zone' feeling, and so I start to think about what else I should write about. I mean, we had the baby; she wasn't the best-looking; I found out that my nose was too big for my face; nearly ended up in the nuthouse with the fear, shame, and guilt... Now what? So much has happened but I'm not sure what to focus on next. Let's see... how about unfaithful husbands? Or slut bosses called Jordan? Or the fact that my whole world is falling apart?

I put my hands on my head and take some deep breaths, forcing the anxiety down. I need to focus. Feeling more grounded, I tap my fingers impatiently on the keyboard.

Time for a glass of water. I drain it and return to the laptop.

Nothing productive happens.

Shit.

My stomach starts to rumble for no reason, given that I have just stuffed sausages, bacon and a fried egg into it, but it reminds me that I really should go to the shops to stock up on some 'necessities'.

Telling myself that a trip to the shops isn't skiving, I grab my bag and keys and then come to a sudden pause by the door. I automatically turn round to call Anna, and feel a pang of anxiety when I remember she's not with me. The thought of it makes me feel physically sick. I reach for my phone and text David to ask him to send a photo of her, of how she looks right now. I need to see her. Even more worrying is the fact that today will be the first time in her four years that she will be spending the entire day with her father – and she hates him these days. What if she doesn't let David help her get dressed or hold her hand when they're crossing the road? Or what if she refuses to eat anything he makes for her? Jesus, she could go on hunger strike. I know I'm being ridiculous and irrational; David is her father, for goodness' sake. He may be a cheating, lying scumbag, but he adores Anna.

After I've sent the message, I grab my coat, fling open the door and on impulse decide to leave the car and carry on down the gravel road on foot to the nearby village I drove through the previous day.

When I reach the bottom of the slope, I turn left towards the village and take the route under a disused railway-bridge tunnel. It feels dark and cool in the tunnel and I am pleased to find the air pleasantly smelling of grass and flowers, rather than shit and piss, which would have most likely been the case in London.

PING! I check my phone and I am relieved to see a picture of my only child fully dressed in her vampire Halloween costume, giving me the thumbs up. David has captioned the photo, 'Off to the cinema!' Tears of relief blind my eyes: not only is Anna alive, but she looks positively delighted.

As I go to put my phone away, I almost crash into a woman hurtling along, steering a pram with one hand and a screaming toddler in the other. I jump out of her way as quickly as I can, but one of the pram wheels runs over my right foot none the less. I give a small squeal of pain, and she comes to an abrupt halt.

She takes one look at my foot and contorted face, and says, 'WILL YOU GET THE FUCK OUT OF MY WAY?'

I am outraged. How dare she? *She's* the one who just ran over my foot with her fucking buggy. Yet all attempts to articulate my rage are drowned by the ear-piercing death-inducing cries of her red-faced toddler, and her attempts to soothe him.

I soften.

There she is, trying to take care of what looks to be like a two-year-old *and* a tiny baby. I remember how hard it is dealing with just Anna; I can't imagine the horror of managing two children who look so close in age.

I want to say something comforting to this harassed mother, who has now plonked the toddler on the ground and is using both hands to search frantically in her changing bag, presumably for something to placate him, but I'm not sure what. The pram starts to slowly roll away and I immediately jump into action and grab the handle before it can go any further.

I wheel it back to where the mum is still crouching on the ground. A blissful silence has fallen now that she has managed to find a lollipop to keep her son happy. She stands up, and looks at me with those sleep-deprived black-bag-ridden eyes I remember so well myself.

'Thanks for getting the pram,' she mutters in a low voice.

Just as I am about to respond with a token 'No problem', we are joined by another visitor to the tunnel.

This time it's an elderly lady, probably in her late seventies, dragging one of those zipped paisley shopping bags on wheels.

'Well, hello, ladies!' she says brightly. 'And who do we have here?'

She drops the handle of her shopping bag and sticks her face right into the pram.

'Would you look at that! A beautiful baby!' she says, in a tone of such surprise that I immediately wonder what else she might have expected to see in a full-size pram.

She pulls her head out of the pram, looks directly at the mum and says, 'Boy, is it?'

The woman sighs.

'No, it's a girl, actually,' she replies. 'She's wearing *all* pink,' she adds, clearly irritated.

The old woman nods her head absent-mindedly and then turns her attention to the toddler, who is sitting on the ground contentedly sucking his lollipop.

She frowns at him for a bit, turns to his mum, takes a deep breath and says with a little titter, 'You must be a very *relaxed* mother. My mother never would have given me a lollipop so early in the morning, and I have to say, none of my kids had sweets in the morning either.'

She leans into the exhausted mother as if she is imparting some vital information and whispers, 'Not good for the teeth!'

Then she gestures to the baby and with sudden watery eyes tells her to 'enjoy every minute'; that 'time goes by so fast'; that 'they'll have flown the nest in no time'; and that 'these are the best years of your life'.

All the while this old biddy is talking, the mother seems to shrink into herself. I watch how her shoulders slump in defeat and see the look of tight-lipped shame, and I can tell exactly what she is thinking because I used to feel the same way. Guilt – terrible crushing guilt – that you're doing everything wrong.

I take a deep breath and fold my arms.

It's time to put an end to all this.

I take a step towards the old woman, fix her with a hard look and tell her, 'No,' in the sternest voice I can muster.

She looks at me in surprise as if she has just noticed me standing there.

'I don't understand, dear,' she says, wrinkling her wrinkles.

'I mean that these *aren't* the best days of a mother's life; time does not whizz by; in fact it goes *more* slowly because you are up all day and half the night.'

The old lady gives me such a poisonous look that I'd swear she has been a nun in a former life. But I'm not finished yet.

'And on another point, don't you EVER judge a sleep-deprived mother for giving her tantruming toddler a lollipop. The problem with your generation is that you FORGET how hard it is to be a mum. Next time, be more bloody considerate instead of waving around your useless platitudes and judgements.'

Now I'm finished.

The elderly lady points at me for a bit, muttering something that sounds suspiciously like a hex, and then grabs the handle of her bag and stalks off, still grumbling.

I look at the mum and she flashes me a weak smile.

'The old ones are the worst,' I say. 'Having said that, she was right about one thing.'

'What's that?' the mum says.

'You do have a beautiful baby,' I say, peering into the pram at the sparkly blue-eyed little doll staring back at me.

'Beautiful baby *girl*,' I clarify.

The mum laughs suddenly.

'Her name is Niamh and I suppose she is lovely,' she admits with all the well-earned pride of a new mum. 'There is a problem, though.'

'What's that?'

'Her brother fucking hates her,' she says, resignedly.

'Ah sure, that's normal,' I reply.

'I suppose. But Conor is such a little prick these days,' she says, looking at her toddler a bit tearfully.

And I take one look at her exhausted face, wild hair, and milk-stained top and I see my own reflection from a few years back. I think about what Bea did for me that day on the bus and suddenly I want to do the same for her.

'What are you doing now?' I say.

'I'm on my way home to tackle a mountain of shitting laundry,' she says ruefully.

'Fancy a beer?' I say.

She laughs as if I'm joking and then stops abruptly when she realises I'm deadly serious.

Her eyes look hopeful and then resigned. 'Come on,' I cajole. 'Your little boy will be grand running around the pub. We'll get him some chips if he's hungry, and your baby looks like a contented little thing.'

She looks at me for a moment, nods decisively to herself, sticks out her hand, and says, 'You're on.'

And so we make our way out of the tunnel into the bright sunshine, me wheeling the pram and her carrying her toddler, all thoughts of shopping, work and laundry completely forgotten.

The next morning I wake up at six o'clock with my heart beating too fast and a feeling of inexplicable euphoria. It's the first time since I found out about David's affair that I've woken up in such a positive mood and it feels exhilarating. I lie there for a moment searching my mind for why I have such a feeling of anticipation and my throbbing head reminds me that I am probably still pissed from yesterday. I groan and turn over, trying to go back to sleep, but it's useless. I am too fired up for sleep. Grumbling, I gently heave myself out of bed, legs first, trying desperately not to move my aching head. My tongue is firmly rooted to the roof of my mouth and I desperately need some non-alcoholic bubbles.

I check the fridge and find it comes up short on pretty much everything I crave for a hangover. Not surprising, given the shopping-dodge I did yesterday.

'I'd kill for a Coke or a 7-Up,' I mutter to myself, slamming the fridge door shut.

I settle for a glass of water instead, but it's not the same as the cool fizz I'm craving. As I sit on the stool at the kitchen island, cradling the water, I spend a few moments trying to remember the hazy events of the previous day. I know that Deirdre, 'but everyone calls me Dee' and I went to McGowan's pub on the high street around midday. Channelling Bea, we started on Prosecco and when that became 'too acidy' we switched to red wine instead. I vaguely remember a man (could have been the father of Dee's children, maybe?) coming to pick up the kids, but Dee staying behind to drink with me. I have no idea what we talked about, what we ate (or even if we ate), or what time I left the pub.

The oven clock tells me it's now 6.10 a.m. and I wonder what I'm going to do with myself. I can't go back to sleep and my jerky stomach tells me it's too soon for food.

It occurs to me that I have no idea where Dee lives or even her last name. If this was London, I'd never see her again, and if I did, we would meet as near-strangers, almost as if our drunken togetherness had been an illusion. I remind myself that this is a tiny village in southern Ireland where everyone knows each other. There is no doubt that I will bump into Dee again.

I finish my water and look guiltily at my laptop, which I had abandoned on the kitchen island a good eighteen hours before. A panicky feeling surges through my upset stomach.

With a huge effort, I slide the laptop over to where I'm sitting and flip open the lid. The white screen of writer's block fills me with horror and before I know quite what I'm doing, I start to type for the comfort of seeing something fill the terrible space.

I write for what seems like minutes but actually turns out to be hours. When I finally stop and read over it, I am pleasantly surprised that it is halfway coherent. It turns out that the tiny part of my brain that hasn't been violently assaulted by extreme alcohol consumption has retained the part about the old lady in the tunnel. I write about the impact of judgement on being a mother, raining verbal blows on old ladies with bad memories and trite comfortless pleasantries, and smug mums who argue for wooden versus plastic toys, organic versus normal food, and full-time mum versus full-time job. Then I end it with, 'After all, the good thing about plastic toys is that they don't get woodworm.'

I spend another hour editing it and when I am finished, I am pleased how it reads. Besides, it feels wonderfully cathartic to blast those who make parenting far, far harder than it needs to be.

Satisfied with an unexpectedly productive morning, I get off the stool to stretch. And then screech because there is an elderly man's face pressed against the glass of one of the sliding doors. When he sees I've spotted him, he steps back from the window and gives me a jovial wave. At first sight, he seems harmless enough but I'm still in my cotton nightie with no pants underneath, and there's no way I'm opening that door. I mime a 'what the fuck do you want?' gesture, and he makes a swimming motion (breaststroke to be exact) in return.

I almost give him the finger but as he is an older man, wearing a saggy old grey tracksuit, I don't have the heart. Sighing, I ease the door open a small way.

'I'm Frank. Kitty told me to get you,' he says, sticking his head through the gap. 'Says you're mad for the swimming!'

I raise my eyes skywards and feel my hands balling into fists.

'I'm afraid Kitty was mistaken,' I say formally. I don't mean to be rude but these people don't seem to get the message.

'Ah, you're British!' he replies. 'Well, that makes sense. The Brits don't like the cold water.'

What? Kitty has accused me of being a 'West Brit' and now this old fella has straight-out called me British. Enough is enough!

'I. AM. IRISH!' I say, speaking like Mr Slow from Anna's *Mr Men* collection.

'Are you indeed?' he says, surprised.

'First generation,' I say, laying on the accent as thick as I am able.

He folds his arms, looks at me appraisingly and says, 'Well, if you're as Irish as you think you are, you'll dive into the Irish Sea, no bother!'

Feeling I have been tricked somehow, I give him a short wave, before slamming the door, sloping back to my room and diving under the covers, where I can hide in the safety of a room with fucking blinds.

I fall asleep and wake up at 3 p.m., feeling a lot less hungover but absolutely starving. There is one voicemail and a text message. I listen to the voicemail first. It's my mother. She begins with 'Do you know who's...?' and then... nothing. Either she's got distracted by her latest eBay auction or her phone has died in the middle of leaving a message. I am not the least bit curious about what she was going to say. I know my mother well enough to finish the sentence without prompting.

Dead.

As in, 'Do you know who's dead?'

Calls like this are a fairly regular occurrence now that my mother has got a bit older. I am rarely sentimental about these deaths because *I have no idea who these people are.* These types of calls usually go along these lines:

Mum: 'Do you know who's dead?'

Me: (sighing) 'No.'

Mum: 'Margaret Murphy.'

Me: 'I have no idea who that is.'

Mum: 'Margaret! Who used to drop you to playschool when you were three? Surely you remember Margaret!'

Me: (hazarding a guess just so we don't have to talk about Margaret any more) 'Did she have brown hair?'

Mum: 'No!'

Dammit.

Mum: 'The hair was straight from a bottle. Dyed it for years. Now that I think of it, I wouldn't be surprised if it wasn't the bleach that killed her.'

Cue the sound of heavy thudding while I bang my head against the nearest brick wall.

As I'm not in a hurry to call my mother back, especially with the remnants of a hangover, I click on the text message. It's from David to say he has left Anna with Bea for a few hours as he needs to go to an important meeting. He signs off with his customary five kisses and I want to thump him. First, it's a Sunday; as long as I have known David he has never gone into the office on a Sunday. A hot flush of anger sweeps over me with the sudden realisation that he is most likely with that slut Jordan. In fact, I would bet my life on it. But what enrages me the most – far more than the thought of him having sex with someone else – is his cavalier attitude towards Anna, binning her off on a Sunday. It's not like he sees her much during the week. The least he could do is keep his fucking boxers on for one weekend.

I pick up the phone and dial Bea.

'Hello? Yes? Is that you, Mum? No, Harry, you've had enough bananas. You don't want to get tummy pains.'

Despite my frustration, I grin.

'Relax. It's me, not your mum,' I say, laughing.

'Oh, good. She's due to call soon so stay on the line as long as you can. I can't face hearing about the latest "juicing diet" for small children,' she says, sounding more like her commanding self.

'I hear David has thrown my child at you for the day,' I say. 'How is she?'

'She's been absolutely fine. Does me a favour, really. She keeps Harry on his toes! Hasn't asked for you once,' she says firmly.

I exhale in relief. I can't bear the thought of Anna crying and wondering why I have abandoned her.

'Can I talk to her?'

Bea calls Anna over and a moment later I hear the heavy breathing of a serial killer on the other end. I greet her and ask her how she is, and she breathes in reply. It's like listening to an anonymous caller. I can hear Bea in the background explaining that it's Mummy on the phone, and to say hello. At last, she starts to speak.

'I want Skype,' she says.

I forget what a child of technology she is, at the age of four.

A couple of minutes later, her big eyes come into view and I blow her lots of kisses. I ask her how her day out with Daddy was, and she gives me a surly, 'Good.' I exhale in relief. 'Good' for Anna means she had a great time. Maybe they are starting to bond after all. Then I ask her what movie she went to, and I get a shrug in return. She stares at the screen for a bit, and says, 'Mummy, why do you have so many spots on your face?'

My hand flies immediately to my face, trying to assess the damage from last night. I tend to get a bit spotty after a night on the booze. Trust Anna to point it out.

'There's a big one on your nose,' she says, touching the screen with her finger. 'Just there.'

Trying to change the subject, I ask her how she's been and what she's been doing, and she warms up enough to tell me that she's been 'having fun with Harry, even though he's a bit naughty sometimes' and she's been eating lots of treats. At this point, Bea sticks her face in front of the camera and reassures me that Anna has not been fed too much shite, but enough to keep her happy.

I wave her away – the fact that she is looking after Anna for me is more than enough to make up for how much crap she's been eating.

A few moments later, Anna wanders off and Bea comes back on again.

'She really is fine, Saoirse,' she says. 'And she seems happy enough with David.'

I frown. 'Did he tell you why he palmed Anna off on you today?'

'Said something about a meeting,' she replies. 'But come to think of it, he was in shorts and T-shirt. I know it's a Sunday, but isn't there still a dress code he needs to stick to?'

I shake my head at David's stupidity; could he not cover his tracks a little better than that? In contrast with other trendy social media firms, where ragged denim and holey T-shirts are the accepted work gear, David's company prides itself on its employees being professionally dressed at all times. The most he can get away with is chinos and a smart shirt. He would never ever go to work in just shorts and T-shirt.

'To be honest, I felt a bit sorry for him,' she continues. 'He looked bloody awful and he seemed so stressed. I asked him in for a cuppa but he told me he was already running late.'

Before I can stop myself, I make a vomiting face.

'What's wrong?' Bea asks sharply.

And I open my mouth to tell her that David is off to a different kind of meeting from what she thinks, and then I close it again. Now is not the time, not with Anna in the background.

Instead, I tell her how grumpy I am about Kitty and Frank, the psychotic swimmers, and how I have become the subject of their mission to plunge me into sub-zero temperatures.

Bea looks at me and hesitates for a moment.

'Oh, yes, the swimming club. My mother swears by it.'

'Yes, I can certainly see how I would be "swearing" by it if I went even as far as dipping my toes in,' I reply smartly.

'The locals always hassle visitors to The Cube about it,' she goes on.

I am flabbergasted.

'Why?'

'It's sort of a rite of passage for us foreigners,' she explains.

I bristle at this. Not her too.

'I'm NOT a fucking foreigner!' I say.

'Well, to them you are. You've deserted the Emerald Isle for the big city and you married a Brit so...'

Before I can reply, she adds, '*And* you're from Dublin, so in a way, that's even worse than being a foreigner.' Her forehead crinkles a bit. 'In retrospect, I'm shocked the locals are talking to you at all,' she finishes.

Before I can express my sheer indignation, she says something strange.

'Did Kitty mention anything to you about me?'

I don't tell her that I suspect Kitty feels sorry for her for being a single mum so I just tell her that Kitty has been asking after her and Harry.

'Good, good,' she says, her expression growing dark, 'because—'

But I don't get to hear the rest because we are interrupted by an ear-splitting scream.

Anna.

Bea jumps up and races off, and I sit and wait at the other side of the screen, feeling bloody useless and extremely anxious.

Two minutes later, Bea comes back holding a teary-looking Anna by the hand.

'They were fighting over the iPad,' she explains.

'Did David not give you Anna's when he dropped her off?' I say, incredulously.

Bea shakes her head.

Fucking useless is what he is. Jesus, fuck that slut Jordan if you want, but at least remember to give Anna the bloody iPad.

Harry comes over and punches Bea on the arm, presumably because she is comforting Anna. 'What were you going to say about Kitty anyway?' I ask, trying to shout over the pandemonium.

'Oh, don't worry about it,' she says, gripping Harry by the wrists to prevent him from smacking her in the face.

Time to go.

'I'll sign off. Thanks again for looking after Anna,' I say hurriedly.

Anna gives me a quick wave and wanders off again. Then the screen goes dark, the call ended.

I think for a minute. There's no fucking way I'm getting into that icy water, even if bestselling children's cookbook author Arianna Wakefield thinks it's the best thing since vegetable ice lollies.

I am distracted by an unattractive growl coming from the region of my stomach. Time to get some food. I jump in the shower, get dressed and, as it's raining, I hop into my little convertible, once again rejoicing in the freedom of having a sporty little number all to myself.

I drive down the windy gravel road to the bottom of the cliff and take the route straight into the village, my stomach churning unpleasantly as I pass McGowan's pub – the scene of yesterday's all-day drinking – and grab a parking space just outside the local newsagent's.

As soon as I'm in the shop, I head straight towards the sweets and crisps section, craving sour, fizzy sweets – the best thing for a hangover. A child's wail goes up and at once I feel a mixture of sympathy for the mother and relief that it's not me. The sweetie aisle is the most treacherous to navigate and only ends one way – in tears.

As I zoom in towards the E numbers, a little hand grabs mine. I look down and there is Conor, Dee's little boy, red-faced and teary.

'Where's your mum?' I ask him, and he bursts into tears again.

Just then Dee runs into the aisle, looking frantic, the pram rocking dangerously. An expression of relief crosses her face as she sees Conor.

'Jesus, Conor! Never EVER run off like that again,' she says, picking up and holding him close. He stops crying and snuggles into her.

She turns to me and sighs.

'I was at the tills when he ran off,' she says.

'That's nothing,' I reply quickly. 'Once I lost Anna in our local park and it took me thirty minutes to find her. Turns out she had disappeared into the woodsy part to look for fairies.'

Dee laughs and her shoulders relax.

'Anyway, how's your head this afternoon?' she says.

'About as good as yours, I imagine,' I reply.

'I'm dying,' she says.

'Yep – me too!'

'Did Ryan see you home all right?' she asks, her eyebrows raised.

I am confused. 'Who's Ryan?'

She bursts out laughing. 'Christ, how pissed were you?'

I think hard. I remember joking with the barman a bit, and there was definitely a live band playing very traditional diddly-aye music, but I have no memory of anyone called Ryan.

I shrug, totally nonplussed.

'I can't believe you don't remember Ryan the Ride!' she says, through more bursts of laughter. 'Sure, you were talking to him for half the night!'

My heart sinks. If I don't remember talking to Ryan, what else don't I remember?

Evidently noting my concern, Dee puts a reassuring hand on my arm.

'Don't worry, you weren't doing anything wrong. I was there the whole time and we were all just laughing and joking together.'

I am relieved but I am still puzzled by one thing.

'Why did Ryan take me home?'

'He was being a gent. You were three sheets to the wind and about to do an "Irish Goodbye" and he didn't want you walking home in the dark,' she explains.

I frown, annoyed with myself, first, for trying to leave without telling anyone; and secondly, for letting a total stranger walk me up that unlit cliff path. Jesus, I'm forty years old, married with a child. It's not good enough to get shit-faced and go off with strangers at my age. That's something you do in your twenties.

'Saoirse, don't beat yourself up. Honestly, I wouldn't have let Ryan walk you home if I didn't know him. He's been coming here for summers for years. And he's pretty easy on the eye, too!' she says, winking.

I laugh suddenly and shake off the guilt. I got pissed, had a bit of craic with a stranger – a good-looking one, by the sounds of it – and that was it. No harm done.

Dee and I chat for a bit longer before making arrangements to meet at McGowan's in a couple of days. We both agree that staying off the booze for at least twenty-four hours is probably a good idea.

When she leaves I turn back to the sweetie aisle and gather a satisfactory selection of the types of fizzy sweets that melt your teeth just by looking at them. Then I pick up some carbonated drinks, a gigantic pepperoni pizza, and head for the tills.

Outside I am pleased to see that the rain has stopped and a hint of sunshine has crept out from behind the clouds. When I get into the car, I contemplate opening the roof, berate myself for even thinking the sunshine is going to last, and get back just moments before the heavens open.

As soon as I am home, I switch the oven on in preparation for the pizza. I am almost giddy with anticipation. David doesn't 'do' Italian food (who the fuck doesn't eat Italian food?) so I rarely have it in the house. I count this pizza, along with all the other rules I have broken, as part of my mission to give David the silent two fingers.

As I pop the frozen goodness into the oven, my phone starts to vibrate in my pocket. It's my mother. Shite, I have forgotten to call her back.

I answer with a sigh.

'Who's dead then?' I say. Might as well get it over and done with.

'What? Who's dead?' she says, sharply.

'Nobody's dead – that I know of,' I reply.

'So why are you talking about dead people?' she says, sounding irritated and perplexed.

'It's just that you left a message earlier,' I explain, feeling slightly foolish. Clearly I had jumped the gun in my attempt to decipher her voicemail.

'Oh, yes,' she says vacantly. 'I did start to leave you a message but then a photo of Betty and her husband, Jim, popped up on the Instagram and I got distracted.'

'Right,' I say, and I'm just about to ask her what she had intended to say in her message when she goes into the story of Betty and Jim, whoever the hell they are. Apparently, Jim and Betty had split up a year ago because Jim had caught Betty 'sexting' some fella she met on an Irish dating website for the elderly, Sean.ie ('sean' meaning 'old').

'And there the pair of them are – taking photos of themselves drinking cocktails together in Tenerife – as if nothing had ever happened,' my mother finishes. I can almost see her shaking her head in disbelief.

'Anyway,' I say, 'what did you want to say to me in the message?'

'Oh, yes. Do you know who's staying just around the corner from you there in Wexford?' she says, with her trademark sniff, triumphant in the certainty that she knows something that I don't.

'I really don't,' I say in a bored voice. Someone who used to pick me up from playschool when I was three? I add silently. My pizza will be ready in two minutes and I refuse to waste any more time.

'Jen!' she announces.

I am stunned into silence.

'Jen! Your best friend from school! She's spending a few days in her aunt Hilda's place just down the road from you,' Mum chatters happily as if she's breaking the world's best news to me.

Of all the people she could have mentioned (dead or alive) Jen is the last person I would have thought of. What the hell was Jen doing in this tiny town in the middle of nowhere? Before I can ask, Mum rushes in to fill the gaps.

'Anyway, it turns out that Jen has been jilted by Liam, that fella she's been seeing for years,' she announces.

Jesus. I haven't been in touch properly with Jen for a long time. Apart from the token 'Happy birthday' texts and a few 'likes' on Facebook, we haven't had a decent conversation since Anna was born. But I am shocked to hear about her spilt with Liam. On Facebook they seemed the perfect couple. Always going away to exotic locations and posting lots of photos of their toes against backgrounds of impossibly blue oceans and dying sunsets, that sort of thing. They seemed destined for a life of togetherness and now it's over.

'I don't think "jilted" is the right word,' I say to my mother, crossly. 'It's not like she's been left at the altar or anything.'

There is a firm tapping and a brief silence. I should have kept my big mouth shut.

'Now, I've just checked the Google, and jilted means rejected, left, dropped, ditched, deserted and abandoned,' she says in her most pompous voice. 'I don't think a wedding is needed just to use the word "jilted", do you?'

I sigh, recognising that I have lost this particular verbal swordfight.

'So, why has Jen been jilted?' I say reluctantly.

'Because of the Big C,' she says with great casualness. 'He can't handle it.'

My stomach dips and mind churns. Holy Christ, my best friend from home is sick – really sick. Her boyfriend has deserted her, and she's all by herself in some old person's cottage in the middle of nowhere. I gulp and try to form the words of my next question.

'How far gone is she?' I whisper.

Jen with no hair. Jen looking frail, with dark circles under her eyes, the blush to her cheeks painfully absent.

'What?' my mother says, sounding impatient. 'What do you mean "far gone"? I told you, she's only around the corner from you there in Wexford, not far at all.'

Irritation and anger replace shock.

'No – I mean how bad is her cancer?' I say, feeling the tears bubble into my eyes.

There is a short silence.

'Jesus, Saoirse. Jen doesn't have cancer! Where did you get that idea?' she says, with an indignant chuckle.

If she was beside me now I'd probably give her a slap.

'You said she had the Big C!' I roar at her, expelling frustration and relief from every part of my body.

My mother gives one big tut, and says, 'I was talking about CHILDREN,' spelling it out as if I'm both a bit deaf and stupid. 'Liam wants kids, she doesn't. That's why they split up.'

Bloody hell, poor Jen. That's terrible. Not as horrific as getting cancer, obviously, but very sad all the same.

'Anyway, she's taking a break from that fashion work for a few days and staying in her aunt Hilda's place,' she explains. 'Have you ever met Hilda?'

'I don't think so,' I say.

'Hilda Snowdon,' she says.

'No,' I say again, feeling tired and impatient.

'Prod,' she replies.

I sigh. I couldn't give a shite if Jen's aunt Hilda is a Protestant or a Catholic. My best friend is heartbroken, for goodness' sake.

'You should go and see her,' she says. 'She needs her friends around her at a time like this.'

I swallow hard and tell her I will get in touch with Jen.

'Ah, good. I'll text you her address,' she says softly, much calmer now.

I've never told my mum the reason why Jen and I lost touch over the last few years but I have a feeling she knows that we're not the friends we used to be.

A burning smell emanates from the oven, and I tell my mum that I have to go and rescue the pizza, and I hang up in a hurry.

Grabbing the oven gloves, I take the pizza out with slightly trembling hands and place it on a big wooden board on the kitchen island. My phone beeps and Jen's address flashes up on the screen. I look at the mass of glistening pepperoni and gluey mozzarella and turn away. I seem to have lost my appetite.

13

It's 10 a.m. on Monday and while I'm grateful my hangover is gone, I still wake up feeling tired and low. My mind is full of Jen. Jen and I doing 'knick knacks' (knocking on doors and running away) at an age where we really should have known better; Jen using free make-up samples in The Body Shop to try out different shades of lipstick on me; or Jen and I drinking 'Fisherman's Fuck' (a concoction made up of a lethal mix of measures of alcohol sneaked from our parents' supplies) on the local green, and then vomiting in miserable synchronisation directly afterwards.

Staring at the ceiling, I think hard about the last time I spent some proper time with Jen. It must have been over four years ago. I was six months pregnant with Anna at the time and Jen had flown over from Dublin to London and taken me shopping for maternity clothes, so I would no longer look like 'a fat bag lady', as she put it. I smile at the memory. It was always handy to have a personal shopper for a best friend.

A text from Maria, Bea's nanny, pops up. It's a photo of Harry and Anna at the local park, each sitting on a swing, both making the types of silly faces that would never make it to a Facebook post. Seeing Anna so happy makes me feel more relieved than I ever imagined.

I reach over for the remote control and press the button to raise the blinds. Might as well get up and start the day.

As the blinds inch their way up from the ground, I am not remotely surprised to see a pair of pale pink runners, attached to pale calves and then as it rises further, two knobbly knees, followed by white baggy shorts, a green polo shirt, and finally Kitty's upturned mouth and raised eyebrows. She shakes her rolled-up swimming towel at me and makes an impatient 'come on' gesture. I wait for the click of the blind as it reaches the ceiling before flinging my legs out of bed, and stomping over to the window, fully armed with a gesture of my own for Kitty. But then I think about David's affair and how much I miss Anna, and Jen's heartbreak... and I turn to Kitty and give her a reluctant thumbs up. What I have got to lose?

Before I can chicken out, I hurriedly put on my swimsuit (which, now I come to think of it, Bea had told me to bring) with a heavy-cotton beach dress over it, grab a towel from the bathroom, and take off my wedding and engagement rings. I feel a flash of pain when I see the bare, lonely ring imprint on my left hand, but as cross as I am with David, I hate the thought of losing those rings to the crashing Irish Sea. I leave the rings on the bedside table and march out the patio doors in the kitchen, determined not to let David's indiscretions get me down.

In fairness to Kitty, she doesn't gloat. She simply makes small talk about the weather – 'There's a wind out that will blow away a few cobwebs' – and gives me advice about the tides and the currents – 'Be sure to swim well behind the set of rocks shaped like a camel humping another camel and you'll be grand' – while we make our way down the steps to the sandy beach below. I ask her if she has any tips on actually getting into the icy and, quite frankly, choppy-looking waters without screaming, and she laughs and tells me to 'stop being such a foreigner'. When we arrive at the bottom of the steps, Kitty guides me towards a small hollow naturally cut out of the rocky cliff face.

'This is our shelter,' she announces, spreading her arms wide.

As I move closer, colourful graffiti across the rocky wall catches my eye, but the letters are illegible.

'Oh, it's a shame that some thug has defiled your swimming spot,' I say.

She looks at me in surprise. 'That's no thug, that's Frank's work!' she replies, somewhat indignantly.

I think about the sweet-yet-persistent old man who had tried to strong-arm me into swimming, and simply can't reconcile this image with a sense-less graffiti artist.

'We were fed up of the young lads pissing and smoking in our shelters, so Frank came up with the idea of spray painting our names on the rocks. Just to show these eejits that this piece of rock is taken,' she says, fondly tracing the letters with her hands.

I look more closely and if I squint one eye just a little, I'm almost sure I can make out a 'K' or maybe an 'F'. There also appears to be a third group of lopsided letters at the bottom and I think I can see an 'R' and an 'N'. Kitty seems pleased when I tell her this.

'Well, I'm glad you can see something, because I can't make head or tail of it,' she laughs. 'Frank made a right balls of it!'

I laugh along with her, relieved she thinks the whole thing is as muddled as I do.

'How many names are there?' I say, refocusing on the jumble in front of me.

'At one stage there were a dozen of us,' Kitty says, sounding wistful. 'But there are only a couple of us now.'

I have a feeling I'm not going to want to know what happened to the rest of the swimmers, so I decide not to say anything. But she tells me anyway.

'Dead,' she says.

I am astonished. Ten out of twelve swimmers dead seems like quite a high number.

Kitty uses her fingers to explain the reasons for the deaths: four heart attacks ('I blame the local chipper'); one drowning ('Eejit went beyond the rocks shaped like camels humping each other – let that be a lesson to you'); four of natural causes ('Sure, they were all in their nineties – what do you expect?'); and finally, a suicide.

I feel my head snap up.

'Suicide?'

'Yes, but we don't talk about that one,' she says sharply.

I get it. Small Irish villages like this one tend to keep local tragedies to themselves. I'm not surprised Kitty won't share this one with me, given I'm an outsider, not to mention a foreigner!

Feeling sad, I look at the mess of letters and wonder which ones belonged to the poor soul who has taken his or her own life.

Kitty turns away to put her beach bag down on the ground, and when she straightens up, her expression is relaxed, almost like she has used the moment to fix it that way.

'I'll tell you what, though,' she says, leaning towards me with a glint in her eye. 'The graffiti bloody worked. Those young eejits haven't dared to set foot in our shelter again. They think Frank's spray painting is a mysterious gang symbol – they're terrified of us!'

She bursts into more fits of laughter and I join in, relieved that the mood has been lightened. Besides, the image of a bunch of young lads being wary of a few harmless pensioners in swimwear is irresistible.

Her eyes move past me, and her mouth sets into a hard line.

I turn round, expecting to see Frank ambling over the sand towards us, but when my eyes come into focus, I stop dead, rooted to the spot.

I have always wondered what it would be like to meet a movie star in real life – what *I* would be like. Would I be cool and nonchalant and do that whole 'Oh, I didn't notice you there – sorry, what's your name again?' or would I immediately presume they were a wanker, purely because they're famous and I'm not, and not even give them the satisfaction of acknowledging their existence. Or would I scream, cry and faint? Apparently, I do neither of these three things because as this movie star gets closer and closer, I become totally and utterly catatonic. It's like being on the Irish ferry during a rough crossing, not daring to move in case you fill yet another plastic pint glass with vomit. Except this time there is no horizon to stare at – just him, straight out of Hollywood and walking oh-so-casually over the sand towards this botched graffitied shelter, where a frozen version of my former self is standing. Mouth open, I turn to Kitty, but she's gone already, walking with what looks like angry purpose towards the thrashing waves. When I look back again, he is right in front of me. He flashes me a perfect white-toothed smile and I take a quick step back as if to shield myself from his beauty. It's all too much. The designer-streaked blond hair, the blue eyes set slightly too close together, the narrow but in-proportion nose, and the full-lipped mouth. Not forgetting the hint of blond stubble on the chin and upper lip. Here is a movie god standing in front of me, in a plain sky-blue T-shirt and beige swimming shorts and there is nothing I can do about it.

Somewhere in the distance, I hear an American accent asking me if I'm going in for a swim. I might as well be underwater for all the good it'll do, for there is no way I can respond. I hang my head in shame. Jesus, at this rate, I'll start drooling out of one corner of my mouth.

When I have the courage to look up again, I see two startlingly blue eyes crinkled in amusement, looking back at me.

'I'm Ryan,' he says, giving me a curious stare.

'Saoirse,' I just about manage. Never has it been so difficult to say my own name.

Struggling to look him in the eye, I simply say one word, 'Gosling,' in a sort of whispery groan, at the exact same time as he says, 'Yes, we've met before.'

What?

My head snaps up and I fix my eyes on him properly now, and with suspicion. Movie star or not, there's no excuse for being a smartarse. I mean, I think I would remember meeting a movie star, especially one as gorgeous as this one.

'At McGowan's? The other night? You're Dee's friend, right?' he says, scrunching up his nose in confusion.

I blink my eyes several times in a valiant effort to focus. So, he isn't Ryan Gosling, even though he looks exactly like him and even has a fucking *American* accent. Not only is he not Ryan Gosling, but it appears that I have already met this version before, and failed to remember him on account of being so outrageously hammered. How could I have forgotten that face? *How?*

With a flush of shame, I realise that this is the Ryan that Dee had told me about. The one we chatted to in the pub for God knows how long. The Ryan who walked me home when I was too drunk to find my own way. Christ knows what I was babbling on about.

I quickly think about my options and realise there is no earthly way of getting out of such an awkward situation without making it even more excruciating. So, with one impatient movement, I turn away from the Ryan

Gosling lookalike, whip my sundress over my head, and march straight into the freezing cold Irish Sea.

14

Kitty is right about one thing. It turns out a voluntary dip into the freezing cold Irish Sea is just the thing to clear a muddled head. I stay in the sea, reaching borderline hypothermia levels, until Ryan is a dot in the distance. There is no sign of Kitty in the water either; she must have gone for a long swim. Part of me wonders about her hostile reaction to Ryan, but the thought goes out of my head as soon as my hands start to turn blue.

Then, with shivering steps, I manage to make my way to the shelter, relieved to find the beach deserted, wrap myself in a towel and hurry up the cliff steps to the safety and warmth of my lovely holiday house.

Dripping dirty puddles and sand all over the cool kitchen floor (David would have gone mental – he hates beaches!), I sit down at the kitchen island, flip open my laptop and check out the latest Vale Mums news feed. I don't know why I do this to myself. The latest victim is a girl called Chantal, who announces that she has just moved into the area and she is posting on Vale Mums for the very first time. I already feel sorry for her. Chantal wants to know if she can borrow a pirate costume for her seven-year-old son's drama performance taking place the following day. 'With all the chaos of the house move, I completely forgot to organise his costume!'

I scroll down through the responses, gratified that most of them are sensible 'welcome to Woodvale' messages, with some accompanied by sad-face emojis for those who either don't have the costume to lend, or who have the costume but not in the right size. So far, so acceptable. But of course, Chantal doesn't get off that easily. Here's Tania, once again sticking the knife in.

WELCOME to Woodvale, Chantal! You're going to LOVE it here. Instead of borrowing the costume, why not make one yourself? My LO looked adorable in the fireman outfit I made him last year, and it really doesn't take long to stitch together. DM me if you need more tips!

Suddenly, I'm really fed up of all this. Why the FUCK would Chantal want to make her own bloody costume when she has just moved house and is probably up to her eyes with unpacking and looking after her kids? Why aren't these stupid women more supportive, instead of constantly trying to outdo each other?

I am so livid about it that I decide to vent my frustration about the impact of social media on motherhood as part of my pitch.

From the moment we have our first child, we are in a permanently vulnerable state. In the early stages, we're sleep-deprived, cranky and often lonely. Although there is no code to crack for child-rearing, we go online for answers anyway, Googling obsessively, desperately trying to find answers that make us feel we're not failing after all. When we're not Googling, we're on Facebook, looking for some sort of comfort and reassurance. For some reason, being validated by a group of total strangers gives us a little lift (the more 'likes', the better we feel), which seem to help us get through an otherwise terrible day.

And this is what social media should be for – a community that supports its members, that recognises when people need help and advice, and gives people a platform to share their concerns without feeling belittled or judged. But rather than reaching out to struggling mums, many people use social media to compete instead.

You see, I couldn't care less if you choose only to feed your child organic food grown in the back garden, or if you make every single one of their meals from scratch, or even if you make every single fancy-dress costume with your own fair hands. What I do care about is whether you are judging others for not doing the same thing; for not understanding other people's choices or situations, and making them feel they are less of a mother because of it. If we were all just to admit that we are all as entirely clueless as each other, and stop the one-upmanship, then surely the world would be a friendlier place. So I propose a call to arms: the next time a mum posts something that implies she is lonely, desperate, and struggling, why not drop her a PM and suggest meeting her for a coffee, rather than telling her what she *should* be doing? Or ask for her number and giving her a call? Surely it's about time that we all embraced the 'social' side of social media and give each other help and support.

Satisfied, I close my laptop, and glance at my watch. I still have enough time to do one more very important thing today. Full of purpose now, I jump in the shower, wash away all the evidence of my first swim in the sea, and throw on some jeans and a T-shirt. Marvelling at the glorious weather, I decide to risk driving with the top down for the journey.

Ten minutes later, the heavens open and I am forced to pull in at a layby and wrestle the top back in place. I complete the rest of the journey with frizzy hair and a dampened mood. Still, when I roll to a stop, my spirits brighten. This is the right thing to do.

Switching off the engine, I sit in the car surveying the house where Jen is staying. It's a small, ordinary-looking 1970s pebble-dashed semi-detached house in an estate of identical semi-detached houses, situated about twenty minutes by car from the sea – basically the opposite of 'just down the road', as described by my mother. All the curtains are closed in that way people used to do to notify the entire burglar community that they are gone on holidays and the house is therefore unoccupied. I look at its ordinariness and for the life of me can't imagine Jen living there. Jen, who lives for high-street fashion and dressing up-and-coming celebrities. This is the type of place she would be mortified to even stand next to, never mind stay there.

A thought crosses my mind: Jen doesn't know I'm coming and I'm not sure if she even wants to see me. What if she thinks the fact that she has been 'jilted' is the only reason I am contacting her? I don't want her to think that this is a pity visit. Maybe she's not even there, I think hopefully, and immediately feel ashamed. It's not about you, I berate myself, it's about her.

Determined now, I push away my anxieties and see this for what it really is: a friend visiting an old friend who happens to be heartbroken. With a heavy heart, I push open the car door and get out. No going back.

I walk up the crazy-paving garden path and press the doorbell firmly. Nothing. I step back a little to see if the curtains have moved even an inch, but everything stays still. I wait for a few more moments before pressing the bell again and decide on a quick peep through the letterbox.

'She's not there,' a woman's voice says behind me.

I pop up so fast that I almost trap my fingers in the slamming flap of the letterbox.

As my eyes come to rest on this figure, my heart thumps faster.

'She's here!' the woman says, cheekily pointing to herself with two upright thumbs.

I stare at her for a moment. For there, standing before me in this dreary old estate, is Jen – my best friend.

And she looks absolutely fucking fabulous.

We embrace like we saw each other only yesterday, and then she unlocks the door and leads me into the house.

I eye her as she walks effortlessly from kitchen counter to kettle and back again, while she makes me a cup of tea. Is this whole heartbreak thing total bullshit? I've never seen the girl look so well. She is wearing some cut-off blue denim dungarees with a white T-shirt underneath. Her feet are clad in simple flat red Converse. She looks the picture of elegance and trendiness.

Putting the mug in front of me, she says, 'You've heard about Liam fucking off, then?'

I give a deep inward sigh. So, it's true after all.

'I'm a shit friend. I only know about Liam because my mum told me. That's how shit I am,' I tell her.

Jen tuts at me before marching over to give me a hug. She tells me to stop being 'such a twat' and that it was her fault that she hadn't told me herself.

'I just didn't want anyone to know, really,' she finishes softly. 'Not until I knew it was definitely over.'

'You look amazing!' I blurt out.

She laughs ruefully.

At Jen's suggestion, we grab our mugs of tea and retreat to the living room, which is decorated in true eighties style. After mocking the brown-and-orange floral carpet and green velvet curtains (with gold tie-backs), we sit down on the mustard corduroy-covered two-seater couch opposite a scratched mahogany coffee table with elephant legs, and face each other.

I suddenly feel out of my depth. It's been so long since we talked properly. How I can summarise the last four years since I had Anna? How do I explain that I'm not the same person she was friends with for most of our childhood and into our adulthood? I'm no longer the care-free 'it'll be grand', living-in-the-present Saoirse. Motherhood has made me more jaded, impatient, frustrated and generally fed up. I can't say all that to her, given we have no shared experience; she'll think I'm a monster. I mean, *I* think I'm a monster half the time. Especially since I've left my daughter behind in London. But looking at her now, I feel a rush of love for my oldest and best friend, and I realise that it's not her fault that she didn't have a kid and didn't go through the same experiences as I did. Maybe things would have been the same even if she'd had children. She could have been one of those bloody organic mums, and I might have ended up falling out with her anyway. Who knows?

'I'm sorry I haven't been in touch,' I say again, feeling helpless.

Putting her mug down, Jen takes my hand and says, 'No, *I'm* the one who should be saying sorry.'

I look at her in surprise. What does she have to be sorry for?

'Listen, when you got pregnant, I knew our lives would take different paths. Please don't get me wrong – I was so happy for you – but you know I have never wanted children, and I just couldn't relate to what you were going through. We had shared so much together for so long, but this wasn't something I felt I could be a part of,' she says, tears glistening in her eyes.

Starting to well up myself, I squeeze her hand in reassurance.

'It's OK!' I say, blinking my eyes rapidly to stop the tears from flowing.

Jen shakes her head vigorously.

'No, Saoirse, it's not OK. Remember that time I called you? It was just a few weeks after you'd had Anna, and I was calling you because I had just bumped into Liam in the pub. I mean, you'd just had a bloody baby and there I was shiteing on about my love life. I mean, how fucking ridiculous,' she says, shaking her head in frustration.

I take a deep breath but before I can say anything, she says something that stops me in my tracks.

'You see, the thing is, Saoirse, I *knew* how stressed out you were – you're my oldest friend; I could hear it in your voice – and I did *nothing* to help.' We're both crying now, and I mean really crying.

'Please don't beat yourself up about this,' I manage to say through my sobs. 'I should have been honest with you about how much I was struggling.'

Jen releases my hand and reaches across to the coffee table to grab a box of tissues. We each take one, and blow our noses in perfect synchronisation. When we have recovered a little, we exchange watery smiles.

'I just felt so useless,' Jen says in a small voice. 'I mean, I haven't a clue about babies. I wouldn't know one end of a nappy from the other, and the thought of trying to calm a screaming child sends a chill down my spine. What good would I have been to you?'

I take a moment to think about it. Even if I had confessed to Jen about how bad things had been, how could she really have helped me?

'Listen, it's my fault for not being honest with you in the first place, but even if I had, I wouldn't have expected you to take care of Anna for me. I barely let David touch her in the early days... But if I had my time all over again, I would have asked you to come over, organised a takeaway and a bottle of wine, and just talked about something other than feeds, nappies, and sterilising. I think that would have made me feel more normal.'

Jen puts her head in her hands, and says angrily, 'I could have done that, Saoirse!'

And I tell her I know. Then we spend a few more teary moments fighting each other for whose fault it was, and grabbing more tissues before falling into an exhausted silence.

'Tell me about what happened with Liam,' I say finally. 'Surely he knew how you felt about not wanting children?'

'That's the thing, Saoirse. He knew from really early on in our relationship that I wasn't into having children. He told me he felt the same way.'

Her head dips for a moment and when she raises it, I notice that her
cheeks are flushed and tears are in her eyes once again. She is deeply hurt,
and my heart aches for her.

'We got on so well, Saoirse. Don't get me wrong, we had our moments,
but we had so much fun together. Why the hell would he throw that all
away?'

I shake my head and squeeze her shoulder. 'So why did he change his
mind?' I ask.

'I think he was getting a lot of hassle from his mother about her
wanting grandkids. Then, of course, his brother had a baby boy, and Liam
really took to him. He started asking me if I would ever consider it. I told
him no way. Then one day, he came home and told me he couldn't live the
rest of his life without being a father. And that was it.'

I wrap both my arms around her while she cries and we stay like that
for a bit. Poor Jen – I feel so desperately sorry for her. She straightens
herself gently and grabs another tissue.

'I wouldn't mind, but since he fecked off, it seems as though I'm losing
the run of myself in the health department,' Jen says.

My forehead creases in concern. 'What's going on?' I say.

'It was a couple of months ago. I had just got a pedicure and was in my
flip-flops walking home. Suddenly I felt like I needed to do a massive fart.
Nothing catastrophic, you know, like the ones you can let out silently
without anyone getting hurt?'

I nod and smile, grateful for a bit of light relief. Despite the grim nature
of the topic, I love Jen when she is in storytelling mode. I remind myself not
to laugh, though. That would highly insensitive.

'So, there I was, trying to let it out gently and suddenly I felt my pants
get a bit damp, and I just thought – no. I have *not* just shit myself.'

Despite the seriousness of her story, I can feel the corners of my mouth
starting to twitch.

'Anyway, when I get home, I leg it to the bathroom, pull down my
skinny jeans and there is just this perfectly round, like, pancake of shit in
my pants, and a small bit on the crotch of my jeans.'

I cover my mouth and try desperately not to laugh.

'So, of course, my first thought is, how the hell am I supposed to take my skinny jeans off without ruining my new pedicure, you know?'

I nod helplessly at this, although I'm not sure I would have given the pedicure the same level of significance.

'So, for starters, I end up waddling into the kitchen, grabbing a pair of scissors and cutting my pants off,' she says.

I feel a bubble of laughter start deep inside me and manage to control it in my throat, letting out a small squeak in the process.

'Anyway, the pants are off, but the jeans are still around my knees and the pedicure needs at least another three hours of drying time so I can't take them off, even though they smell of shite. But then again, I have a wealthy client in half an hour who has hired me to find her a wedding outfit.'

'What did you do?' I say, just about managing to get the words out.

'Sure what else could I do, Saoirse? I pulled up my jeans, sprayed a bit of perfume around the crotch area and went to the job fully commando.'

That is it. The thought of glamorous Jen going to her posh personal-shopper job without wearing any underwear, with the faint whiff of 'eau de poo' cracks me up. I laugh and splutter and gasp until my breath catches and my stomach hurts. I am ashamed of how good it feels – it seems like years since I have had a good laugh like that. Wiping the tears from my eyes, I glance at Jen and immediately sober up when I see her face.

'Jesus, sorry, Jen. I don't mean to be insensitive,' I say, reaching out towards her.

'I don't mind if you laugh – it is a funny story,' she says, waving me away. 'Besides, apparently, shitting yourself is fairly common when you're under a certain amount of stress.'

'All goes down the plughole after you turn forty,' I say grimly, thinking about my own undignified twice-nightly dashes to the toilet.

Then Jen tells me that she has been offered her own permanent segment on the popular Irish television show *Revealed!*, giving viewers tips on how to dress smartly, using fashion inspiration from the high street.

'Oh, Jen, that is fantastic!' I say, clapping my hands. And I mean it. That gig is right up Jen's street.

But she shakes her head sadly.

'How am I supposed to present a fashion show when I'm the type of person who shits herself?' she says.

'Jen, honestly, I'm sure it won't happen again,' I say, feeling helpless.

I look at her long, toned legs and her wingless arms and I feel a flash of envy. We're the same age but she could pass for my much-younger sister.

'You look incredible,' I whisper. Then I take big risk. 'Especially for someone who shits themselves and has just been jilted.'

Jen catches my eye and the pair of us totally crack up, and I'm glad the risk has paid off.

When we have recovered, Jen gives a mock yawn, an exaggerated stretch and declares a subject change, saying, 'The only thing worse than people talking about their break-ups is people talking about their dreams, or their children.' She catches my look. 'No offence.'

'None taken,' I say. And I mean that because even though I have a child of my own, I don't want to hear stories about other people's kids, unless they have done something particularly gruesome, and then it's just entertainment.

Then she asks me about David ('Has he taken the covers off the garden furniture yet?') and Anna ('I can't believe I still haven't met her!'), and with some effort, I answer no to the furniture question, before telling her that she has to come to London and see Anna – and I really mean it. A quiet moment follows and it crosses my mind that I could tell her all about David's affair and my life falling apart, but I don't. I'm not ready to open that little box just yet. Besides, the last thing I want to do is take away from her problems. Instead, I spend the next few minutes telling her all about the Ryan episode – how I managed to get so pissed I didn't remember him, even though he had walked me to my door, and how I threw myself into the sea just to escape the mortification of it all.

Jen snorts into her tea. 'Jesus, Saoirse, only you could get so shit-faced that you would forget someone who looked like a famous movie star,' she says.

'What do you mean "only me"? When was the last time I blacked out from drink, anyway?

'Don't look so shocked, woman!' she says, laughing. 'Have you forgotten what happened with Killian Moriarty?'

I glare at her for a second and flop back on the couch and think. Now there's a blast from the past. Killian was a long-term friend I ended up sleeping with after a Tequila night out but had no recollection of the event itself the next morning. It was the only proper blackout I had ever experienced, and it really put the shits up me. Because of that episode, I haven't touched Tequila since. I can't believe she is even bringing him up, and I tell her so. And then I tell her that the Killian thing is totally different from the Ryan thing, and then she says something that renders us both speechless for a bit.

'Saoirse, the only difference between the Killian episode and the Ryan episode is that you *slept* with Killian after a stomach-full of Tequila but didn't remember it the next morning,' she says.

We look at each other, wide-eyed, and the teasing smile falls from her face.

'You weren't drinking Tequila, were you?'

Fuck, what if I'd had Tequila? Anything could have happened.

15

As soon as I get home from Jen's place, I text Dee with trembling fingers.

Was I drinking Tequila the night we got pissed?

It's 6 p.m., bath time, so I don't expect to hear back from her until she has both kids asleep and a big glass of wine in her hand.

I lean back on the comfiest of living-room couches and take a few deep breaths, terrified of the response.

There is a voice in my head (mostly Jen's, come to think of it) who is berating me for being so ridiculous. Just because I don't remember anything sexual happening with Ryan doesn't mean that anything did happen. I had woken up in my pyjamas so that must mean I had been competent enough to get undressed. Besides, wouldn't I have felt it 'down there' the next day? Given that David and I hadn't been in the sack together for a good year, wouldn't I have felt the effects in a sensitive place that had lain dormant for so long?

'Unless Ryan has a tiny cock,' another voice in my head whispers, and I shut it down. Then I start to think about what could have happened. Maybe penetration hadn't occurred. We might have just kissed or done 'other stuff', like you do when you're a teenager and you don't want to get pregnant. But still, even if I hadn't had sex with Ryan, isn't any form of intimacy a betrayal? Fuck's sake, I'm married. Then I remember that David is banging someone else, which should make me feel better and more justified in messing around with Ryan, but it doesn't. It just makes me feel sad.

I jump as my phone vibrates beside me. It's Dee. I grab the phone and read the message.

Are you taking the piss? They had to call Mexico for an emergency supply of Tequila to be delivered!

I cry out and throw the phone on the couch as hard as I can. After a minute or two of sobbing, a thought occurs to me that puts all of this in perspective. Why the hell would someone as gorgeous as Ryan want anything to do with a spotty, forty-year-old married mother of one with a flabby stomach and an arse that – thanks to acres of cellulite – bears all the markings of an aged rhinoceros?

My phone buzzes again. It's Dee.

Only joking – no Tequila. You told me about that time you blacked out with some fella called Killian. You said you didn't want to go near the hard stuff.

OK, good. No Tequila. That's something. Relieved as I am, I am still slightly mortified at the 'confessional' nature of this conversation with a near-stranger. What else had I bloody said?

My phone rings in my hand. It's David FaceTiming me. I know I have to pick up; I may have spoken to Anna but I haven't spoken to him since I got here. It's awful to think that less than five years ago a call from David would have sent me into an ecstatic demented jig, and now here I am, feeling obliged to pick up. I take a deep breath and press the answer button.

'What's wrong, Saoirse?' he says, scrunching up his face in concern.

I am puzzled for a moment. How would he know if anything was wrong? And then I remember that I have just been crying about the possibility of cheating on him, and probably look like a tear-streaked mess.

For want of a better reason, I tell him I'm upset because I miss Anna, which I do, terribly, but I shouldn't use her as an excuse to cover for my stupid dashes back to adolescence. David isn't looking too hot himself. He has dark circles under his eyes and a nasty cold sore on the left side of his top lip. Must be exhausted from all that shagging, I think, narrowing my eyes.

'Listen, the school places came out today,' David says, running one hand through his hair.

Jesus! The school places! How the hell had I forgotten? I've only been stressing about it for the last twelve months.

'I take it that it's not good news,' I say.

'Well, she did get a place at a local school...' he says.

'But it's the shit school,' we both chorus at exactly the same time.

For a moment we are united in our mutual antipathy of Anna going to a crap school.

I think for a moment. What choice do we have?

'Maybe it's not so bad, David,' I say. 'I was reading about it on Vale Mums and apparently it's up and coming.'

'I'm too old for "up and coming", Saoirse,' David says, looking more defeated than I've seen him in a long time. 'Besides, on an aesthetic basis, it looks like prison.'

I take exception to this.

'Hang on a minute. Anna's nursery looked like a concentration camp, and we still sent her there,' I say. '*And* we had to pay huge fees for nursery,' I add. 'At least this school is free.'

He sighs.

'It's not like we can afford private school,' I say.

'And who's fault is that?' he shoots back.

I feel like I have been punched in the stomach. Is David really blaming me for not being able to pay to send Anna to private school?

'That's a really low blow, David,' I say, tears springing to my eyes.

'Look, I'm sorry,' he says, with a sigh. 'I'm just really stressed with work. People are cracking up trying to make this deadline. And then there's Anna to take care of...'

This annoys me no end. He's barely seen Anna since I left. Didn't he ditch her at Bea's at the weekend so he could go off and have sex with his fancy woman? I don't want to confront him about the affair over FaceTime, but as I am still annoyed over being blamed for not being able to give our child a good education, I spend the next couple of minutes berating him for not spending the whole weekend with his only daughter.

I am gratified to see his face reddening and his mouth tighten. Good, I think. Now you know how I feel. When I have stopped ranting, he glares at me before saying, 'Fucking hell, Saoirse. The one Sunday I had a meeting and you're beating me over the head with it.'

'Yeah, right, David – as if that meeting was anything to do with work,' I hiss.

Then we both freeze.

'What's that supposed to mean?' he says, and his face seems to drain of all colour.

And this is it. This is where I'm supposed to tell him exactly what it means. That while I've been wiping arses and plastering scraped knees, he's been out doing the bloody sexual fandango with that slut from work.

But before I have the chance to say anything, Anna's face suddenly replaces David's and I quickly rearrange my face into a big smile.

'Hi, sweetheart!' I say. 'I miss you!'

And it's true. Looking at her huge brown eyes, I realise I miss her very, very badly. I'm not sure if she picks up on the emotion in my voice, but she says, 'I miss you too, Mummy!' and promptly bursts into tears.

I look away from the screen for a moment to compose myself.

'I'll be home soon, my angel,' I say, trying to keep the wobble out of my voice.

'I want you home now!' she screams, and starts doing that heavy chok-ing-sobbing thing that rips the very heart out of my body.

Tears are falling down my face. I am totally and utterly helpless to comfort her. David's face replaces Anna's and then the screen goes black.

I get it.

When Anna is in full meltdown mode, she needs to be removed from whatever has upset her as quickly as possible. I just can't bear that, in this instance, the thing that has upset her most is me.

I go to the kitchen and pour as much red wine into a glass as I can without it spilling over, and then return to the couch to drink it with the desperation of someone sorely in need of liquid refreshment. Through a blur of tears, I text David to tell him I'm getting the next flight home. This is bullshit. Nothing is worth this – I have to see Anna. NOW. Minutes later, he texts me back and tells me that Anna is fine and busy watching a new episode of *Ben and Holly*. I make him take a photo as proof, and sure enough there she is, glued to her iPad, her little cheeks still bearing the glow of a tantrum, but otherwise looking peaceful enough.

In the midst of all this, Bea sends a brief text:

FUUUUCCKK – the shit school!

I take this to mean that Harry has also been denied a place at the lovely Woodvale Primary in favour of the needle-strewn, condom-infested cesspit that is the local shit school. I quickly send her back a skeleton emoji before sending David another text to say I'm coming home anyway. But a moment later I get one back telling me that there's no need. I have another glass of wine, and welcome the numbness.

Throughout our whole texting exchange, I notice David has neglected to put his five customary kisses at the end of each text. This means he is cross with me. For what? What have I done now? I haven't even accused him of having the affair, for Christ's sake.

During my third glass of wine, I am tickled that David is upset – with me. The irony! The man who's blatantly having an affair and abandoning his daughter. In actual fact, it's his fault she's not going to a decent school.

'Fuck you, David!' I say to an empty room, holding out my glass in a drunken 'cheers' gesture. Then I spend a few happy drunken moments fantasising about Ryan's tongue in my mouth.

* * *

Tap, tap, tap. I curse heavily. It's still dark in the bedroom, so I know it's not time to get up yet. I throw my hands over my ears, but it's no good. I follow the noise and see that it's coming from the bedroom window. Who could be knocking on my window so late at night? Then I have a sudden realisation. It's Kitty. Or Frank. Bugging me to go for a night swim. Either way, I need to find out so I can give them a serious piece of my mind. I reach over for the remote control and press the button with unnecessary force to raise the blinds. I watch as the rising blind reveals a pair of large white trainers, feet too big to be Kitty's, then what looks to be a pair of jeans, followed by a man's white fitted shirt, too slim to be Frank. I take my finger off the 'up' button for a moment, my heart beating in my throat. Because I don't know if I want to go any further.

I watch my finger activate the blind again and now there is no mistaking who is tapping on my bedroom window in the middle of the night. He smiles at me just like he did at the beach, and I walk over to him and open the window.

We stand for a moment just looking at each other, and I suddenly feel very calm, because this feels absolutely right. I take a step towards him and gradually start to unbutton his white cotton shirt slowly and deftly. I leave it open, and slide my hands on either side of his toned waist. Then I pull him into me, and he comes to life. He takes the straps of my satin sheath and slips them off my shoulders. The fabric feels cool against my skin as it slides down the full length of my body onto the floor. I am totally, and gloriously naked.

Shrugging off his shirt, he bends down and slides his tongue over one of my nipples, and then the other. I feel the ache get stronger and my breathing faster. When he rises, I unbutton his jeans and take him in my hand. He feels hard and velvety. My hand starts to move and I grow wetter as I hear him groan with want. His face screws up and I know he is desperate to come and I speed up my movements, watching him all the time, enjoying the control I have over him. Suddenly his face relaxes, and he reaches down and gently presses his hand over mine.

'Stop,' he says, smiling. 'It's your turn.'

Then he gets down on his knees, gently strokes my legs and pushes them apart.

I hold my breath and wait for his glorious mouth to come closer, feeling the heat build and the wetness flow.

And then I wake up.

16

'Seriously, since when have you ever worn a satin sheath?' Jen says, giggling hysterically.

I am glad she is so amused at my graphic wet dream about some guy who I've only met twice in my life – and I can only actually remember one of those times.

Then Dee joins in.

'And who exactly has oral sex any more?' she says, laughing.

It's Tuesday evening and Dee, Jen and I are in McGowan's, getting pissed. After everything that's happened lately, I have badgered my old friend into joining me with my new friend on a girls' night out. I haven't said anything to Dee about Jen's split with Liam; that's up to Jen to share if she wants to. Although this is the first time Dee and Jen have met, they are getting on like a house on fire, bonding over their cruel analysis of the most real dream I've ever experienced.

'I thought you said people who talk about dreams are boring,' I say to Jen, crossly.

'Not this one!' she says delightedly. 'My favourite part is when he tells you to stop pulling him off. Like that would happen in real life!'

'That's when you should have known it was a dream, Saoirse,' Dee adds with a grin. 'No man alive would pull himself back from the brink in order to satisfy his woman!'

I smile, in spite of myself. It was such a ridiculous dream, but it still bothered me that, in that moment, I wanted to have sex with Ryan. How it felt so right and natural to be with him.

'I just don't know why I'm even thinking about Ryan,' I say.

'Because he's a ride, Saoirse!' Dee says.

'If you're worried about cheating on David, you're not,' Jen says.

I take a deep swig of my wine then. The cheating thing is a little too close for comfort.

'You didn't even kiss Ryan or fuck him in the dream,' Dee adds thoughtfully.

That's true.

'Jesus, Saoirse, if you're that much of a prude in your dreams, you must be shite in bed in real life!'

We laugh for a bit and then Dee says something wistful.

'I'd love a good ride,' she sighs, cupping her chin in her right hand.

Jen looks at her with wide eyes and says, 'Are you and Sean not—'

I interrupt her. 'Fuck off, Jen. They're married with two kids. Of course they're not!'

Dee shoots me a grateful look, and says, 'Well, it's not like sex doesn't happen the very odd time – it's just a bit shit when it does. Since Sean has hit his late forties, it takes longer for him to you know... stand to attention.' She whispers the last bit.

Jen and I look at each other with raised eyebrows.

'So how long does it take, then?' I ask, fascinated.

'Too long!' she says, with a bitter laugh. 'I mean before the kids came along we had it down to a fine art – fifteen minutes and job done. Now I have less time, and I'm more exhausted, yet it's taking up to an hour before he finishes.'

She takes a deep swig of her wine. 'I mean, where's the fucking justice in that?'

We shake our heads for a bit, before Jen says, 'I caught my ex, Liam, having a wank on the couch late one night when I went downstairs for a glass of water.'

I burst out laughing and Dee puts her hand over her mouth, her eyes merry.

'Jesus, what was he wanking off to?' Dee asks.

'That's the thing,' Jen says, thoughtfully. 'He wasn't wanking to anything. The telly was off, the laptop was still in its case, and not a magazine in sight.'

'So why was he doing it then?' I say, full of admiration for Jen for talking so matter-of-factly about the man who had just 'jilted' her.

'He said he felt like sex but didn't want to wake me up, so he had a wank instead. At first I was pretty pissed off but then he swore blind that he only thought about me when he was doing it.'

Good answer, I think. Liam was no eejit. But when I turn to exchange a cynical glance with Dee, her mouth is half open and her eyes soft.

'That is so romantic,' she says. 'I wish Sean would have a wank in my honour!'

We all laugh and I know if I'm to follow the girl code, it's my turn to come clean about some unwanted aspect of my sex life, but I can't do it. How could I confess to the fact that David and I haven't had sex in almost a year? I could blame it on his travel, or me being too busy juggling work and Anna, but that really isn't the case. Unlike Dee, I can't do the whole 'lie back and think of England thing', and unlike Jen, I probably wouldn't give a shite if I found David having a wank, but of course he's not doing any of that because he's shagging that slut instead. To me, sex is more than a mechanical act. I need to feel connected on an emotional level before I can even think about engaging in a physical act, and I haven't felt that connection with David in a long time.

'Are you all right, Saoirse?' Jen says, her forehead wrinkled in concern.

And just as I open my mouth to reply, a male voice says, 'Howerya, ladies? Can I join the party?'

Dee looks up at the figure and squeals in the manner of someone who has just had a drink spilled over her.

'Sean! What are you doing here?' she says. 'Who's looking after the kids?'

'Sure, they're grand. I left the pair of them by themselves splashing around in the bath,' he grins.

Dee shakes her head and raises her eyes skyward.

'The kids are with my mother, Dee, don't worry,' he says, ruffling her hair fondly. 'Can I join your crew for a drink?'

With the exuberance of three women who have drunk a bottle of wine each, Jen and I beckon him ferociously to sit down with us, while Dee mouths a quick sorry.

It's hard to look at Sean without thinking about his 'issues' in the bedroom, but on the face of it, he's a good-looking guy – clear green eyes, a narrow face, softened by short, tousled brown hair, and a mouth that goes slightly up at the sides, which gives the impression of being permanently amused. I watch him give a reluctant Dee a quick kiss and put his arm around her and I feel a flash of envy. I can't remember the last time David was that affectionate towards me. He gives me a 'nice to see you again' wink and I smile back, doing my best to give the impression that I remember him from the boozy evening with his wife – which, of course, I don't.

More drinks are ordered and the chat is flowing, and the craic is brilliant, and everyone talks over everyone else and it's one of those nights that I never want to end.

At some point in the evening, I decide it's high time we got more drinks in. But just as I'm about to get up to go to the bar, Jen tugs at my hand, her eyes fixed to a point behind me, her mouth open.

I turn round and instantly freeze.

'Holy fucking Christ,' she breathes.

Somewhere in the distance, I hear Sean saying, 'Jesus Christ, I'd ride him meself.'

And before I can prepare myself, an apparition in jeans and a dark blue slim-fitting polo shirt, slides into the empty seat beside mine and says hello.

I take a deep breath and meet his gaze. Ryan. This time I refuse to go all wobbly around him, but then I remember I performed a sex act on him in my dream the previous night, and look away, feeling my face grow hot.

Dee is the first one to recover from the arrival of our surprise guest. In a valiant attempt to avoid slurring, she introduces Ryan to Jen and then to Sean, who Ryan has never met before. After all the introductions have been made, a moment passes and then another, before Jen decides to use a classic tactic to break the tension.

'SHOTS!' she shouts, elbowing me and pointing to the bar.

'No, no. I'll get them in,' Ryan says, instantly standing up. Jen gives him the drinks order and we all watch that perfect bottom make its way towards the bar.

'Jesus! That's HIM,' Jen says, in the loudest whisper ever uttered in a public place.

'Who?' says Sean.

'Ryan!' Jen says, impatiently.

'I know the fella's name but what's he got to do with Saoirse?'

I give Jen my best 'I'll kill you if you say anything look' but it doesn't even begin to work.

'That's the fella Saoirse had the sex dream about last night!' Jen says.

I groan and put my head in my hands. The cat's well and truly out of the bag now. I wait for Sean to rip the piss out of me, but he ends up saying something both surprising and disturbing.

'I can see why,' he says, thoughtfully. 'He's a looker all right. Reminds me of someone... Even got a round in before he's barely sat down. He's a good lad.'

Jen and I exchange raised eyebrows again.

Dee turns to Sean and asks him drunkenly what the FUCK is he going on about, and does he actually FANCY Ryan or something, and I can see it all turning ugly, and then mercifully the pair are interrupted by Ryan putting eight shots on the table (eight shots for four people – Sean looks at Ryan with such a look of adoration that for a second I genuinely feel worried for Dee), and then everyone shuts up for a bit. I knock back both of my shots in quick succession, and immediately start to feel a bit calmer.

When Ryan laughingly asks me about my record-breaking plunge into the icy sea the last time we met, I don't get embarrassed. I laugh it off easily by telling him that I needed to make my first dip as painless as possible, like ripping off a plaster. When Jen asks him what he's doing in this part of the world, he tells us he's been coming here for two weeks every summer for the past five years. When Sean asks him what he does for a living, he tells us that he is a management training coach who, although based in LA, does a fair amount of travel. And it goes on like that, us asking lots of questions, and Ryan answering them easily and with the odd bit of humour thrown in.

But then it all goes a bit wrong, countless shots later, when Sean suddenly blurts out, 'That's it! *La La Land*!' and slaps the table to wobbling.

Jen, Dee and I exchange tortured glances. Ryan looks up to the ceiling.

Too drunk to pick up on our reactions, Sean stumbles on with the force of a desperate comedian determined to land a joke at whatever cost.

'YOU! You're like that fella from *La La Land*,' he says, pointing unnecessarily at Ryan. Then a puzzled expression flashes over his face. 'Now, what's that actor called?' he asks, frowning.

'Ryan,' Dee hisses furiously.

Sean turns carefully towards her. 'Fuck's sake, Dee! I know his name's Ryan. I'm talking about the fella from *La La Land*!'

Dee sits back in her seat, shaking her head.

When I am pissed enough I thank Ryan for walking me home after the all-day drinking episode, and ask him if I said anything embarrassing.

He smiles, and says, 'No, nothing embarrassing.' And even if he is just being kind, I'll take it. Then he adds something that I wish he hadn't. 'In fact, you didn't talk as much as sing all the way home.'

Oh God. I forgot about the singing. That's a sure sign I've had too much to drink. But if that's all I was doing, I am happy enough.

And in that moment, I know with full certainty that nothing happened with Ryan that time he walked me home from the pub. He is too polite and well-mannered. It wouldn't have occurred to him to try anything on. And I realise that he makes me feel safe.

Just then Sean explodes.

'GOSLING! You're the spitting image of Ryan Gosling,' he stutters, spraying spittle everywhere.

Ryan smiles patiently. I can see that Sean's spittle has landed on his nose, but he doesn't wipe it away.

He's kind, I think, feeling all fuzzy, drunk, and affectionate. Kind and easy to talk to.

'I bet you get that all the time,' Jen says.

Ryan gives a modest smile, and says, 'No, not at all,' with as much sincerity as he can manage under the circumstances. Sean's spittle stays on Ryan's nose until we leave the pub, and I like him all the more for it.

That night, when we all part ways, someone drunkenly suggests that we all go for a swim together the following day in the Irish Sea 'to chase away the cobwebs'. I think that person is me. After I hug everyone goodbye, I hum the songs from *La La Land* all the way home.

17

It's been a long time since I have woken up in a pool of my own piss, but that's just what has happened. Clutching my thumping head in my hands, I gingerly step out of bed, overcome with the shame of drinking to the point of unconsciousness. What the hell is wrong with me? Ever since I've arrived here, I've been caning it with the drink, like a first-year student who's just broken the pledge. I knock back a couple of pills to make the pain in my head go away, and miserably change the wet sheets before stuffing everything in the washing machine. It's been a long time since I felt this low.

With effort, I make myself take a long, hot shower, and it's only when I'm in clean clothes again that I remember my drunken vow about our pre-arranged swim from the night before. Frankly, diving into the sea is the last thing I feel like doing, but I throw on my swimsuit anyway and let myself out of the house... only to find it pissing it down outside. I pause for a moment but then decide to carry on, feeling an odd comfort that the weather matches my mood.

I navigate my way carefully down the cliff steps to the swimmers' enclave below. As I reach the bottom of the steps, I am surprised to see Ryan already there, standing perfectly still with his back to the sea. He looks so focused that I stop for a moment, reluctant to destroy the peace. As I watch, he lifts one arm slowly and reaches it towards the back of the cliff face. For a minute he looks like he's going to do a bout of tai chi, and this disappoints me a little. Tai chi may be trendy on an LA beach, buster, I think, but it's hardly in keeping with a little Irish beach in the pissing rain. But he doesn't practise any tai chi moves after all. Instead, he uses the tips of his fingers to trace something on the wall, exactly in the space where the graffiti is displayed. I am too curious to stand about waiting, so I start walking towards him. As soon as he sees me, he jumps, and swivels round quickly so he is facing the sea once more.

'I'm sorry,' I say. Trust me to ruin someone else's moment. 'Did I disturb you?'

He looks at me with dark eyes and then looks away. Frankly, he seems really pissed off.

'Were you thinking of fixing Frank's handiwork?' I say to lighten the mood.

Ryan musters up a small smile, so I keep going.

'Maybe you can add my name too. I hear they're running short of swimmers these days!'

He rounds on me. 'What the fuck is that supposed to mean?' he says, impatiently wiping the rain from his face.

'Nothing!' I say, totally shocked. Where the hell has nice-guy Ryan gone? 'It's just that Kitty was saying there have been a few deaths around here lately.'

His eyes widen, seeming to turn a much darker blue.

'Did Kitty tell you what happened?'

'No... I...' I stammer.

'What about Dee? Did she tell you?'

I see his fists clenching and unclenching and I start to feel really hacked off. I'm hungover to the point of wanting to throw up and in no mood to be shouted at for no reason.

'No!' I say, angrily. 'Nobody said anything about... anything!'

He bends down and grabs his sports bag and walks away fast down the beach, shouting, 'The gossiping in this godforsaken town is total bullshit.'

I feel my mouth drop open and the rain pouring down my face. What the hell was all that about? I look back at the graffiti and a memory of Kitty pops into my head: the suicide. The death nobody ever talks about. I wait until Ryan is a dot in the distance, and give myself a little shake. Well, fuck him. He's obviously a total weirdo, which is a shame, given his gorgeousness. I march self-righteously into the icy water and plunge headlong into the turbulent sea.

As I swim, a sense of peace and calm washes over me; the cold water washing away hot-tempered thoughts, and a brutal, shameful hangover. I stay in a bit longer today, exhilarated by the personal triumph of withstanding such cold temperatures, coupled by the power and weightlessness of my body as it cuts through the waves.

As I emerge with purple/blue legs and unclenchable fingers, I see Kitty by the enclave, wriggling out of her tracksuit. I greet her with a wave, and she gives me a short wave back. When I get closer, I see that her eyes are red, and her face slightly swollen. She looks as though she's been crying. What is wrong with everyone today?

'Are you all right, Kitty?' I say.

She waves me away, pulling on her swimming goggles.

'I'm fine, love,' she says, and we both pretend not to notice when her voice cracks.

'Ryan's not exactly a happy camper today either!' I say, in an inappropriately jocular tone. This is something I do when I have no idea what to say. As David often reminds me, 'Sometimes it's all right not to rush to fill every gap in a conversation.'

Kitty's head whips around to me. 'You've seen Ryan?'

I nod. 'Not only did I see him, but he bit the head off me!'

She shakes her head vigorously as if she's trying to get water out of her ears, and gives me an indecipherable look. Then with a curt wave, she walks away into the crashing waves ahead.

I am now more flummoxed than ever.

I don't feel calm any more. Now I'm annoyed.

As soon as I get home I call Dee.

'What's today supposed to be?' I say, the second she picks up the phone.

'Wednesday?' she says, yawning. 'The day I murder both my children because they kept me up half the night?'

I swallow hard in frustration and explain what has happened on the beach.

'There's Ryan with a face like a slapped arse, and then Kitty looking all tear-streaked, and I haven't a clue what's going on,' I moan.

Dee is quiet for a moment.

'I've just realised what today is,' she says. 'I can't believe I almost forgot,' she adds, almost to herself.

I'm barely hanging on here.

'Dee,' I say through clenched teeth, 'any chance you could fill me in?'

She sighs, and says, 'I can't. It's not up to me to tell you.'

I swear at her for a bit and, fair play, she takes it on the chin, and then I put down the phone, forgetting to ask her why the hell she hasn't made it to the beach yet. I am still annoyed so I call Jen – not because she'll have any of the answers (she's as clueless as I am when it comes to local knowledge) but because I need a rant.

Jen waits until I have finished venting and then says something that takes the wind out of my sails.

'Let me ask you something. Did you tell Dee or Kitty about my relation-ship breaking down?' she says.

'Of course not!' I say, instantly. 'That's absolutely none of my business. That's your news to tell.'

Then I get it. 'Fine. So, you're saying Ryan or Kitty need to tell me instead, right?'

Jen is so annoying when she's right.

'Bingo,' she says in the world's most patronising voice.

'Fuck you, Jen,' I say.

'Besides, whatever chance I have, as a Dubliner, of the local villagers confiding in me, you have none,' she says, laughing.

'I swear, Jen, if you call me a foreigner too...' I say, my fists bunching. The pills are wearing off and my head starts to thump. 'And fuck you for not coming for a swim today like you promised,' I add.

'Have you seen the weather, Saoirse? It's pissing it down outside,' she says.

Then she hangs up.

After I shower and change, I grab my laptop with the false intention of doing some work, even though I know full well that all my fuzzy mind can cope with is vacuous social media. I click into Vale Mums and a new post catches my eye. It's from Rosalind. She has posted a picture of a child's arm, which looks to have a mild-looking rash ('that fails the glass test') and has asked eight hundred medically unqualified people what they think. I don't even bother to look at the responses: they are too predictable. Tania and her Organics crew will offer all sorts of 'advice' in the form of natural reme-dies ('I find soaking a potato in the morning rain and then rubbing it on the rash in an anti-clockwise motion works a treat') while a more sensible side (albeit few and far between) will encourage her to go to the doctor. I am in the middle of cursing the whole situation when a sudden thought occurs to me. Everything I have written for the pitch so far is about mothers being judged, criticised, and torn down by people like the Organics, but all the while I'm not doing anything to change things, which makes me as bad as they are. So, before I can give it any more thought, I DM Rosalind a quick note introducing myself and asking her if she'd like to go for a coffee sometime.

Then immediately regret it.

Nobody, but nobody, reaches out to a total stranger over Facebook. She's going to think I am a total weirdo.

Sighing, I get up to look for something fizzy from the fridge, but a loud ping stops me in my tracks. I check my phone and my heart quickens when I see Rosalind's name flash up. I take a deep breath and steel myself for rejection. But it's good news. Rosalind says she would love to meet me for a coffee. Hurrah! She asks when and where, and I go to reply, but then I stop myself.

I don't want to look too keen.

Then I make myself a congratulatory cup of tea and think about how much has happened in less than a week. Not only have I written some material for the pitch, but I have reunited with my best friend from school, made a new mum-friend in Dee, discovered the shocking sensations of sea swimming, connected with another mum and... I push thoughts of Ryan out of my head. He was a dick the last time I saw him. So, no, I don't count him as a friend and decide to completely ignore him if I ever run into him again.

Then I spend the rest of the afternoon dragging myself around the house, tidying up for my mother, who is arriving the following day. To be honest, I am genuinely surprised to see how messy it is. When I walk through the rooms and see them through my mother's eyes, all my feelings of contentment disappear and I start to freak out. Jesus, how could I have let it get into such a state? The hallway is strewn with a variety of my shoes, jackets and towels from the beach, which I clearly haven't been arsed to tidy up. Thanks to wearing shoes in the house at all times, the cool marble floors are full of muddy footprints and dry sand. More clothes and towels lie scattered over my bedroom floor. The bathroom is filthy. I spend a good hour wrestling chunks of hair from the shower plug, scrubbing the tiles and bleaching the toilet. The living area is cluttered with post for Bea's mum or junk mail, which I hastily form into neat piles or chuck in the bin. When I walk into the kitchen, a dark smell assaults my nostrils and I gag when I realise the stench is coming from days' worth of unwashed plates in the dishwasher. Did I have fish one night? It definitely smells like it. The oven is like something out of a murder scene except instead of blood it's tomato sauce from all the pizzas I've cooked and overturned accidentally during various stages of red wine consumption. I get out the rubber gloves and start scrubbing furiously.

After three hours of cleaning, I am finally satisfied that the house is a decent enough state for my mother. It is almost 9.30 p.m. by the time I finish, and have my dinner (not pizza). I flop down on the couch with a large glass of wine and I wonder for the first time if all this silent revenge stuff on David has possibly backfired a little bit. I mean, maybe it's not such a bad thing to live in a very clean and tidy house.

On my way to the kitchen for a refill, I take a moment to look out the window to catch the sunset. I shouldn't be surprised when I see a tall figure standing in my back garden close to the edge of the cliff, but I am. I take a large sip of my wine, place the glass carefully on the kitchen island, and slide open one of the glass doors.

As I walk over the steely wavy grass, the figure turns.

'Hi, Saoirse,' he says, smiling.

'Hi, Ryan,' I reply. 'You're trespassing,' I add, folding my arms.

He laughs.

I don't.

'Hey, I'm sorry I was so off with you earlier,' he says, holding up his hands in mock defence.

'Yes, you were a right prick,' I say, determined to show him that I have no intention of being disarmed by his pretty face.

'I have a good reason,' he says, looking suddenly sad.

And I crumble because, of all things, I hate to see anyone looking sad.

'Tell me,' I say softly.

And he does.

Five years ago, when he was on a trip with his girlfriend, he got chatting to a local girl called Frances, who worked as a receptionist at the hotel and she just 'blew him away'.

'I can't explain it, Saoirse. She was warm and funny, and she had these... like really kind eyes,' he says, staring out at the horizon. 'I mean, I had this long-term girlfriend, for God's sake, and I knew I loved her, but I couldn't get this other girl out of my head.'

He turns to me suddenly, his expression agonised. 'I mean, I couldn't stop myself, you know?'

I nod, not because I approve but because I am desperate to hear the rest of the story.

'Anyway, I started getting up early every morning, before my girlfriend woke up, just so I could spend some more time with Frances. By the end of that first week, I knew I had to be with her,' he says.

It turned out that Frances was a member of the swimming club and they arranged to meet at the beach at dawn as often as they could.

'So, you know Kitty,' I say.

He looks away as he nods.

'Kitty is Frances' mother,' Ryan says, rubbing his eyes tiredly.

Things start to fall into place. No wonder Kitty hates Ryan – messing around with her daughter when his girlfriend was mere minutes away.

'It doesn't sound like you were doing much swimming,' I say, crossly. I have no time for men and their supposed 'urges'.

He drops his head.

'How long did it last?' I say.

'Almost two weeks,' he says. 'And then myself and my girlfriend packed our bags and went back home to London.'

Wait a minute. London?

I must look surprised because he goes on, 'Yes, at the time, I lived in London. I moved to LA shortly after... ' and then his voice breaks and I wait for him to recover.

'What happened to Frances, Ryan?' I ask as gently as I can.

He takes a deep breath.

'We had agreed to end things between us before I left. Actually, she was the one who called it off. Said it was a holiday romance, and nothing more. I didn't believe her, but she told me that's what she wanted. She didn't want any further contact.'

He takes a deep breath, as if willing himself to go on.

'But then she knew where I worked, and she emailed me to tell me that she wanted me back – that she would do anything to have me in her life again.'

'So, what did you do?' I say, fearing the answer.

'I made the biggest mistake of my life,' he says. 'I ignored the email.'

I am really trying not to judge him, but it's hard. So he comes to a little Irish town with his long-term girlfriend, cheats on her and then heads back to London, and ignores an email from a girl who had clearly been in love with him, and by the sounds of things, him with her.

'You don't understand, Saoirse. There were other things going on in my life at the time. I had made a decision to stay with my girlfriend, and I couldn't risk losing her because of Frances.'

I fold my arms, raise my eyebrows and stare at him.

'But I didn't ignore the email for long,' he says, pleadingly. 'Only for a week or so until I figured out what I was going to do.'

Ryan tells me that he used that time to break the news to his girlfriend about Frances. Inevitably, she kicked him out of the house. He got on a plane to Ireland to see Frances... and then he pauses once more, taking a few shuddering breaths.

'I go straight to the hotel as soon as I arrive in the afternoon and they tell me she's left work early,' he says, his face screwed up in the memory. 'I spend the rest of the day looking for her, but I can't find her. I talk to Kitty and Frank on the beach, but nobody has seen her.'

I don't like where this is going, and so I close my eyes and focus on my breathing.

'That evening, I'm sitting in the hotel lobby, hoping that she'll turn up for her evening shift, when two policemen come rushing in. I just know there and then something bad has happened to Frances,' he says, tears falling down his face.

'What did Frances do, Ryan?' I say, tears filling my own eyes. But in my mind I am asking, What did you *make* her do?

'She jumped off this cliff, and killed herself,' he says, bent double now.

What? This cliff? Where we are both standing?

I take an involuntary step backwards. I HATE these kinds of tragedies – this is the whole reason I don't watch the news.

'I'm so sorry, Ryan,' I say, and I really mean it.

Yes, he fucked up and he made a big mistake, but nobody deserves to go through what he has.

He straightens up and I give him a little hug. In fairness, even when he's snotty he's bloody gorgeous. Realising how inappropriate it is to feel attracted to him, I release him in order to dig out a raggedy tissue and he smiles weakly.

'Is that why you come here every summer?' I say. 'To remember Frances?'

He nods. 'Yes, every summer for the last five years. I go to her grave and tell her how sorry I am.'

My whole body is covered in goose bumps. I think of Kitty a few days ago staring out over the cliffs, eyes full of tears and I feel desperately sorry for her.

I think of Anna and I can't imagine how horrific it must be to lose a child.

'The worst thing is,' Ryan begins, trying to catch a sob, 'Frances told me she had always struggled with depression and had tried to commit suicide before. And I *knew* that and I still ignored her email.'

He wipes his eyes impatiently with his sleeve.

'But I came back Saoirse,' he says, with unbearable pleading in his eyes. 'I came back to tell her I wanted to be with her, but I was too late. I couldn't save her.'

He reaches out with one arm and pulls me to him, and we stay there in a tight embrace for what seems like hours. Eventually, his body stops trembling and I gently push him away.

There's only one thing to say.

'Wine,' I say firmly.

He gives me a sad smile, and nods.

As we walk towards the house, Ryan puts his arm around me and I don't resist. He's a friend in need, I tell myself. That's all it is. Then we separate while I pour us each half a bottle of wine into the biggest wine glasses I can find.

I lead him to the living room and flop down on the couch. Ryan sits down next to me and we clink our glasses together, and sip our wine quietly for a bit.

'You know, you remind me of her,' he says suddenly. 'Frances, I mean.'

I'm not sure what to make of that, so I just raise my eyebrows in surprise.

'You have the same kind eyes,' he says, reaching out and tracing his fingers over my forehead.

It is such an intimate gesture that I dare not break it, and we stay there for a bit, just looking at each other as he strokes my forehead. The atmosphere becomes thick and dreamlike, and I see his face – his beautiful face – moving closer and I hold my breath in anticipation. And then the doorbell rings.

We both jump apart at the loud buzzing sound. I leap off the couch and bang straight into the coffee table, causing the large glasses of wine to wobble dangerously. Ryan puts one hand out to steady the table. The buzzing continues.

For a moment, I can't think straight. The only thought I have right now is to stop the fucking buzzing.

My legs feel heavy as I walk to the front door. Annoyed now, I fling it open and there, standing on the doorstep, is my mother.

'Jesus, Mary, and Holy Saint Joseph!' she says, marching into the hallway and slapping her travel bag on the floor. 'Don't you ever look at your phone?'

As soon as I find my voice, I say, 'What are you doing here? You're not supposed to be coming until tomorrow!'

'Sure, I texted you, *and* posted it on the Twitter and the Facebook!' she says, in a tone that intimates that this whole thing is all my fault. 'Jesus, you'll be wanting me to put it on the Instagram next!'

Before I can say anything in response, Ryan walks into the hallway.

My mother looks at him and quickly looks back to me with her eyebrows raised.

I feel my cheeks grow hot. Suddenly I am a teenager trying to explain to my mother why there is 'a boy' in my room.

Ryan holds out his hand to my mother, introduces himself, and tells her how happy he is to meet her. My mother looks him up and down, gives him her best sniff and says that it's nice to meet one of Saoirse's friends – she gives me a disapproving look when she says the word 'friends' – and then she drops his hand quickly and walks through to the living room.

Ryan shrugs, and I mouth a sorry, and he gives me a shy smile. When I walk him to the front door, he thanks me for listening, and then bends down and whispers, 'Another time,' before planting a kiss on the corner of my mouth. I watch him as he crunches over the gravel drive towards the path that will take him back to the village. He doesn't look back.

I close the front door and jump when I see my mother standing in the hallway, arms folded.

'Who's that then, Saoirse?' she says, giving me a hard stare.

Yes, who is that? I think. Is he a friend or something more? Did he want to kiss me? Did I want to kiss him?

'A friend who needed a shoulder to cry on,' I say finally, returning her stare.

'What on earth should someone who looks like him have to be worried about? Has he been diagnosed with a serious case of handsome fever?'

Despite myself, I laugh.

'Ah, so you've noticed his looks then?' I say.

Her expression is cross for a moment and she says, 'He's a bit too pretty, no? Besides, his eyes are too close together – mean with his money.'

I let that one go and spend the next hour showing her around The Cube ('It looks better in the photos'), getting her a cup of cocoa ('Sure, it's far too late for wine, Saoirse'), before eventually settling her in the spare room ('This bedroom is awful small').

By the time I get to bed I am exhausted but my mind is whirring with everything that Ryan has told me. What would have happened if my mother hadn't suddenly arrived the way she did? I touch my fingers to the corner of my mouth where he kissed me goodbye, as his parting words echo over and over again.

'Another time.'

18

The next day is Thursday and I wake up with my head full of Ryan. When I peep into my mother's room, she tells me, eyes glued to the screen of her phone, that she is in the middle of a 'make or break auction' on 'the eBay'. I leave her to it and then start feeling guilty that my sixty-nine-year-old mother seems to be working harder than I am, so I pad into the kitchen and pop open my laptop. Writing is always a good distraction and I use it now to still the voice in my head that whispers the promise of 'another time'.

I need to write something light to replace the heaviness in my head from being with Ryan and hearing his tragic story.

For the last couple of days, I have been mulling over the conversation I'd had with Bea about swearing. Bea has challenged me over being brave enough to write the truth, but today I feel brave. I mean, if you think about it; language is everything – the only way we can really be understood. In fact, language is one of the main reasons I love spending time with my Irish friends. You see, *everybody* understands me here. I can say things like 'we had great craic', or 'Anna's taken a real stretch,' or that I'm 'wrecked' without the puzzled expressions on the faces of my London pals. Even Bea has to ask me what the hell I'm talking about sometimes. Best of all, *everyone* here can pronounce my name. Even though I'm still a foreigner who defected to the UK twenty years ago.

But being in Ireland isn't just about being understood, it's also about the freedom of using 'bad' language. *Everybody* swears in Ireland, not necessarily in an aggressive way, but to vent emotion, or add humour or colour to a story. So I write:

> Swearing is cathartic, and, frankly, we should do more of it, especially during those dark times of parenting. And if we let the odd swear word drop in front of our kids, then so be it. Perhaps it's better that they know the words that will get them in trouble at school rather than picking them up from other kids and using them blindly and ignorantly. Overall, swearing is a good way to let off steam and, let's face it, there's nothing like a good sweary rant over a glass of wine in the right company to lift ourselves out of those dark moods.

Just as I finish typing my final sentence, my mother walks into the kitchen fully dressed.

'What are you doing stuck to your laptop on such a lovely day?' she says, irritably.

I don't bother pointing out that she has been doing the same thing. After a quick shower and change, I take my mother for a brisk walk along the beach. We bump into Kitty, who gives me a warm smile, and I return it by squeezing her arm. I tell my mother I'm off for a swim and leave her chatting with Kitty. I haven't told her anything about Kitty or Frances, so I'm pretty sure she can't stick her foot in it.

As I am leaving them together, I hear my mother say to Kitty, 'Saoirse! Going for a *swim* in the *sea*! I never thought I'd see the day. Can you credit it, Kitty?'

I shake my head in annoyance and slow down to hear Kitty's reply, 'Well, she'd have been doing more of it if she'd only stayed in Ireland. There's no sea-swimming in London, Brenda!'

Then they both tut for a bit.

I raise my eyes skyward and quicken my pace towards the shore; I have no chance against those kindred spirits.

As the water reaches my ankles, I allow myself to think about Ryan. I feel both relieved and disappointed when he doesn't make an appearance, but given my mother's suspicions from last night, it's probably better that he isn't around.

After my swim, on the walk back to the house, my mother tells me that she's had a great chat with Kitty. I groan inwardly and wonder what information she has managed to wrangle. Sometimes my mother sees people as wet sponges, just there to be wrung out for every personal confession, admission or secret.

'So, I believe Ryan and Frances had an affair,' she says a few minutes later, casually, stacking the breakfast things into the dishwasher. 'The one who committed suicide,' she adds.

Despite myself, I am impressed. What took me days to discover, she's managed to crack in a twenty-minute conversation. Clearly the locals only see me as a 'foreigner' but have no problem confiding in my mother.

'Yes, I know,' I say, feigning boredom so she won't keep going on about it.

'Ah, Frances was always very troubled. Even as a child,' my mother says sighing, in the manner of someone who has had an intimate relationship with Frances. 'That's what Kitty told me,' she adds, unnecessarily.

Yes, Kitty your best friend, whom you met just twenty minutes ago, I think bitterly.

'I wouldn't say it was just all about Frances,' my mother says thoughtfully. 'There's something about that Ryan fella that I just don't like.'

This is her way of testing my loyalty to Ryan but I don't fall into her trap and defend him. Instead, I busy myself with the dishes and we clear the rest of the kitchen in tense silence. Afterwards my mother announces that she needs her 'eBay fix' and disappears into her bedroom, presumably to flog more marital cures to unsuspecting punters. Just as I'm wondering how I'm going to get through the rest of the day without cracking, I get a text from Jen asking if my mother and I want to meet her for lunch in McGowan's. Jen! That's it! My mother loves Jen – she will save the day!

I tell my mother that we're meeting for lunch and she seems as happy as I am to have some sort of distraction. A couple of hours later we set off for McGowan's on foot, just as it's starting to drizzle. When I suggest we take the car, my mother looks at me as if I've done a particularly appalling fart, and snaps, 'Sure, it's barely raining, Saoirse. Have you been out of the country that long?' And I say nothing lest I get reminded once again of my 'foreigner' status.

When we get to the pub, Jen is already there, looking fabulous as usual in a fitted navy-and-white-striped T-shirt and white skinny jeans. She looks like a really sexy sailor.

Although I have told my mother explicitly that Jen is happy and healthy despite being jilted, she still greets her with, 'Left the wedding dress at home, did you?' which is her idea of a joke. Luckily Jen has known my mother almost as long as I have and she bursts into giggles, and stands up to give my mother a hug.

'Howerya, Brenda?' she says.

We order burgers and chips all around, and a bottle of wine to start off with. My mother entertains Jen with all her internet stories, while I sit back and switch off and think about Ryan. Suddenly, the sound of my name brings me back into the room.

'What's that?' I say, puzzled.

Jen laughs and says, 'Your mother was just filling me in on finding a strange man in your house last night.'

I tell myself not to react but my body betrays me: a slow flush spreads across my chest and cheeks.

My mother eyes me and then Jen.

'A good-looking fella, this Ryan, but there's something off about him,' she says.

'His eyes are a bit too close together,' Jen says.

'Mean!' the pair of them chorus, and then burst into fits of laughter.

I make a face and say nothing. What do I care what they think of Ryan or his 'mean' eyes?

'Is he your boyfriend?' my mum says in her teasing voice, but I can see more than a glint of disapproval in her eyes, and suddenly I am very pissed off.

'Fuck off, the pair you!' I begin, enraged. 'He's just a friend, and even if he wasn't, what does it matter? It's not like David is being exactly faithful.'

Then I stop, realising what I've said. It's the first time I've uttered those words out loud and they sound dreadful... terrifying.

My mother and Jen stare at me, mercifully speechless for once.

Jen finds her voice first. 'Hang on, Saoirse, are you telling us that David – your husband of five years – is shagging someone else?'

I look her straight in the eye, catch my breath, and my voice breaks as I say, 'Yes.'

Wide-eyed, Jen turns to look at my mother and they lock eyes before doing something completely unexpected.

The two of them burst out laughing.

* * *

This is the first time I have been in the sea twice in one day, and it feels colder than normal, but I ignore it by thrashing it with my arms and beating it with my legs. Despite its freezing temperatures, it does nothing to cool down my rage and eventually I stop swimming and start treading water, wondering how far I have come. I am both gratified and slightly nervous to see I have swum well beyond the humping camels and I wonder how far I would have to go to end up like that poor swimmer whose name has been immortalised by Frank's terrible graffiti on the cliff wall.

I brush away angry tears with salty hands and think about what happened in McGowan's not yet an hour ago. It wasn't the laughter that had made me storm out of the pub. It was something far worse. First of all, they picked holes in my story of how I had discovered the affair: 'Sure, that text could have meant anything, Saoirse' – my mother, and, 'People work late all the time, Saoirse – it doesn't mean anything!' – Jen, and, 'Sure, aren't flowers a nice gesture?' – both of them. And then Jen asked me why I hadn't confronted David about it, and I told her because I needed time to process it.

Then my mother looked at me with eyes as narrow as slits and said, 'Saoirse, I think I know why you haven't said anything to David. It's because part of you wants it to be true.'

And that was when I stood up, told them they could go fuck themselves, and raced back to the house for my swimsuit.

I stop treading water and start swimming again, this time towards the shore. Fuck them, I think ferociously. As if I want my marriage to dissolve; as if I want Anna to be without her father – and I swim and I swim to thrash away the niggling voice that comes from deep down and that whispers perhaps part of what my mum has said might be a little bit true. Maybe I want to think badly of David because I want a reason to leave him; one where the blame would solely be on his side, and not mine.

Ten minutes later, I am exhausted, my mind too numb from the cold to think any longer. I switch to breaststroke and start swimming to a place where I can stand. Two figures waving on the beach interrupt my pace. I squint my eyes and can just about make out my mother and Jen standing at the edge of the sea, waving furiously in my direction. I ignore them and continue my breaststroke. As I get closer, I hear them shouting. They want to talk to me. Well, they can feck off. I motion with my middle finger that it would be best to leave me be, but they fold their arms and stamp their feet and shake their heads, intent on staying where they are.

This is annoying. I can't get out of the sea without passing them, and so I choose to stay where I am. A voice inside tells me that it's a bit nuts to choose hypothermia over talking to the woman who gave birth to me and my long-time best friend, but there you have it. Either they feck off and leave me to it, or I stay where I am. This stand-off lasts another three minutes. Eventually, Jen starts making praying gestures with her hands and my mother starts shouting, 'Ah, come on, Saoirse!' and suddenly I come up with an idea.

I feel for the stony surface of the sea bed and stand with the water up to my chest. If they want to talk to me, they can damn well come to me. I do a beckoning gesture, and shout, 'Come in!'

They look at each other and laugh nervously.

My mother cups her hands over her mouth and shouts, 'And how can we come in if we have no swimsuits?'

I give an exaggerated shrug in return. Secretly, I'm hoping that they will piss off and get their swimsuits, leaving my exit clear. But then they do something far more unexpected.

They start taking off their clothes.

Jen goes first, pulling her top over her head in one move, before wriggling out of her skirt until she stands there in a stunning gold bra and pants, looking like a twenty-something Victoria's Secret model. My anger against her increases. We are the *same age*.

My mother hesitates for only a moment and then quickly strips off her polo shirt and tracksuit bottoms until she is down to her big pants, and I am also annoyed with her because for a sixty-nine-year-old woman she looks bloody fit, and seems to possess a flatter stomach and fewer stretch-marks than I do.

I start treading water again to keep warm, comforting myself in the knowledge that this whole charade will come to an end when these two amateurs hit the freezing water. Ha! They'll be lucky to get in past their ankles.

They start walking smartly over the sand and both stop dead as soon as their feet touch the water. I remember doing the exact same thing when I first got in: the shock of something that cold hitting such a small part of your body, and how incomprehensible it seems to subject the rest of your body to the same treatment. It's a real do-or-die moment. My mother shoots a wide-eyed look at Jen but Jen pumps both her fists in the air in a sort of 'we can do this!' gesture.

'It'll be grand once you're in!' I shout, unable to resist the most patron-ising phrase in the English language when it comes to reassuring reluctant swimmers about freezing water temperatures.

Jen gives me the two fingers, before throwing back her shoulders and marching through the water towards me with a steely look on her face. She must be bloody freezing. My mother follows at a more tentative pace, staring down at the water as if she is marginally surprised to see it rising up her body.

As they get closer, I start to feel a little nervous. I hadn't banked on them actually coming into the sea and I have no idea what I'm going to say to them.

Jen is the first to reach me. The water is up to her shoulders. She stares at me for a moment and then splashes water directly in my face.

'That's for making me come in here, you fucking sadist,' she says.

Despite my anger, I can't help laughing.

'See! I told you it would be nice and warm once you got used to it!'

'Don't make me splash you again,' she says grumpily.

My mother joins us, the pain of the freezing temperatures written all over her weary face.

'Well, if Muhammad won't go to the mountain...' she says, hugging her arms to her chest.

'So, where were we?' Jen says, for all the world behaving like someone who is simply carrying on a normal conversation that somehow had been interrupted.

'You were telling me that I actually *want* my husband to have an affair,' I say, and give a sulky sniff.

Jen looks at my mother and sighs.

'Look, Saoirse. We didn't mean to hurt you, but you have this tendency to...' my mother says, and then she trails off.

Tendency to what?

'You have a tendency to put off dealing with difficult situations,' Jen says matter-of-factly.

My mother smacks the water in agreement. 'Yes!' she says to Jen. 'I call it her "little box". She did the same thing when her dad died, and she's doing it again now.'

'It was the same thing with Hugo,' Jen says.

'What about Hugo?' I say, raising my hands indignantly out of the water. What's my ex got to do with it?

'We had plenty of conversations when things started going south with Hugo. I remember that you spent a lot of time thinking about life without him and how much better it would be. Before you even broke up, you had already decided to chuck your job in and flat-share with Joss,' she said.

'So you're saying I should have stayed with Hugo?' I say, folding wet arms across my chest.

'No, you did the right thing, but you never really opened up to him and told him how you were feeling. My point is that Hugo wasn't the right man for you, but David is. I'm worried' – here my mum gives her a nudge – '*we're* worried that instead of confronting David about your problems, you're persuading yourself that life is better without him.'

'That's utter horseshit,' I tell them both.

'What would life without David look like?' my mother says, quietly, reaching out with one wet hand and touching my shoulder. And I don't know if it's the intimacy of the gesture that does it but suddenly everything just pours out.

'Life would be *easier* on my own. I wouldn't feel so bloody trapped. I would finally be free to do whatever I wanted,' I say angrily.

Then suddenly I can't stop talking. I tell them if David wasn't around I wouldn't have to deal with the petty house shit that causes so much resentment between us; that I wouldn't have to keep reminding him of routine stuff for Anna that he should *really* know by now, like what she eats for tea or what toy she likes to snuggle up to in bed. That I could watch all the shit reality TV I wanted without him complaining all the way through.

I wouldn't have to worry about his sheer insensitivity for having a go at me for not changing the towels to clean ones because I've been distracted by one of Anna's horrific meltdowns, or feel beyond irritated when he *refolds* his T-shirts after I've spent ages on them. And I wouldn't have to spend day after day holding my breath just because I don't want to get into yet another argument about all this meaningless shit.

When I finish ranting, Jen waits a moment before saying, 'Do you still love David, Saoirse?'

And the words spill out of my mouth before I can stop them.

'Of course I do!' And then I realise that I really do. For all his flaws and irritating habits, I love my husband. There might be moments of relief that he's absent when he is away and I'm on my own with Anna, but after a couple of days, I start to miss him. It's just sometimes harder to be with him. And then there are all these other feelings I have been experiencing lately. If I really loved David, why was I so attracted to Ryan?

I look at Mum and Jen and they are smiling, and then I ruin it all by saying, 'It's just that I think sometimes love isn't enough.'

My mother's expression darkens.

'Do you think you're the only one who feels this way when the kids come along? I had all this with your father, Saoirse. God forgive me, but he was bloody useless when you were little. In fact, it's a good thing he's already dead because I might have murdered him myself,' she says, wiping her wet hand across her forehead.

I am in shock because my mother has never said anything bad about my father – ever. In fact, throughout my existence there has been no pedestal high enough for him.

Jen pats my mother on the arm, and says, 'Look, I don't have kids but I know relationships are hard enough without kids. There were times when I wanted to smother Liam in his sleep.'

I look at her curiously. They had both seemed so happy together. I'm dying to know why she wanted to murder him as he slumbered.

'Saoirse, you love David. You're meant to be together. There's nobody else on this earth who loves you as much as he does,' my mother says.

But something in my expression must alert her because her eyes widen and she says, 'Saoirse! Tell me there's nobody else!'

And I tut, look skyward and tell her not to be so ridiculous, but I can see by Jen's raised eyebrows that *she's* not convinced.

'So, here's my theory,' she says, glaring at me. 'People who leave the person they are married to in order to act on their fantasies of a particular person eventually end up in the same position but just with a different person.'

I take both hands out of the water and shake them in a 'what the fuck?' motion because I have no idea what she's on about.

My mum says, 'She's saying that if you leave David for Ryan, you'll have great sex for the first six months and then it will be back to the same boring domestic routine and griping as you have now. Except it will be worse because a child will be involved.'

I don't know which shocks me more, the mention of Ryan or my mother using the word 'sex'.

'Ah, for fuck's sake,' I say. 'I'm not going to run away with Ryan. Sure, I barely know him!'

'He fancies you, Saoirse,' Jen says.

'Fuck off, Jen,' I reply, but secretly I'm flattered. I mean, *look* at him.

'It's always nice to get a bit of male attention, as long as you don't act on it,' my mother says, wagging her finger. 'Mind you, if I was thirty years younger, I'd be tempted meself!'

Jen and I burst out laughing at this and the mood lightens. Then my mother starts doing jumping jacks in the water to 'warm up' and the sight is so comical that Jen and I start to giggle all over again.

When we are finally quiet, my mother says, 'Listen. I want you to promise me that you'll talk to David about everything, including this supposed affair.'

I know she's right. It's only fair that I confront David about it.

'Some things don't stack up, Saoirse; there has to be another reason for that text and all the late nights. He's too in love with you to mess around. I mean, he barely even looks at me,' Jen says, giving me a wink.

I know she's joking but it is true: Jen is a total knockout and David has never given her as much as a polite glance. Mind you, neither has Ryan. STOP IT!

My mother's teeth start to chatter and we decide to head back to the shore. As we stumble over the gravelly bits towards the beach, my mother says, 'Ah, Saoirse, you wouldn't survive a day without David. You're bloody hopeless on your own.'

'Well, you did it!' I say, defensively.

'True, but you don't have to,' she says, throwing an arm around me.

And I let myself lean in to the embrace, because she's absolutely right.

19

I wake up the next morning with the usual feeling of missing Anna, but today there is something else there, and it takes me a minute to figure it out. Then I remember the day before and smile. After we came out of the sea, shivering and blue, we traipsed up to The Cube for hot showers and large glasses of wine. The three of us sat there until midnight, drinking and laughing and exchanging juicy stories. My mother cracked us all up with untold and not exactly flattering stories about my father ('He was the type of man who would prefer to rub sticks together to light the fire than spend a few pence on the matches'); and Jen caused even more hilarity by describing Liam's first efforts in bed as 'strictly vanilla'. ('Honestly, the only orgasm he was interested in was his own.')

And as always happens when high quantities of alcohol are consumed, there were the confessional moments too.

My mother: 'I should have given you and David a chance to spend more time together without Anna.'

Followed by Jen: 'I'm sorry I didn't tell you about breaking up with Liam.'

And me to my mother: 'I should have asked more for your help.'

And me to Jen: 'I'll be here whenever you need me.'

And then we all had a little cry and more wine, and then, 'Who wants

Prosecco?' before Jen finally ordered a taxi home ('I like to wake up in my own bed'), and my mum and I retreated into our respective bedrooms.

This morning, with woolly heads, my mother and I sit down in our nighties to an early breakfast of good old-fashioned porridge with a bit of toast. It's time I started eating healthily again after abusing my body with red wine and pizza for the last seven days.

The toast pops up, and Mum springs up to get it. When she puts the plate down in front of me I notice she has buttered it and cut it into four triangles, just the way I used to like it when I was a child. This tiny act makes me feel oddly emotional and, in a rush, I start to tell her about the motherhood book, what I need to do to pitch for it and the ideas I've had so far. All the time she listens in her usual way – with her head cocked to one side.

When I have finally finished, she pushes her plate away from her and wrinkles her forehead.

'I was twenty-nine when I had you,' she begins, 'and truth be told, I didn't know what hit me. As I told you in the sea yesterday, your father was useless, but so were all men in those days. A man's work was outside the house, earning a living, and the woman's was inside the house raising the children.'

'So how did you cope?' I say. This is the first time my mum has spoken to me so intimately about life after I was born and I am breathless to know more.

'I had a group of friends from school, who were all in the same boat,' she says, with a wistful look in her eye.

Then she interrupts herself to ask me if I remember Joan with the lazy eye, and Trish who used to play tennis on a Sunday. I nod, not because I remember Trish and Joan but because I'm desperate for her to continue.

'Anyway, you'd go round to one of your friend's houses with your screaming baby in one arm and a bag of nappy cloths in the other, on your knees from being up half the night, and you'd walk out of there an hour later, crying your eyes out from the laughter,' she says smiling at the memory.

'So, no judgement then?' I say.

'Ah, no, these would be my closest friends. The judgement came from all those snobby cows at mass on a Sunday. They'd bring their babies dressed up to the nines, parading them up the aisle at Communion, desperate to show off the latest fashion. If your baby gave as much as a squeak, they'd give you the biggest glare. And don't get me started on their disapproving views about breast-feeding.'

I am aghast at this. 'What was wrong with breast-feeding?'

'It was a sign of being poor. Breast-feeding meant you couldn't afford the price of formula,' she says, wrapping her hands around her mug.

I shake my head in disbelief. Even over forty years ago, new mums just couldn't win.

'But we didn't give a fig what they thought,' she says, lifting up her chin, proudly. 'We just did our own thing and giggled about them behind their backs.'

I raise my cup of tea in a 'cheers' gesture and we clink mugs.

When she puts her mug down, her expression suddenly grows dark.

'Then of course, your father died suddenly,' she says, twisting her wedding band, 'and I was all over the place.'

I am gripped because she has never told me how she coped after my dad died. I can't imagine her falling to pieces; to me she has always been so strong and confident.

'I couldn't look after you, Saoirse,' she says, through a half-sob.

The sound is so unexpected that it takes me a moment to reach over the table to comfort her.

'It was the shock of it, you see,' she says, giving me a pleading look, and I squeeze her hand to show her I understand.

She takes a few deep breaths, stealing herself to carry on.

'It was Trish and Joan who took you between them. Every day for weeks, they would pick you up in the morning and drop you off at bedtime. I would spend the day crying, put you to bed, and then cry all through the night. I wasn't fit to take care of you.'

A sudden memory shoots through me. 'Was there a house with a green door?'

She bursts out laughing, and says, 'Yes! That was Trish's house! It's amazing what kids pick up on.'

We smile at each other for a bit, and then I ask her, as gently as I can, to tell me how she recovered from my father's death.

'It sounds like a cliché but time is really a healer,' she says. 'Besides, I was running out of money, which gave me the kick up the arse I needed to get some training, which is how I became a teacher.'

My eyes well up as I think about how hard it must have been for her, losing her husband, and having to start her life all over again.

'Grief is a terrible thing, Saoirse; if it wasn't for my friends, I don't think I could have carried on. They gave me hope and the courage to pick myself up and start again. Because of their support, I became a survivor,' she says. 'And because of them, I was able to be your mother again.'

That does it. We sit there holding hands, neither of us bothering to stem the flow of our tears.

'I was so worried about you, Saoirse. You never talked about your father, you know. You packed everything away in that little box in your mind, and never opened it,' she says, wiping away my tears with one thumb, and I suddenly feel about five again.

'You didn't do anything wrong,' I say fiercely. 'I was being well looked after. I don't even remember any of it!'

And it's true: I don't remember being traumatised by my father's death at all, but in hindsight, maybe that's where I learned to compartmentalise.

'Apart from the house with the green door,' she says with a watery smile.

'Apart from that,' I say, through a snotty chuckle.

I let go of her hands and get up to grab a box of tissues. After we have blown our noses and wiped our eyes, I say to her, 'You had such a tough time, Mum.'

But she surprises me by shaking her head.

'Not as tough as it is now. Things are different now, Saoirse. People don't live in close communities like ours any more, or go to church, or make the effort to know their neighbours. That's why people are going on social media, because they no longer have those real-life connections. They are lonely. It's loneliness that's the real killer. And there's nothing lonelier than being a new mum when you don't have your real friends around you.'

Ain't that the truth, I think.

And suddenly, I know exactly how I'm going to pitch my book.

'I haven't thought about all this stuff in years,' she says, with a sigh. 'Just think, I'm almost seventy and the memories are as clear as yesterday.'

My heart skips a beat. Jesus. With everything going on, I've completely forgotten that her birthday is at the end of the month. And it's a big one. But I have an idea. I tell her that she's going to come over to London and we're going to have a family do to celebrate.

Her face brightens.

'I'll do a couple of lasagnes!' she says.

'Mum, it's your birthday! You're not doing the cooking!' I say, although she does do the most amazing lasagne. Even David, who hates all things pasta related, loves my mum's lasagne.

She holds up one hand in protest and I back down.

'Fine, I'll do the cake,' I say.

'Grand,' she says. 'And you'll be inviting Bea.'

As this is a statement rather than a question, I don't bother arguing the fact that Bea isn't exactly family, but seeing how much my mum loves her, it would be hard to say no. Besides, Anna will be delighted to have Harry around to trash our house while we're eating.

'And Jen,' she adds.

My heart gives a little leap. I think a trip to London is exactly what Jen needs to give her some distance from her heartbreak.

'Done!' I say.

'Right, I'm off to check the eBay,' Mum announces, pushing back her chair.

I smile.

'I'm off to call David,' I say.

She looks at me and nods. 'Good girl,' she says. 'He's a good one, Saoirse. Don't let him go.'

I blow out some air in reply. Deep down, I know she's right. We may have lost our way, David and I, but I'm determined to find a road back again.

I grab my phone and head into my bedroom. It's barely 9 a.m. and I am already emotionally exhausted. At this time of day, David should be walking from the Tube station to his office. Just as I'm searching my contacts for his number (I still don't know it off by heart), my bedroom door opens with a crash. It's my mother still in her flowery nightie with a wild look in her eyes. She brandishes her phone at me. I groan inwardly, thinking this has got to be another eBay drama.

'Have you seen the breaking news, Saoirse?' she says frantically.

I look at my phone, but nothing has flashed up yet. I hate breaking news. I'm jaded from it.

She shakes her head impatiently.

'It's another terrorist attack!' she says.

Immediately I feel sick.

'Who have the bastards targeted this time?' I say. In my head I'm thinking poor France, or poor Belgium, or poor Turkey, or poor Spain – because when terrible things happen the countries become as human as their inhabitants.

My mother sits abruptly down at the end of the bed and whispers, 'It's London, Saoirse.'

London. Again.

'How bad?'

'Suicide bomber has blown himself up in the City,' she says. She taps into the news site and says, 'Three dead so far,' and my mind starts to race. Anna will be fine because she is staying in Bea's house, and Bea will be fine because she works miles from the City, in Canary Wharf. My mind stops then and my whole body freezes.

David.

David works in the City.

My mother stares down at her phone and lets out a terrible whimper.

'Where in the City?' I say, my voice trembling.

My mother tells me the place.

It's the street David works on.

PART III

LONDON, PRESENT DAY

He waits for your love
He wants to be your husband
Let him, Saoirse. Please

20

David's phone rings out and goes to voicemail. I call his office but nobody picks up. My mother, still glued to her news feed, tells me that all the buildings on that street have been evacuated. I call the helpline number and the woman on the other end, sounding as hysterical as I do, tells me to call everyone David knows. I do that, and no one knows any more than I do. In desperation, I call Bea at work.

She answers the phone, sounding annoyed.

'Oh, for fuck's sake. I'm NOWHERE NEAR the terrorist attack. London is a BIG PLACE! Now leave me the fuck alone!'

'It's me,' I say, in a quiet voice.

'Saoirse!' she says, immediately contrite. 'Sorry, I thought it was yet another of my South African relatives that my mother ordered to contact me to see if I was still alive. They've been bothering me all day.'

'Is Anna OK?' I ask.

'Of course she is!' Bea says impatiently. 'It's not as though Maria decided to take it upon herself to bring two mental children into the City to see the sights. She's with my little horror, the pair of them causing mischief as usual.'

'Bea, David isn't answering his phone,' I say, a sob catching in my throat.

'Christ, Saoirse. What's wrong with me? I forgot he worked on that street. I didn't think.'

I tell her that I've called everyone I can think of, and nobody has heard from him.

'I left for work before he dropped Anna over this morning,' Bea says, sounding very tired. 'Have you tried Rose?'

Of course! Rose – David's mother. I haven't called her. I thank Bea and hurriedly hang up.

Rose answers the phone, breathless.

'Saoirse, I'm rushing out to a golf match,' she says. 'Can this wait?'

I fight the urge to shout at her. Trying to keep calm, I ask her if she has seen the news. She tells me she never switches on the TV before 7 p.m. (which is a dig at me as she disapproves of my turning on the TV for Anna at any given opportunity).

'Rose, there's been a terrorist attack in the City of London,' I say, my voice starting to tremble. 'Right by David's office. I can't get hold of him, Rose. Please tell me you've heard from him.'

I lean against the door jamb, the tears spilling down my face.

She doesn't say anything for a moment, and I give her this time because I imagine she is in shock, and then she says in this sulky, child-like voice, 'I doubt if I would be the first one he would call in a crisis, Saoirse.'

She is so cold about it that I want to scream at her and tell her what a horrible, shitty, complete COW of a mother she is. So I do.

I start by telling her that she is an ice-cold bitch who should never have adopted David in the first place, and how she doesn't give a *shit* about Anna or indeed anyone else but herself. Then I tell her that she has made everyone else's lives a misery, including her dead husband's, and I finish by telling her that if I *ever* see her again, it will be far too soon. I sign off with, 'Go fuck yourself, Rose,' and then jam the button on my phone until her hateful name disappears from my screen.

I walk into the living room where my mother is staring at a TV screen filled with dazed people in suits covered with silver sheets being rushed off into ambulances. Although the cameras try not to zoom in too much, you can see the stretchers.

'Over twelve people confirmed dead,' my mother says, rubbing her eyes. 'Not to mention those injured.'

I close my eyes for a moment. I refuse to believe that David is on one of those stretchers.

My mother gets up wearily from the couch.

'Did you try Rose?' she says.

'I did,' I say.

'Any sign of David?'

'No,' I say, and I don't bother telling her about the call because Rose isn't important enough to think about.

We look at each other for a moment completely at a loss. Then my mother suddenly clenches her fist and waves it at me.

'I know how to locate David!' she says.

'What? How?'

'I have his phone tracked,' she replies, rushing over to the couch to grab her phone from the armrest.

Fighting the urge to ask her why the fuck she is tracking my husband's phone, I race over to look at the map on her screen. And there it is. The icon of David's phone.

'Where the fuck is it?' I say, crying openly now. 'Please tell me it's not on the street.' Because I know if David's phone is lying on the street, there is a strong likelihood that he might be badly hurt or worse.

My mother zooms in with trembling fingers, and shakes her head.

'No, Saoirse. His phone isn't on the street,' she says.

And I feel dizzy with relief. Maybe David got out after all.

Then she calmly puts the phone down, and takes me by the shoulders.

'His phone is in St Thomas's Hospital in Westminster,' she says.

And I feel my knees collapse under me.

* * *

I never realised how useless I am in a crisis until now. David's in hospital. David is hurt. Probably dead. And I can't even focus enough to phone the hospital, because I don't want to know the answer. My mother leaves me in my place on the floor, and starts to tap her phone furiously. She holds it to her ear and waits, her face creased with worry. My mind clouds over with a comforting numbness; whatever she finds out will not break through the impenetrable mental fog. And then she throws her phone in frustration onto the kitchen island and utters a loud, 'FUCKING CHRIST', which makes me want to giggle a bit, given my mother's staunch stance against both swearing and blasphemy.

'I can't get through to the hospital,' she says, holding her head in her hands. 'The lines must be jammed.'

I say nothing.

She narrows her eyes a little bit and reaches for her phone again. I yawn and practise zoning out some more. It's much better this way.

I'm not sure how long I have been sitting here when I hear a familiar, but decidedly unwelcome voice.

'Saoirse, snap the fuck out of your little box,' the voice says, from somewhere above me.

I raise my head wearily to see Jen – no make-up, sunglasses falling off her head – glaring at me.

She reaches down, grabs both my hands and pulls. I try to make my body a dead weight but I can't. It feels unnatural to be standing. I feel myself wobble and she puts her arms around me and half-drags me to the couch, where she allows me to plonk down once more into a sitting position.

She turns to my mother.

'Brenda, I'll get her sorted out. Book her a flight to London. She needs to find David,' she says.

My mother gives her a quick nod and disappears into her bedroom with the motion of someone who is grateful to be given a task.

Then Jen sits beside me with a sigh.

'Listen, you don't know anything bad has happened yet, OK? You need to go and find out for yourself.'

I manage a nod, because everything she says makes perfect sense, but I'm not feeling very logical right now. If nothing bad has happened to David then why hasn't he called me?

She looks away for a moment and shakes her head.

'The whole thing is bloody awful. I bumped into Dee on the way over here and she told me that Ryan has already left for London. Apparently he has some family there who might be affected.'

At the mention of Ryan, I snap my head up and my mind suddenly clears. Ryan's already gone. No more little box. I need to fucking *do* something.

My mother returns, waving her phone.

'I've managed to book you on the last seat on the next flight from Dublin to London!' she says, breathless.

Jen gives her the thumbs up.

'It's the 11 a.m. flight from Dublin,' my mother continues, flushed now from her little victory.

'Who's Saoirse flying with?' Jen says.

My mother's expression falters a little. 'Ryanair,' she says in a small voice.

'Ah, for fuck's sake, Brenda,' Jen says, tutting.

'No, it's fine,' I say, rising to my feet. I feel a rush of adrenalin swoop over me now there is a plan in place.

'I don't give a shite if it's Ryanair. I'd swim across the fucking sea at this stage,' I say, and then march towards my bedroom to throw some things into a bag.

Jen follows me.

'Look, I'm sorry you have to do this alone,' she says.

'You heard my mother – only one seat left!' I say, and I know my voice sounds far too chirpy but I need to get moving.

My mum appears in the doorway. 'I'll drive you to the airport in my car, Saoirse,' she says.

'And I'll return your rental car,' Jen says.

I open my mouth to protest and close it again. Like it or not, I need the support.

Half an hour later, I'm packed and ready to go.

My mother and I don't speak on the way to the airport and I am grateful for the silence. I look at the news of the attack on my phone but the content doesn't change. Then I stare out of the window and curse the weather. It is the one hot, sunny day of the year and I feel bitter because surely this is the day where it should be cold, dark and damp.

As we pull into Departures, I get out of the car, my legs feeling heavy and stiff. My mother hurries round to the boot of the car, hands me my suitcase and gives me a quick hug. Then she grabs me by both shoulders and brings her face close to mine.

'Saoirse, I need you to listen to what I'm about to say,' she says.

I force myself to meet her gaze.

'This is your time,' she says with force. 'I grew up in the terrible grip of terrorism. People in my day were terrified of going into central Dublin. Every car might have had a bomb in it; every department store the same. And when you finally started to relax, some prick with a clipboard would march over to you, cocky as you like, and try and persuade you to 'join the cause'. We were just kids, Saoirse. Kids desperate to do a bit of shopping or go and take in a film at the cinema, but we had all these fears...'

She lets go of my shoulders and stares at the ground for a moment. Then she lifts her chin and says quietly, 'In our case, the situation became salvageable. Eventually, there were two sides that were ready to put down their arms and negotiate. It was never going to be perfect but peace was possible.'

'And in this case?' I said, hoping whatever she says next will provide some sort of comfort.

'I don't know, Saoirse,' she says, her voice catching. 'How do you negotiate with a group of people who place no value on human life?'

And I feel like all the wind has been knocked out of me again.

'Listen to me. No situation is hopeless. This is your time. You will get through it. You will find David. You are NOT going to lose your husband, like I did.'

The strength in her voice fills me, and I feel the energy flowing back into my body. David is alive and I am damn well going to find him. My mother and I hug for a few quiet moments and then she gets back in the car. I don't watch her drive away.

The airport is strangely quiet. I check in and wait at the gate for my flight to be called. Out of curiosity, I bring up Vale Mums on my phone and hope that nobody they know has been injured in the attack. The very first post that flashes up is a request from Rosalind for party-bag ideas for a six-year-old's birthday. One daring mum has suggested ordering pre-filled party bags online ('Save yourself the hassle!') but has been quickly shut down by another who tells the mum to give seeds for the kids to plant in the garden. Yes – seeds instead of sweets. I'd love to see how Anna would react to *that* party bag. Tania ends the entire discussion with two damning sentences:

I don't give out party bags. Instead I tell the parents that the cost of the party bags will be donated to our local children's hospital.

The smug cow.

I scroll down and down, looking for any mention of 'ONE OF THE WORST ATTACKS IN RECENT HISTORY' but for ages all I can find is the usual chat about schools. Finally I see a meek post from Rosalind, simply saying that she hopes everybody is OK after the terrible attack in the City. Tania has responded with a curt, 'Let's not discuss. That's exactly what the terrorists want.'

I think about that for a moment. Why does Tania think she knows what the terrorists want? Does she really think a discussion over a suburban Facebook group is really 'giving in' to the terrorists? I wonder what it really means to 'give in' and I think about how these attacks make me feel: the places I feel are no longer safe; the countries 'too dangerous' to visit; the places too crowded to be considered safe (football stadiums, concert arenas, theatres, cinemas). The world is shrinking. I am afraid. I am afraid because I have a child and a lot more to lose. Living in fear. Is my mother right? Is this 'our time'? The first time our generation has experienced real fear for our lives? Maybe living in fear is what 'giving in' to terrorists means, but I am loath to admit that anything Tania Henderson says is right.

Minutes go by and then a full hour. I overhear people on phones talking about the attack in London, and how terrible it is. Nobody seems to have any links to the dead or the injured and I feel relieved on their behalf. The flight is clearly delayed but nobody confirms this. Passengers, previously strangers, all start bonding over their mutual hatred of airlines that don't bother telling you when things go wrong. While everyone seems to agree that passengers should always be kept informed about delays and so on, there is the usual trickle of people who dare to defend the airline: 'Sure, you get what you pay for!' and 'Imagine what this would have cost if you'd flown BA!' These are the least popular passengers and are soon ignored.

Eventually, a seventeen-year-old boy who looks as though he has merely shrugged himself into his uniform and left most of it behind (including his top three shirt buttons) appears, holding a clipboard. He looks exactly like the type of 'youth' – minus the hoodie – my next-door neighbour Joseph would have tutted at for simply looking at his house. A balding man in his sixties, carrying an old-style black briefcase, marches over to him. He asks the boy impatiently how long the flight is going to be delayed.

The boy looks skyward, and replies in a thick Dublin accent, 'Jesus, you're in an awful hurry to get to a burning city, arnt'cha?' Then he turns round and goes back the way he came, leaving the man standing stock-still with two bright red spots on his cheeks.

Ten minutes later, the flight is called. As there is no reason left to grumble, the bonding is forgotten as everybody races onto the plane as if by moving quicker they'll help the plane somehow make up the time it has lost.

Exhausted, I lean my head back and try not to think about David, lying alone somewhere, injured. I glance at my watch and see that it is just after 11 a.m. The attack happened a mere four hours ago. Already it feels like the longest day of my life.

21

I dive into a black cab and instruct the driver to take me to St Thomas's Hospital, half-expecting him to tell me the roads are closed, but he simply nods and puts the car into gear. I ask him about any roads that have been blocked, and he says, 'Just the ones closest to the attack. This is London, love. We don't start blocking off half the city because of some fuckwit terrorists.' I hear the measure of pride in his voice and my eyes fill with tears, because he is right. That's the thing I love about London. In the face of great adversity, it will always brush itself off, get back on its feet and carry on. And much as I love Ireland, at that moment I feel like I'm home.

As we get closer to St Thomas's, I feel sick. My news feed tells me that people are using Twitter in a desperate effort to find missing friends and relatives. It's hard to fathom how one person can cause this much devastation.

About five minutes from the hospital, the traffic starts to get bad. Six ambulances block our path. I hand over some money and tell the cab driver I will walk the rest of the way. But panic grips me and I start to run. As I approach the hospital, the pavement becomes crowded with dozens of people. People hugging, people crying, people screaming. People with dazed stares, waving their phones around to nobody in particular, 'Have you seen this woman?' and worse, 'Have you seen my little girl?'

Tears stream down my face as I weave my way towards the big grey building. People being killed is always dreadful, but there is something even worse about attacks involving children. I think about Anna and what I would do if something happened to her, and I remember the overwhelming feeling of protectiveness when I first saw her battered little face after her birth. Becoming a parent makes potential murderers out of all of us, because I know that if anybody hurt her, I would have no hesitation in putting a bullet in that person's hateful skull. I feel a terrible ache inside.

My phone buzzes violently in my pocket. My heart leaps – maybe it's David. But the name flashing up is not his, and my stomach lurches in disappointment. It's Maria, Bea's nanny. 'Anna wants to talk to you,' she says, sounding flustered.

I walk a few steps away from the crowd to hear her better, taking deep breaths to calm down.

'Hi, Mummy!' she says, her cheerfulness incongruous against the gloom of the day. The thought that she has no idea what's going on comforts me.

'How are you, sweetheart?' I say, trying to keep my voice as steady as possible.

'It's rude to sniff,' she says.

'Mummy has a bit of a cold,' I say lightly, deciding that she doesn't really need to know the reason for Mummy's tears and stuffy nose.

'Are you behaving yourself for Maria?' I ask.

'I don't like Maria any more,' she says in her grumpiest voice.

When I ask her why, she tells me that Maria is 'a meanie pants' for not letting her and Harry have ice cream 'with sprinkles on' for breakfast.

Before I can respond, she suddenly says, 'When are you coming back, Mummy?' and suddenly I'm dissolving in tears again.

I tell her I'm going to pick her up later that day, which is true. Even if I don't find David today, I will still pick up our daughter.

She doesn't say anything for a moment, and then comes out with two words that break my heart.

'With Daddy?'

And I don't know what to say to that, so I reach deep inside for the courage to tell the biggest lie I can, and I say, 'Of course! I'll bring Daddy with me to pick you up too.'

I tell her I have to go, adding, 'And make sure you eat your...' and I pause because a sob has started to push its way up through my throat and I need to stop it from getting out.

'My what?' Anna says.

I take a deep breath, and force the word out. 'Vegetables!' I say as brightly as I can.

'Oh,' Anna says, sounding puzzled. 'I thought you were going to say, eat your *fucking* vegetables.'

What was just a sob is now a hysterical guffaw, because dire though the situation is, there are fewer things funnier than a four-year-old swearing like a fishwife. I tell her I love her and I hang up. Talking to Anna has given me renewed energy and a solid deadline. I promised her both her mummy and daddy would pick her up, and that is one promise I will bloody well keep.

I grab my suitcase and haul it up to the hospital entrance. A man in a neon jacket waves an arm around, pleading for quiet. In his hand is a clipboard. Cupping his other hand over his mouth he announces that some of the injured have been moved to another hospital, due to the number already admitted to the burns unit here. People still looking for their loved ones must report to him immediately. In spite of the panic, people form an orderly line, with me third from the top. I bring a photo of David up on my phone and ask the people in the queue if they've seen him. Some of them shake their heads and others show me the pictures of their loved ones. Then it's my turn, and with shaking voice I give David's name to the man in the neon coat, and watch him as he taps his pencil down the page. His shoulders drop and before he raises his head I know he has bad news.

'He's not on the list, ma'am,' he says, his voice heavy with sympathy.

That means he's not on the list of people who are alive. I don't want to ask for the list of the dead. Not yet.

I show him the photo of David on my phone, and he shakes his head again.

'But he's here!' I say, in a pleading voice I don't recognise. 'His phone is here.'

The man gives me a helpless shrug and I turn to the people in the queue, who give me sympathetic looks mixed with impatience because they too are waiting to hear news about the people they love, so I just turn and walk away.

David is somewhere in this building. I know it. Spying a fire exit, I race up the stairs two at a time – adrenalin pumping now. Fuck the man in the neon. I will find my husband. I forget how big hospitals are, and it takes me long minutes of running through corridors and trying to make sense of signs, before I come to a desk with a real-live human behind it. The sign behind her says, 'Burns Unit'.

Breathless, I wave a photo of David at her, and clutch my stomach when her face frowns a little. She knows him.

'I have seen him,' she says, taking my phone for a closer look. 'He's been here all day.'

'Where?' I say, relief flooding through my core.

'Are you a relative?' she says with a frown.

'I'm his wife!' I say.

She looks at me as if I've just told her a very complex riddle.

'But I thought...' she starts, but she sees the murderous expression on my face and just sighs.

'He's in Ward B,' she says, pointing to a set of double doors at the end of the corridor. Grabbing my phone back, I push through the double doors and find myself in a room crowded with beds.

Forcing myself to slow down, I make a big effort to look at the patients, but they all seem to be covered in bandages. I see glimpses of nurses and doctors working behind closed curtains, changing dressings and calling instructions, and they don't see me when I walk past. My stomach plummets: everyone seems to be covered in bandages. How will I be able to recognise David? I reach the end of the row of beds and peep in the final curtain. There I see the long brown hair of a girl with her face turned towards the wall, with someone's hand holding hers, and I start to withdraw, embarrassed to intrude on this couple's privacy.

Then I hear my name. The curtain whips back.

It's David.

I feel my hands fly to my mouth but no sound comes out. My mind works at an inexorably slow pace. David. In hospital. Not hurt. I feel his arms around me, and I try and hug him back, but every muscle in my body feels tired and weak.

He loosens his grip on me and says, 'It's OK, it's OK. I'm OK.'

And I look at him, and try to take him in.

He tells me how he'd been running late for work and had missed the whole attack. He'd found out about the explosion the same way I had, through his news feed.

'Why the fuck didn't you call me to tell me you were OK?' I say, teary now. Now that I know he's not dead, suddenly I'm really pissed off.

'I'm so sorry,' he says. 'I must have dropped my phone somewhere. I was trying to help her.' His eyes move in the direction of the bed, where the brunette lays prostrate.

Now I take another look at the figure and I notice half her face is covered in a white bandage, and I start feeling a bit ashamed of myself. Maybe David hadn't called but he had good reason. You know – like saving someone else's life.

'Will she be all right?' I ask.

'The force of the explosion knocked her backwards,' he says. 'She has a nasty burn on her right cheek, but the doctors tell me she will make a good recovery. There won't be too much scarring.'

I look at her again and feel an icy chill start to form in the pit of my stomach. Because suddenly I think I know who this wounded girl is. It's Jordan. The slut. Weeks of pent-up rage and hours of terrible anxiety and fear roll themselves into one gigantic ball of fury.

'You let me think you were *dead* when all the time you're with that slut!' I hiss, clenching my fists in an effort to avoid lashing out.

Somewhere beyond the red mist, the woman starts to stir, but I ignore her. She may have been caught up in an explosion but she's going to be *fine*. My marriage, however, has been destroyed forever because of her and my stupid weak husband.

David opens his mouth to an 'O' shape and holds up his hands in surrender.

'Hang on a minute, Saoirse!' he says.

'Don't come over all innocent!' I say. 'You've probably been fucking that slut Jordan since we've been married.'

'What? Jordan?'

He says it with such disbelief that doubt flashes through me.

'Saoirse!' he says, turning me by the shoulders. 'That's not Jordan! Jordan's in Mauritius, on her honeymoon.'

As if on cue, the figure in the bed sighs before turning over. And David's right. It's not Jordan at all.

It's my old flatmate, Joss.

Before I can say anything else, David leads me out of the ward and downstairs to the hospital canteen. We sit opposite each other at a plastic table. I try to make sense of what I have just seen. Joss – whom I haven't laid eyes on since I moved out of the flat five years ago.

'There is something you should know,' he says, looking down at his hands. 'For the past few months—'

And I finish the sentence for him. 'You've been having sex with Joss.'

He whips his head up. 'Joss?' he says, as if I have just accused him of having sex with a goat.

I nod, lips pursed, but even as I'm nodding I'm thinking that something about the two of them together doesn't add up. But what else could it be?

'What are you talking about? Are you insane?'

His response is so utterly indignant that I instantly believe him. But I still need to get to the bottom of whatever it is he is trying to hide.

'I can't believe you think I'm shagging Joss,' he says, running his hand impatiently through his hair. 'In fact, I can't believe you think I've been shagging *anyone*.'

'OK, fine, you're not shagging Joss, but you've been hiding something from me all the same,' I snap back.

And then he tells me everything and I am right – he has been hiding stuff from me but it's not what I suspected.

By the time he stops talking, I'm not sure what to think any more.

* * *

'MUMMEEEEEEE,' Anna cries, and throws her little arms around my neck, smothering me in kisses.

In reality that doesn't happen at all. When I knock on Bea's door at 6 p.m., Maria actually has to go and forcibly extricate my daughter from Harry's iPad in order for her to greet the woman who gave birth to her, whom she hasn't seen in a week. Anna walks sulkily to the entrance of the front door where I am crouching low with open arms and burning thighs.

Despite the dangerous look in her eyes, I am so happy to see her.

'Hi, sweetheart!' I gush, and move to put my arms around her.

She pushes me away and says two words that she has only ever uttered around three times in her life, and only then when she wants something, like sweets.

'Where's Daddy?' she says.

'I'm here, Anna,' David says, behind me and with astonishing role reversal, Anna races straight past me and into her daddy's arms.

'I've missed you, Daddy!' she cries, burying her head into his shoulder, as I straighten up.

What? Anna only saw him this morning! Not to mention every single day since I've been gone.

She raises her head, looks David directly in the eye and says in the world's most angelic voice, 'Did you bring my sweeties, Daddy?'

David gives me a furtive look. He knows that I disapprove of giving Anna any kind of sugar before bedtime because it sends her into a lethal hyperactive state. God knows what time she has been getting to bed.

Balancing Anna with one arm, he uses his free hand to reach into his pocket and stops as soon as he sees my death stare. He looks desperately from me to Anna, presumably wondering which one of us is less hassle to piss off. I don't know who he's kidding.

Moments later, Anna has a packet of chewy sweets in her hand (an adult packet – the ones I usually tell her have wine in them to put her off) and a big smile on her face. She wriggles out of David's grip and tells us it's time to go home.

I want to thank Maria properly for taking care of Anna so I tell him to walk ahead and I'll follow on. David gives me a nod, and walks away, Anna trotting happily beside him shovelling E numbers into her mouth as fast as her sticky hands can manage. I turn to Maria, who is still standing in the doorway wrestling Bea's lipstick from Harry's pudgy hands. Eventually he lets go, and gives her a kick before running off upstairs.

I thank her profusely for looking after Anna, and she waves her hands in a 'she's no bother gesture,' which is a standard response from someone who is being paid to look after small children. Still, she looks tired and I comment that she must have had her hands full over the last week.

She wipes a strand of hair from her face, crosses her arms, and says, 'Well, today it's not the kids who are the problem. It's—' And then she stops dead.

'What is it?' I say, because Maria isn't the type to look ruffled.

'Let's just say Bea has a visitor,' she says, raising her eyes skyward. 'They've just gone out for dinner.'

Judging by her frustration, I'm guessing Bea's mother, Arianna, is in town. I'm not surprised Maria is irritated by having the ultimate Organic fussing over every bite of food Harry eats. But when I say this to Maria, she shakes her head.

'No, it's not Arianna,' she sighs. But before she can tell me anything else, Harry comes barrelling through the door holding one of those shit polystyrene toy aeroplanes that well-meaning parents give out in party bags, and heads straight towards the garden gate. I get there first, successfully blocking his innate intention to kill himself. Maria lifts him up battering-ram style and gives me an apologetic smile.

I thank her again and walk home slowly, thinking about Bea's mysterious guest, but mostly wondering how I'm going to face David when I get in.

22

It is 10 p.m. Thanks to the sugar rush from 'Daddy's sweets', Anna has gone to bed late. After the trauma of the last twelve hours, I am exhausted and think about cutting my talk with David short, particularly as we appear to keep going around in circles.

'It's still a betrayal,' I say.

'It's not!' he says, shaking his head vehemently. 'I just didn't mention it because I wasn't sure if I wanted to go through with it.'

'You could have talked to me about it!' I said, and I feel my voice getting a bit wobbly. 'I'm your wife!'

He puts his head in his hands and stays like that for a bit. I watch him – the man who used to tell me everything – and wonder if we will ever be that way again.

David was telling the truth. He hasn't been shagging anyone else, but he has been hiding something: his search for his biological mother.

He got in touch with Joss a couple of months ago after rediscovering her business card in his wallet. As she works for the government in the field of missing persons, he thought she would be able to help him track down his biological mother. It was Joss he was texting. Joss with all her kisses and hearts ('She's an emoji freak, Saoirse. She thinks it's ironic'). Joss who he had been meeting while I was away. I still can't believe it. Joss – my disdainful flatmate, who I haven't thought about in years – knows more about my husband's movements than I do.

This morning, Joss texted David to tell him she was pretty sure she had some information about his biological mother. She was on her way to meet David to pass on what she knew when some total scumbag decided to blow himself up right outside David's building. The impact of the explosion knocked her backwards, but she was still conscious when David found her moments later. He rode with her in the ambulance when she passed out, and stayed by her bedside until I arrived.

'All these years, David, you've never mentioned a thing about finding your biological mother. Why now? Why not five years ago, when you had that conversation with Joss?'

David raises his head and says, 'At the time I was just curious about how it all worked. I wasn't sure if I would ever go through with it, so I didn't see the point in talking about it. But over the last few months, I have just felt so out of control. Work is crazy, we're struggling financially, and Anna doesn't even have a decent school to go to. I know this sounds nuts, but I thought that maybe if I found my real mother, I would feel more grounded; that things would make more sense.'

His face is so filled with anguish that I can't help but feel terribly sad for him. I feel the same as he, and probably have done so for longer; I just manifest it in a different way. When he feels out of control, his compulsive behaviour kicks in. It makes sense to him – ensuring his home, his sanctuary, is neat and clean gives him peace and a level of control that he doesn't have over other aspects of his life. Whereas when I feel out of control, I want to shout and scream and throw things.

So I tell him all this, and he asks how we are going to manage it, and I like the way he says 'we' because it might mean we have a future together if we both want it.

'You need to start telling me things,' I say, feeling teary. 'I can't have secrets between us. I mean, finding out that you've been searching for your biological mother is a huge thing to keep from me.'

He wraps his arms around me and says, 'I'm so sorry,' over and over again until I begin to feel calm again and a wave of exhaustion rushes over me.

'I miss us, David,' I say, into his shoulder.

And he tells me he misses us too.

'I love you,' I say, drawing back for a moment. 'But you're so fucking hard to live with! Sometimes I feel that you don't *see* me any more. That I'm just a person that fucks up everything domestic in your life, as though I'm just a really shit maid that you can't fire.'

'I know!' he says, raising his hands helplessly. 'I know I've been getting worse. Sometimes, I don't even know I'm doing it. And I'm sorry for taking it out on you.'

While I am relieved he recognises that his behaviour is unacceptable, I still can't let go of everything I have put up with over the last few years. 'I just don't get why the cutlery has to be arranged "just so" in the drawer, or the shoes lined up in perfect symmetry or...' and once I start I can't seem to stop.

When I finally finish, David replies, 'I know you think I'm petty and these things don't matter... but they matter to me. And I know it sounds stupid but every time you don't wash a dish properly or leave old vegetables in the fridge it makes me think you don't care about me.'

I grab a tissue and blow my nose, all the time trying to take this in. My husband thinks that I don't care about him if I don't clean out the fridge regularly. And much as every part of me wants to fight it, I have this uncomfortable feeling that there are things that make me think he doesn't care about me either, which could be considered just as petty.

'Technology,' I say, continuing where I left off.

He looks at me, forehead creased.

'You're always on your smartphone or your laptop or work phone or iPad... I can't go into one room in our house without something whirring or flashing or buzzing,' I say, my stomach tight with frustration.

He nods in a patient way before saying, 'I get it, but you know I have to work in the evenings.'

I tell him I know that, but surely there needs to be some sort of cut-off time? A time where we both abandon technology to actually spend some time together? And before he can say anything, I say, 'Remember when we used to shout at the TV together? We never do that any more. I know it sounds silly but I miss shouting at the TV with you.'

'I miss that too,' he says, and gives me another hug.

I return it, finally feeling we are getting somewhere. It's been a long time since we really listened to each other.

We end up agreeing that no matter what, we will meet in the living room at 9 p.m., technology-free and spend some time together – whether it's watching TV or listening to music.

Then David says we should go away for the night, just the two of us, and I tell him I love the idea apart from one tiny problem: we can't afford to pay someone for a whole night's babysitting. He thinks for a moment and his response makes my heart stop.

'We could ask my mother,' he says. 'She really should spend more time with Anna.'

Rose.

Rose, who I abused over the phone in Ireland when I thought David was dead.

FUCK.

Evidently David sees the look of horror on my face, and asks me what's wrong.

I say, 'Nothing!' as cheerfully as I can. 'Rose! Great idea!'

Sod her – I'm not letting her ruin this. I'll confess another time.

David gives me a serious look and then asks if I can do something for him.

Eager to change the subject, I give a firm nod.

'Is there any chance you could even *try* to arrange the cutlery in the dishwasher the proper way?'

My stomach drops. In some respects, I'd be happier 'fessing up about Rose. I really want to meet him halfway on this but I feel the familiar irritation rise. I try to keep my voice controlled and say, 'David, I have successfully run the dishwasher plenty of times without arranging the cutlery in the right way. I just don't understand why you think it makes any difference.'

Now it's his turn to mask his irritation, and I appreciate the effort.

'It's just that it wouldn't be in the dishwasher instructions if it didn't make sense to arrange them that way,' he says in a quiet, measured voice.

I can't help myself.

'Jesus, David, who the fuck *reads* the dishwasher instructions?'

He gives me a sad look and turns away and I burn with resentment, but I can't give up now. We've come too far.

I take a deep breath and apologise for losing it.

'If it means that much to you, I will have a look at the instructions and follow the guide,' I say, every word hurting as I utter it.

His face lights up. It's as though I've just announced I'm about to give him an unexpected blow job.

'Can I talk you through the instructions?' he says, with an enthusiasm I haven't seen in months.

'If it turns you on!' I say, jokingly.

Jesus, I hope this stuff doesn't turn him on.

Then we smile at each other, and a sense of warmth and relief rushes over me. We have a long way to go but it's an overwhelming sensation when you realise you're still in love with your husband.

'So,' he says, through a yawn. 'How was Ireland?'

So I tell him all about my reunion with Jen, and meeting Dee, and my mother's views on The Cube, and my progress with the pitch. But I leave out the part about Ryan because, let's face it, some things are just not worth sharing.

He laughs when I tell him about Kitty and Frank, and them bullying me into almost succumbing to hypothermia, and expresses mock horror when I tell him how they finally succeeded in getting me into the sea.

'I'll be taking you in the sea with me next time!' I say, and I laugh when he answers, 'No fucking way.'

Then I tell him about Mum's birthday and her trip to London at the end of the month, and before I can raise the subject of having a party for her, he suggests it first.

'It's about time we had a good knees-up!' he says, and I smile at him, pleased to see a glimpse of the old David back.

But despite the lighter atmosphere, there is something I need to ask David that's been preying on my mind.

'Are you going to meet your real mother?' I say.

He rubs his eyes with both hands, and tells me he doesn't know yet. 'I think I need more time,' he says.

I agree that sounds like a good idea, and when we both start yawning we agree to call it a night. David calls the hospital to check on Joss and she's much better: slight concussion but she'll be allowed out tomorrow.

While David's on to the hospital, I call my mother. I have already texted her, not to mention Jen and Dee, and Rose (reluctantly) to let them know that David is alive and well, but I know my mother will need more than just a few lines on a small screen to keep her going. She answers on the first ring.

'Hey, Mum!' I say. 'Do you know who's *not* dead?'

'Jesus, Mary and Holy Saint Joseph, wouldn't you think you'd have called earlier?' she says crossly.

'Sure, I sent you a text!' I say, indignantly.

'Well, a text doesn't give me the whole picture,' she says. 'I have been plagued all day by the Facebook with people wanting to know exactly what happened to you and David, and don't get me started on the Instagram. And I haven't been able to tell them a thing!'

So that's why she's so annoyed. She's in the spotlight without a story to tell. I signal to David that I might be some time, and he mouths back, 'Your mother?' and I nod. With a pang of envy I watch him as he settles down on the couch in front of the news. Knowing my mother, it'll be a while before I get to join him.

After a good hour of 'What? It wasn't Jordan-the-slut in the hospital? Now, remind me who's Joss?' followed by much crowing: 'See? I TOLD you David wasn't having an affair...', I finally manage to get her off the phone by yawning in such a way that even she can't ignore it. I go into the living room to complain to David about the unnecessary length of the call, but the muffled sounds of a podcast tells me that he has retreated to the downstairs bathroom. I contemplate waiting until he comes out, but I'm not quite sure I have it in me to wait the requisite forty minutes.

With heavy steps, I climb the stairs, dragging my suitcase behind me. When I get to our bedroom, I throw the suitcase on the bed and unzip it quickly. Just as I'm pulling out my toiletries bag, a plastic bag containing two small boxes drops out. I pick up the first box. It is made of flimsy cheap pink cardboard, decorated in yellow flowers. It has the words 'Marital Miracle' written on the top. I burst out laughing. My mother must have sneaked the boxes into my suitcase before I left for London.

I open it and spill the contents out onto the bed. Sure enough, there is a small white sheet of paper, like the ones you might use to jot down a shopping list, a small pair of nail scissors and a tiny pebble. My eye drifts towards a folded piece of yellow paper, which I imagine is another one of my mother's attempts at a haiku. And tickled as I am by such nonsense, I find myself reluctant to open it. The last time I had seen one of these I believed my marriage had fallen apart.

Telling myself not to be so silly, I reach for the folded paper and open it. It says:

> He waits for your love
> He wants to be your husband
> Let him, Saoirse. Please.

I rub the tears away with the back of my hand, and try to stem the tickling feeling in my nose. Despite everything that has happened I know deep down that David loves me. Now all I have to do now is let him. Quietly, I put the boxes away in the drawer of my bedside table. Maybe I will give David his box one day (blue with no flowers – very gender specific) but tonight, I need to sleep away the trauma of the last twenty-four hours.

I brush my teeth, get into my nightdress, climb into bed and try to keep my eyes open until David joins me. If this was a movie, we'd probably be having 'make-up sex' now, but nothing could be further from my mind. Besides, we're married. With a child.

Five minutes later David climbs into bed beside me, childishly triumphant about his bathroom experience. He kisses me good night and we say our 'I love yous' and then turn over, our backs to each other, wriggling as far away from each other as possible for fear we might touch during the night – just the way we like it.

23

The next day, David receives an email telling him to work from home for the next few days until the anti-terror squad has swept the area for explosive devices. I hate this. Now every time he goes to work I'm going to worry that he won't be coming home again. Still, on the plus side, as things have quietened down on the work front he is spending more time with Anna (who is now his biggest fan), which gives me more time to focus on finishing my pitch. But before I start work, there's something I need to do first. I grab my phone and message Rosalind, asking her if she can meet for a coffee today. If I have any chance of writing a book about motherhood, I have to stop being such a hypocrite and try to be a supporter of other mums rather than a silent observer. My phone pings almost immediately. She suggests our local coffee shop (the one where the entrance is permanently obstructed by prams and buggies) and we agree to meet there in twenty minutes. I ask David, who is plugging away at this laptop, if he can keep an eye on Anna for a bit, and he looks uncertain.

'She's on her iPad,' I say, and his face immediately brightens, secure in the knowledge that he's not going to be disturbed for at least an hour.

On the walk to the coffee shop, I think back to how nervous I felt when I first contacted Rosalind, but now I'm actually meeting her, I feel totally calm. Mind you, given the trauma of yesterday's events, I'm not sure if anything would rattle me now.

The smell of coffee hits me several yards from the café itself. The café occupies the lower half of a terraced house that looks exactly the same as mine, which I like because it breaks up the uniformity of the stifling rows and rows of identical houses.

As I squeeze myself past one double buggy and two triple buggies, I see Rosalind is already there (I recognise her from her Facebook photo), sitting at a small table by the window. She gets up to greet me (she must know me from my photo too), and gives me a little wave. Rosalind is tall and very thin, with long, loose limbs that look as though she has yet to grow into them. Her slight figure is clothed in a loose-fitting V-necked green-and-blue speckled shirt tucked into dark blue skinny jeans. Although it is twenty-eight degrees outside, she wears a cream knitted woollen cardigan over the shirt. She has black curly hair tied up in a barely contained bun and her blue eyes are encircled by big, round black-framed glasses.

She looks like a bird, I decide. Like a very fragile, anxious peacock.

When I reach the table, she claps her hands excitedly and says, 'Ooooh!'

I'm not sure what to do with this so I just smile and say, 'Hello.'

'Sit down, sit down,' she says, gesturing her hand wildly towards the opposite chair to her.

Just as I sit down, she jumps back up immediately, startling me a little.

'Coffee! I'll get you a coffee!' she says, and before I can stop her, she is waving over the waiter and putting in an order.

I thank her, and she sits back down.

'So, how are you?' I say.

'Ooooh, I'm all right,' she says again, resting her hand under her chin.

I ask her about the terrorist attack, and she tells me that nobody she knows has been hurt.

Our coffees arrive and we sip in awkward silence for a bit.

'So, I see you have three boys,' I say.

'Ooooh, yes,' she says, sighing. And then the floodgates open: how she has been really struggling since number three came along, how her husband is away all the time, how her nanny dumped her by text... basically a summary of everything she has posted already on Vale Mums.

When she has finished, she peers at me through her big glasses and says, 'Ooooh, I'm sorry. You don't even know me and here I am going on and on about myself. I mean, I *love* my kids but—'

And that's when I cut her off.

'Please don't feel you have to justify your love for your children, Rosalind,' I tell her firmly. 'We all love our children, but let's face it, they are bloody hard work at times.'

She nods and her shoulders slump. When she raises her head again, her eyes are watery.

'I mean the first two boys, Ben and Ethan, are a handful, but the two-year-old, Jacob, is a real challenge,' she says, shifting a little in her chair, a flush beginning to grow on her cheeks.

Jesus, if it's one word I can't cope with it's 'challenge'. I take a deep breath and ask her gently to think of a better word than 'challenge' to describe her difficult toddler.

She looks a bit nonplussed for a moment, before tentatively suggesting, 'Little monkey?'

Not quite what I had in mind.

'How about little shitbag?' I say.

She laughs as though for the first time and, as if surprised by the sound, stifles it by covering her mouth guiltily.

'Ooooh, I couldn't call him that,' she says, but she is smiling all the same.

'Have a think,' I say, feeling more encouraged.

She brushes a stray curl behind her ear, and says, 'I suppose if I really had to think of the most accurate word to describe him, I would say he is a little cock.'

This time it's my turn to be surprised. I wasn't sure she had it in her.

After that, we have a joyous time trying to outdo each other with our war stories about tantruming toddlers.

Rosalind: 'The worst was when I lost sight of Jacob when I was dropping Ben off at school, only to find him firmly planted with all the other kids on the big rug in the classroom. I had to drag him out of there kicking and screaming in front of Ben's teacher, who looked extremely unimpressed.'

And me: 'That's nothing. Once, I had to crawl under a whole row of cinema seats to retrieve a "special stone" that Anna had dropped by accident. It was the only way I could get her to stop screaming.'

Once our supply of terrible tales has been exhausted, I move on to the topic of Vale Mums. I am curious to see why she feels compelled to post, especially considering the hammering she gets from the Organics.

'Since I had kids, and with my husband away, I really don't have time to socialise. I'm an only child, and my mum died ten years ago... I guess I post on Vale Mums for company,' she says, twisting her hands.

'And what makes you think Vale Mums have all the answers?' I say, trying to withhold my rant about the Organics and how hideous they are.

'I don't,' she says. 'But sometimes it's nice when people care enough to reply to my posts.'

Even though what some of them do say knocks your confidence as a parent, I add silently. She takes a sip of her coffee, almost shrinking into herself. I honestly think she is one of the loneliest people I have ever met, and I immediately feel guilty that I have judged her for posting so prolifically on Vale Mums, when all she really needed was a good friend.

Suddenly, Rosalind glances at her watch and stands up abruptly.

'Ooooh, look at the time! I have to go and pick up the boys from sports camp!'

She pays the bill and we head out into the hot sun. As we say goodbye, I tell her I will be in touch again with some more days and times for coffee, and I really mean it. She says, 'Ooooh, lovely,' before she goes, legs and arms flailing as she runs. As I'm walking home, I think about how kids bring people together: people you may not have immediately bonded with prior to having kids. Not to be mean, but if I had met Rosalind at work, I probably would have dismissed her for being a little kooky. Just before I reach my street, my phone beeps and flashes. It's a text from Bea. She says that she's glad David isn't dead and wants to know if I can come around for a cup of tea and a chat. I would love nothing better than a catch-up with Bea so I text David to let him know that I'm heading to her house and won't be long. I add a few kisses without any sense of duty or obligation and feel happier than I've felt for a long time. I decide that tonight, after Anna goes to sleep, I am going to make a pass at my husband and at the very least put on matching bra and knickers.

As I knock on Bea's front door, I already have a smile on my face. I can't wait to fill her in on everything's that's been happening with David and me, and his supposed affair and all the gossip from Ireland (well, almost everything – I'm keeping the Ryan stuff to myself), and about my coffee with Rosalind. I hear the key turn in the lock, and the door suddenly opens and I wave my hand in greeting and stop halfway because it's not Bea.

It's Ryan.

My mouth drops open to match his. It can't be him. It can't be. I am frozen just the way I was on the beach when we first met. We lock eyes, and the air fizzes with electricity.

Then suddenly Bea is there, nudging Ryan out of the way so she can give me a hug while I look at Ryan over her shoulder and blink a couple of times, because he *cannot* be here.

Bea draws away, and looks at me with puzzled eyes. Then she slowly looks from me to Ryan and back again.

I hold my breath in my throat.

Ryan is the first to move. He steps forward with his hand out, grips mine firmly, and says, 'Nice to meet you.'

It takes me a moment to digest what he is doing. He is pretending we are strangers. Why? However, I have no choice but to follow his lead. His touch shoots a little bolt of electricity through me, which I try to pretend isn't sexual, and I squeeze his hand just as firmly in return, find my voice and tell him it's nice to meet him too.

Bea shakes her head slowly.

'Honestly, it's like you two are in some kind of executive meeting,' she says. She gives herself a little shake and says grandly, 'Saoirse, meet Ryan, the father of my child.'

What the FUCK?

'Well, don't just stand there, come in!' she says, as if she hasn't just dropped the world's biggest bombshell.

My mind is reeling. How the hell could this be? Ryan is Bea's ex – Harry's father. My mouth feels dry and my legs feel heavy as I walk down the narrow hallway to Bea's kitchen. I am flooded with relief when I see Ryan's back retreating up the tiny stairs to Harry, who is waiting at the top with what looks to be some kind of plastic gun.

Bea fills the kettle with water while I flop into one of the least-stained kitchen chairs. While the kettle is boiling, Bea joins me at the table and we both start talking at the same time. She asking me about David and I ask about Ryan.

She holds up her customary one finger, and we both fall silent.

'You first,' she smiles.

My head is still spinning from seeing Ryan but I manage to talk about David instead. I put a half-coherent story together and tell Bea what happened as best I can. I tell her about Joss and how she's been helping David find his biological mother, and she crosses her arms and looks thoughtful for a moment.

'It makes sense that David would want to find his mother eventually,' she says. 'It might help him feel more grounded.'

I nod, once again appreciating her insight on how David's mind works.

'You look pale,' she says, getting up to make the tea. 'You're probably still in shock.'

I am in shock, I think, but not about David.

'So, what about you?' I say, trying to keep my voice as steady as possible. 'How did Ryan end up here?'

Bea grimaces a little, and crosses the kitchen in two long strides to the fridge.

'It's all a bit strange,' she says, looking at the milk in her hand as if wondering how it got there. It's the first time I have ever seen her composure slip.

I get up from the chair, quickly grab the milk from her, and balancing two teacups in one hand, guide her over to the kitchen table. I bring the kettle over and pour in some hot water, while she looks at her hands for a bit.

'I'm not sure where to start, Saoirse,' she says.

So I tell her to start from the beginning, which she does.

Bea tells me the whole story of why they split up five years before. How Arianna had paid for the trip to Ireland to get Bea to scout out a particular plot just outside Wexford as a potential location for a summer house, which of course would end up becoming The Cube.

'We were having such a lovely time,' Bea said, with a sigh. 'The plot was perfect, so we didn't have much to do apart from laze around the hotel and take walks along the beach. Although the weather was pretty shit.'

Well, obviously.

'We met Kitty and Frank at the beach and they persuaded Ryan to take a dip in the sea. I was too pregnant at the time, but Ryan really took to it. Every morning, he would get up early and go for a swim – or so I thought.'

I nod along, mainly because I know most of it, although she doesn't know that. But I didn't know all of it, because for all his guilt and repentance, Ryan never told me that his long-term girlfriend had been six months' pregnant with his baby when he cheated on her with Frances.

'I mean I had *no idea* he was fucking someone else. It just didn't register at all. I feel so stupid now, looking back,' she says, sipping her tea. 'Anyway, back in London, when he finally told me about Frances, I knew that was it for us. It's horrific what happened to her but I couldn't bring myself to feel sorry for him. So I cut him out of my life completely.'

I stay quiet for a bit so it looks like I'm trying to process what should be new information but inwardly I'm livid. How could Ryan not tell me that he had cheated on his girlfriend while she was pregnant? The total scumbag.

'So you can imagine my surprise when he rocked up at my office – apparently he Googled me – demanding to see Harry and wanting to know if he was safe.'

'So, what did you do?'

'Well, naturally I told him to fuck off,' she says casually, dipping half a digestive in her tea. 'And then he sits down on the chair opposite and spends a good half an hour telling me how sorry he is about everything, and how the terrorist attack made him realise what he'd lost and that he'd never forgive himself if he didn't at least try to see Harry,' she says.

'And what did you say to all that?'

'Well, I'll admit that it made me think. There may be nothing between Ryan and me any more, but perhaps Harry does deserve to see his father.'

'Wow,' is the best I can come up with.

'The whole area was being evacuated as a precaution anyway, so we just hopped in a taxi and came back here.'

'So, what did Harry think?' I say.

'This is the best part, Saoirse,' she says. 'I let us both into the house and Harry comes tearing down the stairs, and he's all delighted that I'm home unexpectedly. Then he comes to this sliding stop in the hallway when he sees Ryan.'

'Go on!' I say, because, despite it all, I'm a sucker for reunion stories.

'So he clocks Ryan and goes, "Who's that bloke?"' she says, laughing.

I laugh with her because Harry is fucking hilarious at the best of times.

'I tell him that his name is Ryan, and he just gives him this long stare, and he says, "But he looks just like me," and then Ryan kneels down and explains who he is.'

'Jesus,' I say, because I can't think of any other way to react. 'What was Harry's reaction?'

'Well, I think it's fair to say that Harry didn't exactly appreciate the gravity of the situation. He kicked Ryan in his left knee, and ran off to find Maria and Anna.'

'It's a lot for Harry to take in,' I say.

'I know. They're getting on better today, but it's a long road, for Harry and for me,' she says, thoughtfully. 'Anyway, after that Ryan and I went out to dinner. Thankfully Maria agreed to stay a bit later. Unsurprisingly, Ryan wants access to Harry, so I need to think more about that. Maybe we can keep things civil and work something out.'

Then I ask her the question that's been sticking in my throat this entire time.

'Are you getting back with Ryan?' I say, busying myself by clearing away the empty cups so she can't see my expression.

'Gosh, no!' she says. 'I may have shagged him last night for old time's sake – more convenient than Tinder – but there is no way I would ever get back with that ratbag. But sex is sex, and he was there, so...'

Then her forehead creases.

'Besides, his American accent is killing me. He's from South Africa for goodness' sake!'

Despite myself, I feel a twinge of jealousy. That just last night my Ryan fantasy had become my best friend's reality. I shake off these ridiculous thoughts, reminding myself that he is a lying, cheating scumbag, and do my best to focus on what Bea is saying.

She looks thoughtful for a moment. 'Besides, Maria would murder me.'

And it suddenly twigs that this must have been the visitor Maria was telling me about yesterday.

'Does Maria not like Ryan?' I say.

'She knows the history so, she was never going to welcome him with open arms. Besides, she reckons his eyes are a bit close together, or some nonsense,' Bea says.

'How long is he staying for?' I say, because if this is only a flying visit, I think I can just about handle it.

'I told him he needs to leave later today, and find a hotel or something. He mentioned something about moving to be closer to Harry, but who knows, Saoirse? He's hardly Mr Reliable.'

I think about what it would be like to bump into Ryan on the street and my stomach lurches. To my frustration, I realise I'm not sure it would be such a bad feeling.

Bea suddenly gives an impatient wave to indicate that she wants to change the subject. 'Anyway, enough about me and the ex! What are your thoughts on the whole school situation?'

Despite everything that has happened, I take a small measure of comfort in the knowledge that Bea and I are in exactly the same boat when it comes to bloody schools. Both lumbered with the shit school unless we dig deep for private-school fees.

'Sure, we're fucked, Bea. Can't afford private, and David refuses to send Anna to the shit school, even temporarily,' I say, and sit back and sigh.

'You never know, Saoirse. I see from Vale Mums that some kids on the waiting list have been getting places at Woodvale. That might happen for Anna too,' she says.

'Ha! I doubt it,' I say. 'She's too far down the waiting list. It'll be probably another year before she gets in and by that stage, she'll be in a juvenile detention centre.'

Bea doesn't smile. Instead she looks down at her hands and taps her fingers on the table. She takes a deep breath, hesitates, releases it, and takes another deep breath. Her expression is grim.

'What the fuck, Bea? Spit it out!' I say.

'So, I'm sending Harry private,' she says, in the same voice I imagine she would use if she had been diagnosed with cancer.

What?

'My mother is paying for it,' she says.

I know I should be happy for Bea. There are some lovely private schools in the area – apart from St Enda's, which is frankly insufferable. But Bea would never send Harry there. The news makes me sad. Our kids won't be going to school together. We won't be able to stand in the playground and slag off all the other mums. I'll be all by myself. The new girl at the school gates. I hate being the new girl.

'What school is it?' I say.

'St Enda's,' she says, and her hands fly to her glasses, which she adjusts for no discernible reason.

Any chance of being happy for her goes straight out the window.

'St Enda's?' I echo. 'The school where all the kids wear boater hats, and hold galas and fundraisers for hippos over actual starving humans? The school we've been taking the piss out of for the last two years? Are you fucking kidding me?'

I feel my whole body clench. How could she be such a hypocrite? St Enda's is the Organics' school of choice, which tells you all you need to know. It's elitist, snobbish, ultra-competitive, zero diversity; it's a school that hammers small children academically, assaults them with too many extra-curriculars and hours of homework, and then moulds them into little toy soldiers.

She heaves a big sigh and shrugs her shoulders. 'I know, Saoirse. I've been battling my mum over it for the last year, but she wore me down,' she says. 'Then when he got a place at the shit school, I thought maybe I should take her up on her offer. Besides, a good old-fashioned dose of English discipline might turn him into a functioning member of society.'

I can see by the line of her mouth that her mind is made up and I cry inside because I don't want to do this without her. We have been insepa-rable since we met on that shagging bus four years ago. I had just assumed our kids would go to the same school. Whatever has happened (or not happened with Ryan), I can't face the thought of losing my best friend. To St Enda's of all places.

'Well, that place is full of snobby cows and dads shagging their secretaries,' I say. 'You'll never fit in.'

I know I'm being a cow, but I am hurt and angry and I want her to feel the same way.

'I don't care if I fit in or not, Saoirse,' she shoots back.

And that makes me even angrier.

'That's not the point, Bea!' I say, and I'm bloody furious.

'What *is* the point then?' she says, shaking her head in frustration.

'I don't want to do the school thing all by myself!' I shout.

I am dimly aware that I am over-reacting but for now I don't care. If I want to behave like a child, I damn well will.

Between David almost getting killed, the shock of seeing Ryan again, and Bea's massive 180, there is nothing I want more than to scream and shout.

Thankfully, before things escalate further, Ryan walks into the kitchen.

'Harry needs a drink,' Ryan mumbles. He has probably overheard Bea and I arguing. Well, he can go fuck himself too.

Bea gets up immediately, finds a clean cup for Harry and gives it to him. Without warning, a memory of Ryan and me standing on the clifftop flashes through my mind. I keep my head down when he passes by and I'm pretty sure he pretends I'm just as invisible.

Bea sits back down at the table just as I announce that I'm leaving. I'm pissed off and I just want to go home.

'Fine,' Bea says, huffily. She doesn't see me out.

On the walk home, I try to process what just happened. Ryan. My best friend, Bea's ex. Ryan who told me I had 'kind eyes', who I'm pretty sure wanted to kiss me, and then whispered a promise of 'another time' when we were interrupted by my mother. Ryan, who never told me that he had cheated on my best friend when she was pregnant. Ryan, who after pouring his heart out to me, had made out at Bea's house that we were strangers. Ryan potentially 'moving closer' to be near Harry and Bea. Oh, and let's not forget Bea's decision to send Harry to St Enda's – the ultimate betrayal.

Well, fuck her, and – because I am in the mood to be irrational – fuck them all.

My mind is spinning so hard that I walk slap-bang into Tania Henderson, leader of the Organics. Her blond hair is animated-princess curled and she is wearing a dress so flowy and flowery that she looks as though Laura Ashley has just thrown up on her.

'Whoops!' she says in that overly loud way people use to indicate that it's entirely your fault.

I refuse to apologise even though she's right.

She recovers from the stand-off first. I am dimly aware that she is holding a loaf of bread in one hand.

'Saoirse!' she says, giving me a warm embrace with her free arm, as I stand stock-still.

She looks down at the bread, hugs it to her and says, shame-faced, 'I know! White bread! So much sugar! It's not for me, it's for a friend.'

I don't bother telling her I couldn't give a fuck about the 'dangers' of white bread.

'How's Anna? Is she still keeping you up at night?' she says, laughing.

The bitch. It's been three years since Anna regularly woke in the night, but Tania still uses my 'failure' to crack the sleeping code against me.

'Sleeps like a log!' I say, but because I'm not a big enough person to ignore it, and I'm in a bad mood, I can't resist following up with, 'Do you still have a night nanny?'

Boom! Her mouth drops open.

I'm not supposed to know her 'shameful secret' – how, after all her boasting about cracking the sleeping code, she had to resort to a night nanny to rock her precious Heath into dreamland. I silently thank David for handing me that grenade a few years ago.

She gives me a tight smile and mutters something about the night nanny being in the past, and I just cock my head and pretend to listen. She starts to go on about her second child, Daisy, who is *so different* from Heath, and has the whole family regularly in stitches with her two-year-old antics. She clearly prefers Daisy to Heath but I don't say anything.

Then she shocks me about asking me something about myself.

'Do you *still* have just the one?' she says, looking at my stomach.

'Yes, just Anna,' I say, and I can't help but feel defensive as people always ask this question when you have an only child. Usually they go on to sympathise with you – if it turns out you can't genuinely have another one – and the child – because the child must be lonely and feel deprived without any siblings to beat the shit out of. What people don't like to hear is that you only want one, especially when you are perfectly healthy and capable of having another.

Just as I'm hoping that Tania won't continue the 'only child' questioning further, she utters the immortal line, 'Do you think you'll have another one?'

I say no. She asks why.

Well, let's see. Because I'm happy enough with the way things are, because financially it would be a struggle, and more importantly, because Anna would likely smother the child in its sleep out of sheer jealousy. But since it's none of Tania's business, I say nothing of the sort and just reply: 'Because I'm dead inside.'

She laughs in a 'poor you!' sort of way. As if I'm so devastated by only having one child that I need to make jokes to cover it up. Just as I'm about to make my excuses, she says one word that forces me to stand my ground.

'Schools!' she says, with the enthusiasm of a Mary Poppins imitator.

Here we go. It's all over Vale Mums that her little darling is going to an exclusive boarding school outside London, and I imagine she just wants to rub it in. So you could have knocked me down with an underweight model when she told me how pleased she was that Heath has got into Woodvale Primary, my favourite school. The one that rejected Anna. The FREE school.

'What?' I say. 'I thought you were going private?'

Her voice drops to a whisper and she tells me that given that the economy isn't doing so well, she can't '100 per cent rely on Giles' to pay the fees for both Heath and Daisy.

'Does that mean you're going back to work then?' I say. If she's worried about money issues, why doesn't she get up off her flowery-patterned arse and start earning instead of spending all day tearing other mums down on social media?

I watch as an expensively manicured hand flies to a fairy-pink lipsticked mouth.

'Oh, I couldn't go back to work! I mean, the children are so young,' she says.

I feel my eyes rolling to the back of my head.

Then she asks me about schools and where I'm going to send Anna.

'Well, she got a place at the shit school,' I say. 'But she's not going.'

Tania scrunches up her face.

'You know, some of my *best friends* are going to send their children there. I think if enough *decent* people send their kids there, it will weed out the rougher elements eventually,' she says, lowering her voice.

'Would you send Heath and Daisy there?' I say, just to watch her blush and cough and splutter her way out of it. She shakes her head and splutters something about the shit school being a bit too 'urban' and a little too centred towards 'sports' and Heath isn't the sporty type. Bored with the total bullshit coming out of her mouth, I tell her I have to dash.

As I am walking away, she calls after me, 'How's Bea?'

Now she's just being a cow because she has hated Bea ever since that antenatal class meeting. I pause for a moment, then turn, and say, 'Bea? Bea's fine! In fact, she's fucking Ryan Gosling.' Then I walk away before I can see her expression change. As much as I am annoyed with Bea, I'm not letting anything slip to the likes of Tania Henderson.

As I turn the corner into my street, a flash of relief rushes over me: Anna may not have got into Woodvale Primary, but at least I won't have to put up with that organic-munching judgemental bitch for the next seven years.

I open the front door and almost bump into Anna, who is standing far too close to the letterbox, with her hands behind her back. She fixes me with a look, and says, 'The postman has been, Mummy.'

Despite my whirling mind, I can't help but smile at her serious expression.

'That's great, Anna,' I say, with as much enthusiasm as I can under the circumstances. 'Anything interesting?'

She takes a piece of paper from behind her back, and waves it at me.

'Daddy says it means I don't have to go to the shit school now,' she says, jumping up and down.

'"Shit" is a grown-up word,' David says, walking down the stairs with a big smile plastered all over his face.

He comes to a stop in front of me and gives me a big kiss.

'The letter arrived this morning. A space has opened up in Woodvale Primary. The council say the place is Anna's if we want it!'

My heart jumps in my chest. This is FANTASTIC news. We don't have to pay for Anna's education. No more poring over spreadsheets trying to work out how many years of eating beans on toast we will have to endure if we dare to go private. No more stress about waiting lists. She's IN. We're safe for the next seven years. David and Anna are doing a little dance now, while singing along to Anna's favourite song, 'Uptown Funk', and I want to join in but I can't. I try to tell myself it's because I don't want be stuck with that bitch Tania Henderson for the next seven years, but it's really because I'm going to have to face school without my best friend.

Suddenly I feel a little hand slip into mine. 'Come on, Mummy!' my beautiful daughter smiles. 'Family dance!' David and I join hands, and we form a little circle, and I can't help but laugh at Anna's sheer strength and determination to keep us all in time to the beat of her own singing.

I squeeze the hands of the people I love most in the world, and catch David's eye. 'It's about time we had a family dance!' he says.

Before I can reply, Anna looks up and says, 'You're damn right, Daddy!'

I lean down and give her a big kiss on one of her soft, downy cheeks. Bad language or not, that child knows what she's talking about.

24

It's one week on from the terrorist attack and life is beginning to return to normal. David is back at work, and I try my best not to agonise about his safety. Things are getting better between us, partly stemming from the relief of Anna getting into Woodvale, as well as David opening up about his true feelings.

Over the last few days I have been inundated with texts from Dee and Jen, who have created a WhatsApp group especially for the purpose of harassing me. To my delight, Jen has agreed to come over for my mother's seventieth birthday party, and Dee has promised a trip after she gets through the mania of 'shitting Christmas' – 'I'll be in even more need of a break then.' I can't wait to see them again.

I haven't heard from Bea since she broke the news to me about Ryan, and her decision to send Harry to private school, but in a way I am glad to have some time to myself to think everything through. While I am in reflective mode, I should really focus on finalising the pitch, but having Anna full time doesn't make life easy, and the iPad only goes so far.

I bribe Anna to come to the shops with me to pick up a few bits and pieces for the party with a promise of going to the playground afterwards. I hate the playground. Every time I go there, I fully believe that I should be decorated with medals for patience and bravery as acknowledgement for the extreme suffering I go through as a mother to ensure my daughter is entertained.

The second we walk through the playground gates, Anna heads for the 'spinny thing', the whirling hell of steel that she likes to spin in until she turns green. I put her in it and give her my most violent push as a passive-aggressive way of getting out all my frustration in the guise of giving my child a great time. After I push, I turn away to avoid watching her whirl round and round. Just watching her spin so fast makes my stomach churn. I focus on a tree for a bit instead, before I hear a voice that makes me turn cold.

'Gives you vertigo too, hey?'

My stomach drops and my temples start to pulse because he is the very last person I want to see right now – or ever again. I take a deep breath and turn round slowly.

Ryan stands three feet away from me with Harry wriggling in his arms.

'Hi, Harry!' I say brightly, deliberately ignoring his father.

Harry, in turn, ignores me, and announces that he wants to go on the spinny thing with Anna. Ryan turns to put Harry in with Anna, who is delighted to see her best friend, and they both beg for Ryan to give them the 'biggest push ever'! Laughing, Ryan uses one arm to effortlessly push them much faster than I could, and when they are a mere blur, he turns back to me, the smile fading from his face.

He runs a tanned hand through his hair.

'Where's your ex-girlfriend?' I ask, pointedly, hating myself for sounding so bitter.

His shoulders drop and he tells me that Bea has taken a day off and plans to join him and Harry a little later.

I glare at him for a bit and then look away.

'Look, I'm sorry about what happened at Bea's house,' he says.

'You pretended not to know me,' I reply, flatly.

'I just couldn't believe it when I saw you standing there. I didn't know what else to do,' he says, his eyes pleading now.

Well, fuck him.

'How about, "What a coincidence! Saoirse and I have already met!" That way, we could at least have told Bea the truth.'

Ryan looks away for a moment and then turns his blue eyes back to me.

'Saoirse, I spent the entire night apologising for what happened with Frances and begging Bea to let me see my son. What would she have done if she knew about us?' he says, taking a step closer.

'What about us?' I say, feeling a flush growing from my neck to my cheeks. 'There is no "us"!'

He takes another step towards me and I freeze.

We stare at each other for what seems like minutes, until somewhere behind me I hear two shrill voices complaining about the lack of spinning. Grateful for the distraction, I turn away from Ryan, and give Anna and Harry the biggest push I can muster, matching their spins with the whirling thoughts in my head.

He is behind me now – too close. I can feel his breath on my ear.

'I know you feel it too,' he says.

A spark of outrage ignites within me. Who does this idiot think he is? The arrogance of him! I whip round to give him a piece of my mind, but before I can even form the words, his mouth is on mine.

My first thought is, 'Ryan is kissing me.' My second thought is, 'How the hell did that happen?' and my third thought is, 'Is he wearing flavoured lip balm?'

Suddenly, the whole situation seems utterly ludicrous. Here I am, a forty-year-old married woman standing in the middle of a playground being kissed by someone I thought I was attracted to. Not only that, but he's someone who's just slept with my best friend, and before that, he cheated on her when she was pregnant with his child. When he tries to slip in the tongue, I burst into giggles and push him away. The relief is overwhelming. To know that I have no feelings for this man after all is incredible. He may be gorgeous to look at, but it's like being kissed by a wax version of him. In fact, I'd be better off kissing one of those replicas of the real Ryan Gosling in Madame Tussauds.

'What's the matter?' he says, head cocked, mouth in a straight line. I see a flash of annoyance cross those blue eyes: I have hurt his ego.

Out of the corner of my eye, I see Harry and Anna have moved on to the swings, clearly fed up waiting for us to give them another push. I take a step towards them, but Ryan grabs my hand and tries to tug me back.

A familiar voice causes us both to freeze.

'Get your fucking hands off my best friend, you utter prick.'

Ryan looks over in surprise and lets my hand drop.

It's Bea and she looks and sounds exactly like she did that day so many years ago when I was trapped on the bus with Anna.

Absolutely fucking livid.

Ryan whips around, his hands raised in surrender. I stay frozen to the spot.

'Harry, come here NOW,' Bea says in her most formidable voice. Clearly picking up on the murderous tone, Harry scrambles off his swing and runs over to his mum. Anna lets out a wail at Harry's sudden departure, and I immediately rush over to the swing to comfort her. Minutes go by as I try to calm her down. When she finally stops sobbing, I turn round to find that Ryan, Bea and Harry have already gone.

I walk home with a very sulky Anna, trying to process what has just happened. I feel sick. Why hadn't I told her the truth about meeting Ryan in Ireland? What must she be thinking?

As soon as I get back, I give Anna a bag of crisps, and call Bea, but she doesn't answer. To be honest, I don't blame her. Then I text her and hope and pray she texts me back.

I spend the rest of the day and the day after that staring at my phone but nothing happens. I'm constantly on edge and I know I'm taking it out on David and Anna. What makes it worse is that I can't talk to David about it, without admitting my previous attraction to Ryan.

After three days of no contact, I take Anna's hand and knock on Bea's door. This is usually the day she works from home, but to my disappointment, Maria answers and tells me that Bea has been called into the office. She invites Anna in to play with Harry but, much to Anna's fury (and Maria's surprise), I decline. It wouldn't be right for me to leave Anna in Bea's house under the circumstances. Instead I bribe Anna with an ice cream on the way home.

At some point during the evening, it occurs to me that I haven't finished work yet; in fact, I haven't looked at it since Bea froze me out of her life. I tell David that I'm going to work for a bit, and he grabs my hand.

'Are you all right, Saoirse?' he says, and his voice is so full of concern that my eyes immediately fill with tears.

No, David, I'm not all right. I am a horrible person because I have betrayed you and my best friend by fancying a man I barely know.

But of course I don't say any of this. I just tell him I have PMT, which always does the trick. He gives my hand a sympathetic squeeze, which makes me feel worse than ever.

When I reach my desk, I try to make sense of all the material I have written, but it's no use, I can't focus. I idly click into Vale Mums and notice that Rosalind has posted something about swimming, which appears to have attracted a number of responses.

Anyone have any idea of a good age to stop swimming lessons? My eldest boy is a good swimmer already, and wonder if I should continue.

Tania has replied:

Of COURSE he should continue! Swimming is a life skill! Why would anyone give it up?

Inevitably, Tania has received a whole host of 'likes' and 'thumbs ups', while Rosalind has been the brunt of both pleading and crying emojis.

My heart quickens.

Deep down, I know I have no business getting involved in this discussion. You see, I have a real problem with the overblown emphasis on swimming for kids. Granted, it's a life skill, but surely they don't need to start so young or need the lessons to last for ever. But I'm not in the most rational frame of mind, so I place my hands on the keys and type.

If a child is a good swimmer FINISH the lessons. I mean, what's the end goal here? The Olympics?

Then I add a thinking face emoji, which I always thinks looks the most sarcastic, and head upstairs to bed.

When I wake up the next morning, I find thirty notifications to my swimming post, but I barely glance at them because something glorious has happened. Bea has sent me a text. She wants me to come over.

As soon as Anna has finished her breakfast, we leave for Bea's house. I am nervous but I am determined to sort this mess out. Bea greets Anna and sends her off to upstairs to play with Harry, who is apparently in the middle of mashing a large cardboard box into a 'car'.

With the kids out of the way, we look at each other, and she beckons me to follow her into the kitchen. It's the first time I have ever felt awkwardness between us, and it feels dreadful. We sit down opposite each other at the kitchen table and I clasp my hands together to stop them from shaking.

'So,' Bea begins, looking at me with stern eyes through the glasses perched at the end of her nose. 'What the actual fuck?'

And without really knowing how, I spill out everything I have been keeping from her over the past few weeks. How I had suspected David of having an affair; the strong attraction I had felt for Ryan in Ireland; everything I knew about Ryan and Frances; the conversations I had with Kitty; how Ryan had kissed me in the park and how relieved I was that I felt nothing for him after all. Everything I thought I had swum out of me in those ice-cold Irish waters comes brimming to the surface once more and I can't seem to stop. Bea stares at me throughout, her expression unreadable.

'Look, Bea, I'm sorry. I had no idea he was your ex or Harry's father. I have been so bloody stupid,' I say, feeling hot with humiliation. I duck my head to hide tears springing to my eyes.

When I look up a few seconds later, Bea is still staring at me with the same cold look, her arms folded across her chest.

'I'm going to ask you a few questions now, Saoirse, and I want you to tell me the truth.'

'Of course!' I say immediately, just grateful that she has finally broken her silence.

'Did you at any stage link Ryan to me when you were in Ireland?'

'No!'

'Did Kitty not say anything about what happened?'

I shake my head vigorously.

She drums her fingers on the table. 'Actually, that makes sense. Kitty would never confide in an outsider.'

At least she doesn't say 'foreigner', I think.

'Why didn't you tell me about your attraction to Ryan right away?' Bea says.

'I was too ashamed,' I say. 'I didn't think it was fair on David to tell you about it. He hasn't a clue about any of this. Besides, I thought it was just a harmless fantasy at first, and then it all got a bit real...'

'Did you act on any of those feelings?'

'Absolutely not!' I shoot back. 'I was tempted, no question, but nothing happened, I swear.'

'Why didn't you tell me you had already met Ryan when you came over to collect Anna?'

That's the one I have been dreading.

'I'm sorry, I should have told you, but he pretended not to know me and I was too shocked to react the way I should have. I'm so sorry.'

She sighs and takes off her glasses, holding them to the light, inspecting them for dust, before putting them back on again. Then she gets up and walks over to the sink, and just stands there with her back to me.

'Bea?' I say, tentatively.

She doesn't answer, so I push myself up from the table, and put my hand on her arm. She turns round slowly, and I am shocked to see tears in her eyes. I have never seen Bea cry – she's not the crying type.

'This is all my fault. I'm so sorry,' I say, welling up myself.

'I should have told you about Ryan before,' she says, wiping her hand fiercely across her eyes.

'And I should have told you what was going on with David,' I say. Maybe if I had confided in her, then she would have made me see sense.

'Tell me honestly,' I say. 'Do you still have feelings for Ryan?'

She shakes her head furiously.

'Don't you get it?' she says, throwing her hands up in frustration. 'Ryan isn't the reason I'm upset, Saoirse. I couldn't give a shit about him. *You're* the reason I'm upset.'

'I'm sorry, Bea!' I say, crying properly now. I don't know what else to say.

She takes a gulp of air and looks away.

'Listen, Saoirse, when Ryan told me about Frances, it was the worst thing that had ever happened to me. We had been together since we were teenagers in South Africa; he wasn't just my lover, he was my best friend. When he left me, there were days when I genuinely felt that I couldn't go on. It was only Harry that kept me going.'

'Oh, Bea...' I reach out to give her a hug, but she holds one hand up to stop me, and my arms drop uselessly to my sides.

'And then I met you, Saoirse,' she says, and her face crumples. 'And I could see you were struggling too, and for the first time I didn't feel so alone.'

My mind is reeling. I had no idea Bea had ever felt his way. She had never confided in me about Ryan, and I now see why: it was simply too hurtful to her to talk about him. I open my mouth to say something, but she's not finished yet.

'Then when I saw you and Ryan kissing in the park, I felt sick to my stomach. Not because of him, but because of you. I have already lost one best friend, Saoirse. I can't lose you too, do you hear me?'

Then she lets me put my arms around her and we hug for a moment.

When we pull away, I grip her by the shoulders, look her directly in the eye, and say slowly and deliberately, 'You are not going to lose me, Bea.'

She sniffs and sighs.

'OK,' she says finally, giving me a weak smile.

'OK,' I say, firmly.

'Cup of tea?' she says.

I smile and nod.

When we're finally sitting down at the table again, she takes a sip of her tea, and says, 'I can't believe you thought David was having an affair. I mean, David! Of all people!' and bursts into deep-bellied laughter that seems to go on for minutes.

'For fuck's sake,' I begin, indignant now. 'Why does everyone think my husband is so unlikely to have an affair?'

But as I look at her, she is red with mirth and before I can stop it, hysterical laughter explodes out of me and we both laugh and laugh until our sides hurt and tears start falling from our eyes.

When we recover, I tell her there is one more thing I need to talk to her about.

'Uh-oh,' she says, with a frown. 'What now?'

'Anna got into Woodvale School,' I say.

'Oh, that's brilliant, Saoirse!' Bea says, clapping her hands.

'She'll be in with the Organics' offspring, though,' I say, gloomily.

Bea makes a vomiting sound.

'Listen, Saoirse, they won't all be Organics in the class. All you need to do is find one friend – one person to whom you can text about homework, slag off the Organics, and bitch about the PTA.'

I nod. I know she's right, but my heart still breaks a little because as far as I'm concerned, I have already found that one friend, and it's her.

'I owe you an apology for the way I kicked off about St Enda's,' I say. 'I was being a knob.'

She laughs.

'Listen, Saoirse, St Enda's may not be the right school for Harry, but I promised my mother I would at least give it a chance. If he starts asking for a tenner from the tooth fairy, or demanding to go to Mauritius over the school holidays, I'm whipping him out.'

I tell her that I think that's fair enough, quietly relieved that St Enda's may not be a permanent measure.

'Besides, we will have a great time swapping tales about annoying mums at the school gates,' she smiles.

I smile in return, and I realise that I don't care as much about going to school without her, because no matter what happens, Bea and I will always have each other.

When I get home, a notification from Bea pops up on my Facebook post on swimming. It says:

I would give all of you swimming die-hards an Olympic medal to shut the fuck up.

I clasp my hand to my mouth and burst out laughing.

'What's so funny, Mummy?' Anna says, crossly.

'Mummy has just got her best friend back,' I say merrily, picking her up and giving her a crushing hug.

She wiggles out of my arms and glares at me, before saying, 'That's not funny.'

That night, when Anna is in bed, and David is working quietly on his laptop, I finally find the words I need to summarise all the themes I have written down for the pitch. It's one of those glorious writing moments where my fingers skip merrily over the keyboard without stopping.

When I first had my daughter, Anna, I thought I would die of loneliness. On the face of it, I had plenty of support – a husband, a long-time best friend, and some family that weren't a million miles away. What I hadn't bargained for was my husband being as clueless as I was when it came to babies, or how much I would resent him for it. I couldn't talk to my best friend from childhood because she had never wanted children and couldn't relate. And forget about making friends with the mums in my baby group; they seemed to know exactly what they were doing, which made me feel even more isolated.

What I really needed was someone that I could vent to without judgement; have a cry over without feeling foolish; and share guilty thoughts and feelings without fear of reprisal. Someone who would swear alongside me; comfort me when I was doubting my abilities as a mother; and perhaps someone who could take care of my child when I needed a break. Someone who could speak my language.

And it's hard to find that person – it really is. It involves being vulnerable enough to share your true feelings with someone new, even though you're already feeling like an emotional basket case; being willing to put your trust and faith in someone else; and being there for someone else just as she is there for you. But when you find that mum, hold on to her. Friendships may come and go, but friendships forged during motherhood are the parachutes that bring you safely to solid ground.

Then, inspired by my mother, I have a go at writing a haiku of my own.

Friends come in and out

> As a mum you need them more
> Keep the ones that count

I finish the draft, edit it and send the pitch to Harriet, before going to bed where I dream about the ebb and flow of that icy temperamental Irish Sea.

25

It's the last Saturday in August and the house hums with the sound of party preparations. Jen and my mother flew in together this morning (My mum: 'Ryanair isn't *that* bad, Saoirse!' and Jen, privately: 'It was a fucking nightmare, Saoirse'). At the moment, my mother is in my kitchen making two lasagnes from a new recipe she had saved on her Pinterest, and Jen is furiously spreading garlic butter on endless slices of baguette. When I make the mistake of questioning my mum on the necessity of so much food for very few people, she says, 'There's only one thing worse than running out of food, Saoirse: running out of alcohol, but sure, there's no danger of that.'

She's not wrong – the stocks are full.

Leaving the pair of them to it, I go to find Anna who is busy 'draw-wing' in her 'woom' – the iPad cast aside on her bed. Another flutter of panic runs through me at the sight of the forlorn iPad. What am I going to do without you? I think sadly, looking at its battered screen.

Then I spend a fairly frustrating few minutes with Anna trying to persuade her to toast my mother's big birthday when the time comes.

'When you see everyone raise their glasses, like this' – I demonstrate the motion with one of her little doll's cups – 'just say as loud as you can, "Happy birthday, Nana!"'

Anna gives a great big sigh in a 'why do I have to do EVERYTHING?' sort of way, and slumps back over her drawing of... whatever the hell it is.

'So, you'll do the toast then?' I say, fervently hoping at least an eighth of what I have said has gone in.

'Fine,' she shouts from behind her hair.

Well, that's something, I think. But just as I turn towards the door, I hear her mumble, 'I don't even *like* toast.'

I find David in the spare room refolding the guest towels I laid out on the bed for Jen and my mother earlier in the day ('Sure, we'll be grand sharing a bed!'). Normally this would bother me, but since our talk, I have decided to try to let go of the little things. I give him a kiss and thank him for arranging the room so nicely. He looks at me a little warily, but when he realises that I'm not taking the piss he puts one arm around my shoulders and gives me a little squeeze. A feeling of contentment rushes over me – we're going to be all right, me and David. I just know it.

Just then my mother rushes into the bedroom, brandishing my phone. I notice she has a smear of Bolognese on her right cheek.

'It's *buzzing*, Saoirse!' she says, thrusting it into my hand.

'That's all right, Mum,' I say, with a smile. 'It doesn't matter if I miss a call!'

She looks at me as if I've just told her I've taken up heroin.

'Would you answer it!' she says, twisting her hands nervously.

I shake my head in amusement, and stop dead just before I press the answer button.

It's Harriet Green. My agent. Calling me on a Saturday.

I turn away to answer the call, dimly aware of my mother hissing, 'Who is it?' to a clueless David.

Harriet greets me with an exhale.

'Searcy, you got it. The motherhood book is yours. I'll send over the contract on Monday.'

I've done it. I am now officially an author. It may not have started out to be the book of my dreams but now, more than anything, I really want to write it. I gulp down a wave of emotion and manage to whisper a thank you.

When she hangs up, I turn round to see the expectant faces of my mother and David.

'Well?' my mother says.

'I got it!' I manage to say. 'The motherhood book. It's mine!'

And then there's hugs and kisses and cries of congratulations, and then Jen runs up to hear what all the fuss is about and then everyone is dancing around, and it feels absolutely fantastic.

In the middle of it all, Anna stomps in and tells us to stop being 'so noisy' and I kneel down and tell her the good news – that Mummy is going to write a book, with her own name on the front.

She puts her head to one side, and says, 'Is it a pwincess book?'

And I say, 'Well, not exactly.'

To which she replies with a frown, 'Next time write a pwincess book.'

I give her a kiss on her little soft cheek and tell her I'll do my best.

Then the doorbell goes.

'That must be Bea and Harry!' my mother calls in a panicky voice.

Anna lets out a squeal at the sound of Harry's name and charges in front of me and David as we all clamber down the stairs.

When my mother reaches the bottom, she has a wild look in her eyes.

'You'll have to get the door, Saoirse. I have to take my apron off. THE STATE OF ME,' she cries, running back to the kitchen.

'I'll give her a hand getting the Bolognese off her face,' Jen says, with a laugh.

David and I look at each other and shake our heads in amusement.

'Shall we open the door in our own house then?' he says, wryly.

'Let's!' I say, and I swing open the door, and welcome Bea and Harry with a quick hug, over the moon to have my friend back in my house again. David greets Bea with a kiss and together we walk into the living room where I tell Bea the good news about the book, and she squeezes me so hard I can barely catch my breath. Jen, now apron-free, joins us, looking fabulous as ever in high-waisted thigh-skimming flowery-patterned shorts, topped with a smart white shirt. I make the introductions, and Bea, who is no slouch to dressing well, immediately compliments Jen on her outfit, and just like that, they're off to the races, exchanging tips on all the latest high-street fashion.

I haven't told Jen anything about seeing Ryan in London or the link between him and Bea. It doesn't seem right, somehow, given that David doesn't know anything about it. Besides, as far as I am concerned, that's all in the past now.

Harry and Anna start playing catch around the glass coffee table, and despite David trying to put an end to it by desperately shouting the word 'iPad' over and over again, there is no taming them.

Just as the hysteria reaches fever pitch, my mother finally appears from the kitchen, Bolognese- and apron-free. With her hands behind her back, she herds Harry and Anna into a corner of the living room, bends down, and whips out two lollipops.

'Lollipops,' they shout hysterically, and immediately race to the couch to open them.

'That'll keep their mouths occupied for a while,' she says, clapping her hands.

I think about that old woman in Ireland who gave Dee such a hard time for giving her little boy a lollipop and I feel grateful that I don't have a mother that judgemental.

I catch her eye and mouth a thank you.

She waves me away, and heads back into the kitchen, muttering something about the lasagne being 'rubbery' if she doesn't get it out soon.

I leave Bea, Jen and David together as I go to sort out some drinks.

When I reach the kitchen, the lasagne is already on the table accompanied by a mountain of garlic bread.

'Jesus, is it time to eat already? I haven't even served the drinks yet!' I say.

'Well, it's your oven, that's the problem,' Mum says, folding her arms defiantly across her chest. 'It's never cooked this quickly in my oven at home.'

As there is zero point in arguing with her, I go back to the living room and tell David and Bea that dinner is on the table.

'So soon?' David says.

'Don't ask,' I say, nodding my head towards the kitchen.

David grins.

I look at Harry and Anna, contentedly sucking their lollipops.

'Don't disturb them when they're so happy,' Bea says, through gritted teeth. 'They can eat later.'

So we back away slowly and make a break for it, each of us hoping we can bolt down at least one course of our meal without interruption.

For once, we succeed. We manage to have a glass of wine each and even an actual adult conversation, mostly led by my mother. ('Did you hear Steve Jobs never let his kids have an iPad?'. David: 'Yes, loads of the Silicon Valley lot have banned tech from their kids,' and Bea: 'Easy for them to ban it when they have a million staff to look after their kids twenty-four seven.)

As the last scrap of lasagne leaves our plates, Harry and Anna rush into the kitchen, shouting for birthday cake. David gets the champagne for grown-ups and apple juice for the kids, while I bring out the baking masterpiece.

Everyone oohs and aahs over it, even though the most generous person would agree that it really doesn't deserve even a fraction of the attention. Under pressure from Anna to decorate it, I have skimped a bit on beating the mixture enough, which means it hasn't risen and now looks like a large, messily iced biscuit. Nevertheless, David lights the candles and we all sing 'Happy Birthday' to Nana.

After the last 'hip, hip, hurrah!' I kneel down beside Anna who is happily sipping her apple juice, and whisper gently, 'Sweetheart,–remember what I told you about giving a toast to your nana?'

'Oh, yeah!' she says, with more enthusiasm than I've seen her display in ages.

Everyone smiles as Anna climbs down off her chair and carefully holds up her cup. I exchange a warm smile with David, and everything seems right with the world.

Anna toasts her nana exactly the way I taught her, and we all laugh and clink glasses. As I bend down to kiss her soft little cheek, Anna whispers, 'I want to say something else, Mummy!'

'Of course!' I whisper back, and give her hair a little ruffle.

'Anna has something more she wants to say,' I announce, and smile at her in encouragement.

'Hawwy's daddy kissed my mummy in the park,' she says, proudly.

My hand flies to my mouth and it takes me a moment to realise that Bea has done the same thing.

David looks from me to Bea and back again, and judging by the hard set of his mouth, he knows it's true.

And this time there's no sea to dive into and no holiday home in which to escape. My mother looks at Jen and shakes her head slowly, and I know just what she is thinking: I will need more than one of her Marital Miracles to get out of this one.

ACKNOWLEDGMENTS

Writing fiction has been the hardest thing I've ever done, but the most worthwhile and joyous. This book would not exist without the faith, love and support from my friends and family. I owe you a debt of gratitude that I can realistically only repay in the form of booze and the odd free dinner, but knowing you lot, that will be more than enough.

First, I want to thank Yoav Segal for listening to me whinge about my desperation to be a novelist and recommending Heather O'Connell, my brilliant career mentor, to put me on the right path. I also want to thank my fabulous friends-for-life nursery mums who have been, and continue to be, a source of unfailing support during these perplexing early child-rearing years. A huge thank you to my childhood friend and former literary agent, Emma Walsh. Emma was the first person to read the novel and gave me the push I needed to persevere. A special mention also goes to Claire-from-Pilates who read an early draft of the book and strongly advised me to remove the first 10,000 words. Without her advice, the manuscript may not have caught the eye of my brilliant editor, Sarah Ritherdon, and her stellar team at Boldwood. But of course, it would never have reached Sarah at all without the help of my lovely agent, Bea Corlett, one of the most patient people I have ever met, who took a chance on a completely unknown fiction writer and never once lost faith along the way despite the plethora of rejections (urrggh).

As for my family, I have to thank my parents for discouraging me from pursuing my childhood dream to be a novelist after finishing university ('Sure, there's no money in it, Emsie!'). Although it pains me to say it, they were right. I wasn't ready – but I am now.

Finally, to my husband, Sam. I cannot put into words how grateful I am for your love and support over the years. Without you, I would never have had the confidence to become a full-time writer, not to mention a novelist. Having said all that, I really don't think this book is your thing. Really. Don't read it. Ever.

BOOK CLUB QUESTIONS

1. What themes are dealt with in TIME OUT?

2. Did you relate to Saoirse? As a mother, as a friend and as a wife?

3. TIME OUT is partly about a woman who takes time out from her family. Is this a selfish or a totally understandable and necessary way to act?

4. How well does the author portray David's domestic fussiness and the impact this can have on a relationship?

5. What does Saoirse really see in Ryan? Is he simply a distraction from the negatives in her own relationship or does she actually have feelings for him?

6. Are there any elements to the story you would have liked the author to delve into more?

7. How well does the author capture the essence of Ireland?

8. Does this book hold most appeal for a mother or, because of the wit, intelligence and insight into the way humans *really* are, can it speak to anyone?

9. Do you feel the novel ends on a cliffhanger?

10.Would you want to read another novel by this author?

MORE FROM EMMA MURRAY

We hope you enjoyed reading *Time Out*. If you did, please leave a review.

If you'd like to gift a copy, this book is also available as an ebook, digital audio download and audiobook CD.

Sign up to Emma Murray's mailing list for news, competitions and updates on future books.

http://bit.ly/EmmaMurrayNewsletter

Discover *The Juggle*, the second laugh-out-loud instalment of Saoirse's story.

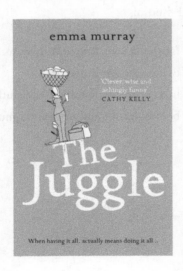

ABOUT THE AUTHOR

Emma Murray is originally from Co. Dublin and moved to London in her early twenties. After a successful career as a ghostwriter, she felt it was high time she fulfilled her childhood dream to write fiction.

Visit Emma's website: http://www.emmamurray.net/

Follow Emma on social media:

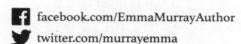

facebook.com/EmmaMurrayAuthor
twitter.com/murrayemma
instagram.com/emmamurrayauthor
bookbub.com/authors/emma-murray

ABOUT BOLDWOOD BOOKS

Boldwood Books is a fiction publishing company seeking out the best stories from around the world.

Find out more at www.boldwoodbooks.com

Sign up to the Book and Tonic newsletter for news, offers and competitions from Boldwood Books!

http://www.bit.ly/bookandtonic

We'd love to hear from you, follow us on social media:

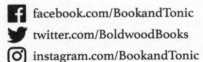

facebook.com/BookandTonic

twitter.com/BoldwoodBooks

instagram.com/BookandTonic